The Right Way to Hire Financial Help

The Right Way to Hire Financial Help

A complete guide to choosing and managing brokers, financial planners, insurance agents, lawyers, tax preparers, bankers, and real estate agents

Charles A. Jaffe

The MIT Press
Cambridge, Massachusetts
London. England

This book was set in Stone Sans Semibold, Stone Sans by Northeastern Graphic Services, Inc.

Printed and bound in the United States of America.

Library of Congress Cataloging-in-Publication Data

Jaffe, Charles A.
    The right way to hire financial help: a complete guid to choosing and
 managing brokers, financial planners, insurance agents, lawyers, tax preparers,
 bankers, and real estate agents / Charles A. Jaffe.
        p. cm.
    Includes index.
    ISBN 0-262-60043-9 (pbk. : alk. paper)
      1. Financial planners.   2. Investment advisors.   3. Finance, Personal.
    4. Financial services industry.   I. Title.

HG179.5 .J34 2001
332—dc21

                                                                        00-050089

For every consumer who has signed up with a financial adviser expecting answers, but come away with self-doubt and more questions.

And for my girls—Susan, Thomson & Whitney

Contents

Acknowledgments   *ix*

1   Starting your search for help   *1*

2   A pocketful of money beats a mouthful of excuses   *9*

3   Recruit advisers before you need them   *17*

4   Overcoming the sins of commission   *23*

5   Do you want your mother's decorator? A guide to referrals   *29*

6   Friends don't let friends become clients, most of the time   *37*

7   Defining a match made in heaven   *43*

8   Your first meeting with an adviser   *51*

9   Swimming through alphabet soup   *61*

10   They're smarter than I am; how do I keep control?   *67*

11   Getting blood from a stone; how to get good answers
     from references   *75*

12   Can my computer replace traditional advisers?   *83*

13   Hiring a financial planner   *91*

14   Hiring a broker   *113*

15   Picking an online broker   *141*

16   Hiring an insurance agent   *149*

17   Hiring an accountant or tax preparer/tax planner   *167*

18   Hiring a lawyer   *187*

19   Hiring a real estate agent   *207*

20   Hiring a banker   *233*

21   How to get a bunch of individuals to function as one unit   *247*

22   Utility infielders; can one adviser handle two jobs?   *257*

23   Breaking up is hard to do   *263*

The Last Word   *269*

Appendix 1: State and federal securities regulators   *273*

Appendix 2: State insurance commissioners/independent insurance agents associations   *283*

Appendix 3: Tax preparer/CPA organizations   *295*

Appendix 4: State bar associations   *301*

Appendix 5: State Boards of Realtors   *307*

Appendix 6: Online consumer resources   *313*

Index   **319**

Acknowledgments

Just as most people can use a team of advisers to secure their financial future, so did it take a team of people to make this book a reality. Several teams, actually.

In almost everything I have done in my career, first credit has gone to Ripley Hotch, my one-time editor, long-time mentor, role model and friend. Ripley helped me start my career in newspapers, then helped me start writing for magazines, then convinced me to do *The Right Way* as my first book. I'm not sure if I should thank him or beat him up, but he kept promising me that reaching the finish line would be worth the journey and he has not yet been proven wrong.

Next, comes the team from *The Boston Globe*, most notably my editor Cheryl Appel, who I insisted on working with in revising this book. She is as fine an editor, person and friend as I know in business journalism, and my columns and *The Right Way* both benefit immensely from her involvement.

Also at the *Globe*, business editor Peter Mancusi (and his predecessor Larry Edelman, who encouraged me to start this project when he was my boss) gets credit for giving me the freedom to do work that I believe in, and for letting me tackle an effort of this scope without fear that my day job would suffer for it. Anne Eisenmenger, Alison Bethel and Maria Shao—my editors during the time the first edition was written—also were instrumental in keeping my work on track.

Then comes the MIT Press team, most notably Victoria Richardson Warneck, editor of the first edition of *The Right Way* and the one who got revisions rolling (before she moved on). I never got to work with Ann Sochi, who left MIT Press soon after convincing me to sign on, but

I am forever indebted to her for offering me the chance to write about whatever personal finance subject I thought most needed coverage. The rest of the crew at MIT Press also is superb; when I hear horror stories from author friends about their publishers (and such stories are common), I am reminded of how lucky I am to have the support of such a fine company.

Of course, no journalist comes without a team of sources. I am privileged to talk every day with the brightest minds in the investment and money management world. I have quoted many of these experts throughout the book, but many more helped form the opinions and ideas you will read here. This legion of people is too big to mention individually; suffice it to say that if you talked with me about financial planning from 1995 and 2000, you are likely to see yourself in here somewhere, and I thank you for the input.

Then there is the home team, my friends and family. My father, father-in-law and brother are my test audience, the designated readers who let me know if my projects are on the right track. The first edition of this book never would have been completed had it not been for Jenny Lamont Johnson, who let me use her Harvard apartment (once the home of T.S. Eliot) so that I could go on long uninterrupted writing-and-cigar binges.

The single biggest contributor to this effort—or any of my work—is my wife Susan, who is most affected by the strains of my additional, not-for-the-Globe writing projects, but who shoulders her burdens without adding pressure to the process. Her contributions are intangible—except for the phone numbers and web sites she fact-checked—yet also crucial and cherished.

Lastly, I owe a special debt to the people who read my columns (as well as those who read the first edition of this book), people who write or call me with feedback, who stop me to talk at the mall or in the airport, and who generally share their stories with me every week in the hope that I can impart some wisdom that might help them navigate choppy financial waters. Along with the people who have heard me talk on the subject of choosing financial advisers—an audience I am grateful to have, and one that has contributed mightily to improving this book—those calls and letters put a face to a problem that had been unaddressed, which made me realize that a book like this one was necessary. I am forever grateful to those readers for their voice, inspiration, insight and dedication to my work; they make all of the effort worthwhile.

1   *Starting your search for help*

From the time we are old enough to spend money, we start picking financial advisers.

It starts with emulating our parents' habits, or deciding not to. It goes on to school days, when we caucus with the other kids about what is cool and on what we "must" spend our money.

By the time we reach adulthood, there are plenty of direct and tangential influences on how we manage money, ranging from the media to friends and family to the people we meet every day.

Each of those connections is a *de facto* adviser.

The lone person with the responsibility for managing your affairs, however, remains the same. It's you.

So take a good look at your needs, interests and lifestyle. Over the course of a lifetime, at the very least you will need to manage investments; secure and work out loans; buy or sell a house; insure that home, your property and family against catastrophic losses; develop a plan to pass that home and your investments along to heirs; and pay taxes on the whole thing.

A lot of that you can do on your own, so long as you have the interest and can develop sufficient expertise to represent yourself. Between Internet sites, personal finance books, seminars and adult-education classes, there is no shortage of knowledge available to help you develop your own expertise.

Yet even that pool of information may not be enough to make you feel comfortable doing all of your financial chores without expert supervision, even if that consists of no more than a routine examination of your strategy to be sure it is on track and covers all the bases.

Say hello to a broker or financial adviser, banker, real estate agent, insurance agent, lawyer and/or estate planner, and a tax preparer or accountant.

Given the likelihood you will need some or all of these advisers at some point during your lifetime, it's important you learn the right way to hire them.

The hiring process starts with the idea that you will "shop" for financial help, the same way you shop around for a car, refrigerator, home or any big-ticket item.

I'm always amazed that people spend more time researching a new microwave oven than checking into the background of the person who will determine a big chunk of their financial future. Presumably, the difference is that no one fears offending the microwave with tough personal questions.

Shopping for financial services, from tax preparation to investment advice, is no different than purchasing any other commodity. There are certain key factors to consider:

Price

It's not the most important factor on everyone's list, but it is always a key consideration. No one, no matter how wealthy, has the ability to say "cost is no object" when it comes to his or her financial affairs; that is how large fortunes unravel in lurid tales of greed, fraud or ineptitude.

No one thinks twice about eyeballing a can of peas for a price check, or even about getting an estimate before hiring a contractor to do some home repairs. Yet people get scared about whether they can ask a lawyer or financial planner how he bills for his services, as if somehow that professional would explode into an "If you have to ask, you can't afford me!" rage.

Well, maybe you can't afford him. Or maybe you simply don't want to. But if you ask the question and a financial adviser gets angry about it, then you know right away that this is not the person for you. Smart financial advisers of all stripes are happy to explain their charges and justify the reasons behind their rates; it is up to you to decide if you want to pay the freight.

A price check also is important because fees and payment structures can vary tremendously from one adviser to the next. I have seen two financial planners in the same town, both providing similar sample plans and advice, charge rates that varied by hundreds of dollars per hour. The difference, in cases like that, may be the overhead of the planning firm (someone has to pay for the fancy office), the years of experience and building up the practice for the more costly adviser, or it may simply be they are charging what they think the market will bear.

What's important is that you seek out a price that you feel good about paying—because that encourages you to use the services regularly and develop a relationship with the provider—and that you understand exactly how the adviser will be compensated and are comfortable with that means of payment.

Quality

The toughest area of financial advice to assess, it is quality that requires doing the bulk of your work in order to be happy with the outcome.

There is a natural tendency to equate high price with high quality, as in "this broker doesn't deal with low net worth clients, so he must be good." Conversely, any adviser who comes on the cheap must be suspect.

Not so fast.

Those are assumptions, not truisms.

There are many big-dollar advisers with a slew of unhappy customers in their wake. The size of their fees is more the result of their time in the business and, in some cases, overblown reputations that allow them to charge as if they are providing exclusive service.

At the other end of the spectrum, there are plenty of lower-paid advisers whose biggest crime is inexperience, lack of time developing a client base or simply poor marketing. It's important to remember that almost everyone in financial advisory roles today started out doing grunt work such as cold calls or posting business cards on bulletin boards to get customers.

The quality of financial advice is not a quantitative issue, although many people try to make it one. You can not measure the quality of expertise simply on the highest rate of return on your money or more deductions on your tax return, because those goals can be accomplished in bad ways such as taking on too much risk or deducting items the IRS is likely to disallow. Empirically speaking, advisers who make huge claims about the numbers they can deliver on your behalf tend to be advisers with a high number of dissatisfied customers in their past.

You will determine the quality of a financial adviser in several ways: professional accomplishments and credentials, satisfied customers, a record of integrity, the perceived value of the work and gut feeling. Paying for advice boils down to purchasing trust, and your gut feeling about someone will go a long way toward determining how comfortable you are with him in the future.

In financial services, as in refrigerators, there is some name-brand consciousness that gives big-name accounting firms recognition that a sole practitioner won't get or makes H&R Block more trusted than "Joe's Tax Service." But the difference between large and small firms often has to do with size and advertising budget more than with quality; you will be better off focusing on ability than on pre-conceived notions.

To find advisers who really are worth keeping, you will have to sort through all kinds of fancy packaging. Some of the dumbest financial advice I have ever heard has been dispensed in the most posh offices in the country, the personal finance equivalent to having a fancy Italian restaurant serve you a frozen pizza.

Need

A critical factor in most of your other purchases, need plays a direct role in your choice of advisers. The more advanced your needs, the more you will tilt your decision-making process to paying the full ticket price.

That's why you must do a real needs assessment, a self-examination of what you want in an advisory relationship and what you expect from your banker, insurance agent or other counselor.

This is particularly important in financial services, in which so many products are "sold," rather than purchased based on the consumer's knowledge. I have yet to meet anyone who says they woke up one morning knowing they **needed** to buy "variable life insurance." Most were looking to increase their coverage safety net and, perhaps, find a savings vehicle, when they bumped into an adviser pushing the policies. Only years later have they started second-guessing their decisions.

I equate purchasing financial help to the first time I bought a computer, when a young salesman simply could not stop pushing the "fast printer," which would knock out my papers more quickly, all for just a few hundred dollars that I could not afford to pay. Faster printing sounded great, but I simply didn't need it; paying for it might not have been a waste of money, but it would have made me less comfortable with the overall deal I negotiated, and that loss in satisfaction might have made the entire experience a downer.

Knowing your needs and being able to explain them to an adviser will go a long way toward ensuring that you hire people who can remain good advisers for the rest of your lifetime.

Affordability

This is different from price, because here you decide how an adviser's costs fit into your budget, and look for low-cost alternatives.

Most people don't realize there is financial assistance at virtually every price point, from ultra-discount to through-the-nose chic.

On the low end, it might be free advice offered by a public agency such as the Internal Revenue Service, or a consultation using toll-free hotlines that hook you up with a financial planner or accountant who bills you on a per-minute basis for the advice provided. The upper end of the scale includes some of the top planners in the country, who charge hundreds of dollars just for an initial interview—regardless of whether you hire them to work for you—and money managers who take a big slice of the assets they run for you each year.

It is not enough to simply look at what you are being charged, you must see how it fits into your budget. If you want ongoing financial planning services but can not afford a $300-an-hour planner, then you will have two shopping choices: either you change your expectations about how often you actually work with this adviser, or you set your sights on a lower-priced adviser who can meet your quality expectations and still deliver the service you need.

If neither of those options is pretty, then consider doing it yourself or using a service that is less customized for the individual, such as those offered via many financial-advice Web sites. Remember, too, that if you decide to be your own adviser after you have an established need for the services of others, it may be too late to go it alone.

You may lust after your neighbor's financial planner—the one who helped him buy the BMW and put in the swimming pool—but you may not be able to afford that adviser, and you will be a lot better off picking someone whose price is better aligned with your budget.

The product itself

In the case of financial services, it's not quite as static as purchasing a computer, when you can see the hardware. Still, whenever possible, examine the hardware that is available.

For example, if you are working with an insurance agent, you will want one who deals only with high-grade companies. In the stock arena, if you are paying for a full-service broker, you want to know how many top-flight analysts—called industry all-stars—are with the firm. Similarly, you will want to know if brokers are discouraged from using anything but house opinions, which means they might stifle their own intuition and knowledge so that they can sell the stocks in which the brokerage firm is a market-maker. (They may get paid extra for selling those stocks, too.)

If your selections are limited, you must review the available products to see whether the firm is realistically capable of meeting your changing long-term needs. Nothing is worse than feeling your adviser can't deliver—or isn't delivering—because he doesn't have the kind of high-quality product you need to succeed.

Services/Features

Here you determine what to expect for your money, not from a qualitative standpoint but in simple "here's what you get from me" terms.

Unless you have a lot of money savvy, the adviser will be educating you on what he offers. Even if you think you know what to expect from an adviser, learn about everything available. Most people consider a banker simply the person who holds deposits, for example, without knowing that some bankers offer valuable trust services.

Just as you would want a refrigerator salesman to explain the different ways the removable shelves can improve your life and allow you to decide whether it is worth paying for a second "crisper," so can you talk to a prospective financial adviser about what the relationship is going to be like and what you can expect. Will it be regular phone calls and the ability to chat without receiving a bill every time you need a consultation because you anticipate a major event in your life? Will the broker accept your calls whenever the market makes you nervous? Does the accountant or financial adviser offer a regular newsletter to customers, and is that publication merely a pass-along from a national office or does it reflect the adviser's feelings about the market, economy, law changes, investment strategies and more?

Before signing up with any adviser, determine what he is offering and match that against your needs and desires.

All of that research—determining what a financial adviser's services cost and what you can afford to pay, what the services are and what you need, and whether he has the ability to deliver on his promises—simply requires that you think of financial services like every other good or service you buy, no different from hiring a plumber or a television repairman except that you feel a bit out of your league.

To ease that problem, do your leg work in advance of your need, so that you will have plenty of time and won't have to rush a decision.

Robert Clark, editor-in-chief at Morningstar Inc., once told me most people deal with a lot of financial counselors over the course of a lifetime, typically taking advice from one, then moving to another and another, without ever establishing a cohesive plan. Bouncing between advisers leads to short-term thinking and mistakes, creating a hodge-podge of holdings and sabotaging the investment portfolio.

If people did the work up front, Clark noted, they could pick one adviser with whom they could work comfortably for a lifetime.

If you want advice and advisers who last you a lifetime, it's time to get to work.

2 *A pocketful of money beats a mouthful of excuses*

Life is what is speeding by us while we put things off.

Nowhere is that more true than in our finances, where time truly is money.

You can see that in virtually every advisory relationship. If you save or invest a little bit today and let it grow, you will need to put away a lot less tomorrow. If you take care of your insurance needs today, you avoid the risk of having no coverage in your time of need. If you talk to a tax preparer in June, you can turn tax preparation into actual tax planning. Talking to a lawyer or estate planner can assure that your heirs don't lose a fortune to inheritance taxes or suffer through emotional times burdened by demanding financial decisions. If you meet with a real estate agent, you can find out how to get the most from your home while you own it, instead of making savvy property moves only as you prepare to sell.

There are plenty of excuses for not doing any of those things right now, but there is no excuse for not hiring the help needed to manage money wisely. Putting off today for tomorrow is not a fair trade when it comes to your money; your investments have a day less to compound, and you spend another day playing without a financial safety net.

So now you have purchased this book and are either about to hire advisers or are evaluating the ones you have.

The right way to pick advisers requires a lot of discipline and attention to detail. It is a subjective decision in which your gut will determine a lot but your brain has to know enough to figure out what makes your stomach queasy.

It can be a daunting task.

That is why most people put it off, far beyond the point when they know they need help. They have a pocketful of excuses for why they haven't hired someone, often using these alibis to overcome the internal knowledge that they really need help.

So here are the most common excuses I have heard for NOT hiring financial helpers. If one or more has been part of your thinking, you'll soon see why you need to change your tune:

"I plan to do that stuff myself—when I need to"

This is a hard-to-overcome alibi, because we all like being self-reliant and believe we can do things ourselves. Plus, this raises the why-should-I-pay-for-help issue.

No one really *wants* to pay for financial help, especially when there is so much readily available information out there designed to help us manage our affairs. Invariably, we have neighbors or friends who seem to be living proof that everyone can manage money on their own (and do well at it) provided they commit the time and effort.

Likewise, plumbing is something everyone can do.

You can buy do-it-yourself books on fixing leaky pipes or replacing copper tubing, get all the necessary tools—if you don't already have them—at the local hardware store, watch experts on the Home Improvement Channel and probably save a lot of money taking care of the problem on your own.

But for some reason, there is neither stigma nor second-thought attached to calling a plumber when the sink is stopped or the shower won't drain. In time of need, most people may pull out a plunger, but they will pick up the phone if the problem can't be solved in just a few minutes.

Just as a plumber can save money by fixing things before leaks and clogs force major repairs, so can an adviser help clean up money problems before they become major.

Another key reason why many people try to do their financial work on their own is that they want "ideal" services.

To the average consumer, the ideal financial plan (or insurance or tax plan) has three qualities: it is cheap, easy and successful.

You can get all of those things in your financial relationships, but almost never more than two of them at any one time.

You can get hassle-free, no-time-involved planning that carries you toward your financial goals, for example, but it won't be cheap. Conversely, if you do all your own planning, it will be free and might be successful, but it won't be easy.

It is very easy to let things slide, to stick with what you know and are comfortable with and to avoid mounting problems that you have never before addressed.

A perfect example is life insurance. Most people starting out don't need it; you should only insure what you can't afford to lose or replace, and singles or young marrieds without a lot of assets frequently don't require coverage.

But that has a way of changing as marriage, a home, family and other issues creep into the picture.

The result is a person who knows he needs insurance, but hasn't done anything about it—until he gets a call from a salesman or bumps into someone at a business lunch. He takes this chance meeting as a sign that Providence has smiled upon him, giving him someone who can address his insurance concerns just at his time of need.

Hundreds of people have told me their personal version of this story, usually with the same ending: disaster.

Hiring help does not mean giving up on doing it yourself; it means shoring up the areas in which you lack the confidence to make decisions. If you know you need to work on one area of your finances, ask why you aren't doing it right now—or at least educating yourself so you will be ready to do it on your own when the time comes.

And as for waiting until you have a need to hire an adviser, the issue is whether you will be smart enough to recognize that moment—and whether you can get appropriate service in that moment of need. It's pretty easy to figure out when you absolutely must have a relationship with a real estate agent, because you have taken a new job or decided to uproot the family or are being transferred.

It's a lot harder to recognize just how your insurance needs have changed or how your investment strategy is inadequate.

Studies show, for example, that the vast majority of people with retirement savings in a 401(k) plan are too conservative for their own time horizon. That means they may be saving "enough money," but they have not invested it aggressively enough to build a sufficient nest egg.

Presumably, many of these people feel they do not need help allocating their retirement savings. They expect their time of financial planning need to come five or 10 years before they retire, when they need to figure out how to protect what they have and save enough to retire on their own time schedules.

What they will find out when they hire that adviser is that they have fallen short of their goals, and that they will have to save more aggressively or perhaps put off their retirement date in order to secure the future.

If you haven't hired financial help because you intend to do it yourself, consider how long you have had that intention. If you have not done real financial planning—developing a clear program of setting goals and managing assets to meet them—you should consider whether you really are a "do-it-yourselfer." Assembling a portfolio of investments is not planning, nor is reading magazines or newspapers; if the financial chores, the real groundwork, has remained undone for a while, you're procrastinating. (You're not, as one consumer tried to explain to me "positioning [yourself] to start tomorrow.")

If you expect to hire help "when I need it," then chances are you need help now but the situation has not turned desperate.

"I don't know enough and am afraid of being ripped off"

Scams are a legitimate fear. And it's always scary hiring an adviser against whom your level of knowledge may make you feel inadequate.

If anything goes wrong—even if it is the kind of simple investment misjudgment that periodically impairs the greatest stock-picking minds—you are likely to feel taken.

But the chances are slim that you will hire a scoundrel, especially if you know enough to remain in control of the situation and have all of your choices spelled out to you. The rule of thumb in financial relationships is very simple: Never do anything you don't understand.

That being the case, you are hiring someone to explore your options. You are then making choices from the menu prepared by the adviser. As in a restaurant, if your waiter can't adequately explain the way a meal is prepared or describe how it tastes, you should stick with something you feel certain will be satisfying.

If the waiter suggests you are making a bad choice—that he or she knows a lot more about this menu than you do and knows exactly what you should eat—then he is trying to control your behavior. That's when it's time to find a restaurant where the staff has better table manners.

If you maintain an active role, regardless of your expertise, you greatly reduce the risk of being swindled. But not having a world of financial knowledge doesn't mean you can't manage a team of experts. It simply means you have to be more pro-active and possibly more demanding of the players you select.

Not hiring financial advisers is indeed a great way to ensure you don't get scammed. But falling short of your financial goals because of your own mismanagement is almost as painful as being ripped off; careful preparation and background checks can virtually eliminate the chance of being suckered by a rogue adviser.

"Those people wouldn't be interested in working with me right now"

The other version of this excuse is "I'm not wealthy enough to afford (or need) help."

This excuse is debunked as follows: You never know until you try.

No one has ever said financial help must be expensive. It certainly can be, but it depends on the level of service you are looking for and the mindset of the adviser.

These days, there are many discount providers, pre-paid plans, employer-sponsored assistance programs and more than can help you out. But whether you are paying a flat rate of $69 for a "fiscal physical" offered by a financial planner or $400 an hour for detailed, individualized service, or a fee equal to 1 percent of your assets annually, there is probably an adviser who can help you regardless of your current financial situation.

"There is help out there for everyone at every income level," says David H. Diesslin, former president of the National Association of Personal Financial Advisors and head of Diesslin & Associates, a Houston-based financial planning firm. "But it is not always easy to find the right match—the person who does what you want and need, who thinks you make an attractive client and who will do it at a cost you consider reasonable. If you are flexible, you will be able to find people who can do a good job for you."

You can bet that the hotshot broker with the $100,000 minimum account is not interested in placing your first-ever $500 purchase of stocks. But there will be brokers in the very same firm for whom that order would represent an inroad to a relationship and a start toward what they hope will someday be a $100,000-plus client (namely, you).

There are plenty of established advisers out there who take on small clients at reasonable prices. And while experience is a wonderful thing, it is also important to remember that every star adviser started out as a raw rookie and worked up.

As a result, if you have a concern about an area of your finances and worry that you can't take care of it yourself, you can both afford and find someone who will help you.

There are financial professionals—in all areas of expertise—whose interest is in building a clientele. Just as you are looking to develop financial relationships, so are they—and that means they value some things a bit more highly than the money you can put in their pocket today.

The smart real estate agent, for example, doesn't just want to sell you a house now, but wants to be in on the deal the next time you decide to move. The local banker doesn't just want your checking account and credit card business, he wants your mortgage, college savings, trust funds and your children's birthday-gift money.

One of the first rules that applies to any financial adviser: if he or she loses interest when you "run out of money," dump him for someone who cares. Anyone who you feel you can't "afford" to work with or who loses interest in you because you don't generate enough money obviously is not a good fit.

Even small clients represent big opportunities for advisers. If your money and earnings potential grows, it translates to future business and enhanced opportunities for the adviser; if you are satisfied with his service, your referrals could become future clients.

Don't undervalue yourself.

"I don't want people meddling in my business"

Good advisers don't mess things up for you, they work with you.

Ironically, most people get advice from meddling-but-well-meaning friends and relatives, as opposed to a financial adviser who is paid to come in and analyze the situation.

There are stock tips from people you meet at cocktail parties, the post office, the hairdresser, and the supermarket checkout line, and from strangers on the Internet. You can call a radio station or write a newspaper columnist or detail your situation to friends and family, all of whom will offer advice that is less-than-individualized and that may not be expert.

These people aren't considered meddlers because you still make the decisions.

Hiring advisers arms you to make those choices yourself. The adviser makes sure you understand the options, the potential consequences and, hopefully, the alternatives.

The chances of making a mistake are, therefore, significantly reduced.

That's not having people meddle in your affairs, it's having them counsel you—and it's worth encouraging.

"My father (or friend or other relative) will tell me whom to go to"

Every financial situation is different. What works for your neighbor or Uncle Bob or the person at the next desk is not necessarily right for you.

Chances are pretty good that your financial situation is a whole lot different than that of your parents (or children). Say, for example, your father is in retirement. His stockbroker has a lot of clients who are retired; you, on the other hand, are just entering your prime earning years and need to be more aggressive than the rest of the broker's clients. Just because he is a good broker for a conservative set does not make him right for you.

Most people find their financial advisers through word-of-mouth, and referrals are a big part of the process, but you have to do the legwork yourself.

Again, think in terms of services with which you are more familiar. Would you go to your father's barber or mother's hairstylist? Would you trust your brother's mechanic, even if he doesn't normally work on the type of car you own? Would you let your neighbors decorate your home?

Probably not.

Turn to others for referrals and ideas, but be prepared to go your own route. When it comes to financial advice, one size does not fit all.

"I don't have time to interview people right now"

This discussion has come full circle, back to time being money. In this case, if you don't have the time to hire financial helpers the right way, you run the risk of losing money to people who either are frauds or just aren't good at this stuff.

With the exception of lawyers, every other realm of financial advice requires virtually no specialized training and knowledge. If you want to be a tax preparer or a financial planner, for example, you need only hang out your shingle (and, maybe, complete a registration form with a state agency). Some states require that certain types of advisers pass an exam to gain their license, but even this is no guarantee of formal education.

The investment in picking the right adviser will be rewarded not only with a good relationship and sound money management, but also with time savings. In the future, you won't be wasting time trying to resolve disputes, pick a different adviser or clean up for the mistakes of the adviser you picked in a hurry.

"I don't know how to select an adviser"

Well, that's what this book is for. Keep reading—or keep the book handy when hiring new counselors—and this excuse should evaporate.

The problem with all of these excuses is that they become the rationale for future failure. They are the reason someone who doesn't get the right selling price for a house blames the agent—"I signed up with her because Joe and Marge had such a good experience"—or why someone who discovers he made bad financial-planning decisions blames his insurance agent ("He said he could advise me on investing, and I didn't want to have to go out and hire someone else").

What we want to avoid most is the failure to reach our goals and control our life's savings. If you fall short in those arenas, no alibis will be satisfactory.

3 *Recruit advisers before you need them*

Mark Twain once wrote that a banker is a fellow who "lends you his umbrella when the sun is shining and wants it back the minute it begins to rain."

That description is apt for a lot of financial relationships. There are plenty of people who are happy to deal with you when it will make them a quick buck, but who aren't going to be there for you when the time comes to make tough decisions.

With that in mind, shopping for financial help becomes more difficult when you have a pressing need.

If you have just inherited a large sum of money, for example, every financial adviser in your neighborhood is likely to be clamoring after you. When you don't have that money—or maybe don't yet know how much you will someday inherit—finding a planner to help you devise an investment strategy is not nearly so easy.

One common reason for troubled advisory relationships is the selection of an adviser at the wrong time in a consumer's life, either when the pressure is on because a large sum is involved or a deadline looms, or when there isn't time to do adequate research on prospective advisers.

But think of the consequences of forging a relationship with an adviser in the crucible of an immediate need for service:

▪ You could learn that you disagree with your real estate agent on the pricing of your house once the first offer has been received.

▪ You could discover that your bank relies exclusively on formulas to make its decisions, right at the time that you need money and your finances don't fit into the bank's equation.

▪ You could find out that the broker whose eyes lit up at the prospect of investing your inheritance has taken more risks than you are comfortable with.

▪ Your tax preparer could play a little fast and loose with the rules, a strategy you might not discover until you are on your way to the audit.

Choosing any type of financial adviser the right way means interviewing at least three candidates. In some cases—most often financial planners, tax preparers and insurance agents—it could easily take five interviews before you find someone with whom you are comfortable.

It's impossible to do that kind of work in a hurry, which is why most people never do it at all.

Instead, they go out and talk to, say, a financial planner, hear a bunch of stuff that sounds good and figure they have heard enough. Almost every planner I know is willing to let potential clients come in for an interview, but I know of almost no financial planners who have gone through these interviews and then didn't get the client.

That tells me one of two things: Either the planners I know are more impressive than their peers during interviews or, more likely, the clients never bothered to talk to other candidates.

When I get a chance to talk to readers, invariably they want to know the name of the one planner I would recommend. I don't give that name for several reasons:

1. By contract, I am not allowed to work with a financial planner in New England—it could be perceived as a tacit endorsement and, therefore, a conflict of interest—so while I have reviewed the work and checked the background of the advisers I use as sources, none has ever handled my money.

There is a big difference between talking to the media and performing for a client.

2. No matter my selection, the adviser may not be appropriate given the circumstances of the person asking for my help. Since I am never intimately familiar with the finances of readers, there is no way I could make a match I could feel comfortable with.

Personally, I would pick one adviser for my mother, a different one for my father and a third adviser if the job were to manage their money together.

But the important thing isn't why I don't recommend planners, it's why people ask for names in the first place. Invariably, they want to skip the background checks—figuring my endorsement means the adviser is okay—and take the fast route out of the selection process. I have heard more than a few groans when I say that the right way to choose a planner is to start by interviewing three of them.

By failing to forge relationships in advance—when there is no sense of urgency—and instead hiring an adviser in a pinch, they are likely to find that they have applied a Band-Aid to their financial woes rather than discovered a cure.

The time to develop a rapport with an adviser is when you have little or no need for service, when you can ask questions without fear that the counselor will take offense and leave you in a lurch.

Your multiple interviews don't have to be within one week. You can network with friends, family and current advisers to get an idea of which specialists to call and then spread the selection process over a month or two; keep notes on the first interviews so you can remember how you felt after the sessions.

Similarly, you should always be able to make an excuse to visit or interview or chat with potential or current advisers. When my wife Susan and I moved from Pennsylvania to Massachusetts, we knew we would need to hire a local attorney to handle our eventual home purchase, update our wills and more. We have a terrific attorney in Pennsylvania, but even he acknowledged we would want someone local to handle the basics.

Throughout the course of our transition to the Bay State, we had a few papers that needed to be notarized. Susan used that paperwork as an opportunity to interview various local attorneys, who would notarize the documents for free; while she had a moment with them, she asked a few questions about the type of work they do, how they handle certain issues and so on.

As we got closer to actually needing a lawyer to review our home purchase contract and refresh the wills, we had a short list of candidates. We did the requisite background checks, arranged for me to ask some questions either by phone or in person and—despite needing a lawyer quickly to review a sudden home offer—didn't rush into a decision.

Not surprisingly, the lawyer we chose was the one who spent the most time visiting with Susan and talking to me. What is surprising— especially because we live in a very small town—is that he was not the attorney recommended to us by friends. They had suggested the other people who made the short list. Had we been rushed into a decision, we probably would have chosen one of those attorneys; in the long run, we would not have been as satisfied to have that lawyer on our team. (From now on, by the way, the new attorney will notarize our signatures whenever necessary, if only because it gives him a reason to chat about any life changes that might require legal maneuverings. In most states, plenty of people can notarize paperwork; we turn a chore into part of our advisory relationship.)

Managing a financial team—and that is essentially what happens once you hire a financial planner, an insurance agent, a tax preparer, lawyer, et. al.—and having relationships with various advisers is not difficult. It's about stepping inside a branch to meet with the banker about financing options on a car or to ask how the Federal Reserve Board's movement on interest rates might affect your ability or desire to refinance your home in the future.

With a broker, it's a call or two inquiring about stock tips you heard, at times when you're not anticipating making changes to your portfolio; with a financial planner, it might be a moment to talk about a mutual fund that both sounds good and seems to fit into your portfolio. With a real estate agent, it is any time you consider making major changes to your house, or when a house sells on your street or in the immediate neighborhood. You should contact your attorney and insurance agent any time there might be a major event in your life, ranging from additional children (or children leaving the nest) to the purchase of new valuables to a change of address.

And in each instance, asking for a breakfast or lunch meeting—especially if the person knows you value him as an adviser—is a great way to develop a rapport. It may be a once-a-year get-together—"Take your broker to lunch" is an old bit of stock market advice—but it gives you an opportunity to talk and brainstorm without the pressure and immediacy of having work in progress.

Throughout the financial services business, specialists break down into two basic categories—"relationship-oriented" and "transaction-oriented."

Later in this book, in Chapter 7, there is a brief discussion of the difference between these two genres of adviser. For now, suffice it to say that recruiting advisers early virtually eliminates the entire group of "transaction-oriented" helpers. Transaction-driven advisers want to make a deal, not chat about what they can do for you at some unnamed point in the future.

These are the folks who lose interest when they find out you can't deliver something for them right now. I call it the "Brendan Byrne" syndrome, an inside joke that dates back to my high school days.

When I was in high school in New Jersey, then-Governor Brendan Byrne came to visit during a campaign run. He flew in by helicopter; it was a big deal for the school and the community. The build-up preceded him for weeks.

Byrne was rushed into the auditorium, where the upper classes were assembled; the lower classes were listening over the intercom. After settling in at the podium, the first thing Byrne asked how many students would be eligible to vote in the next election.

Seven kids raised their hands.

Nine minutes later, Byrne's speech was over and he was out the door.

Byrne, obviously, was transaction-oriented. When we couldn't deliver the votes, we got the five-cent talk instead of the dollar's worth the students and administration hoped for.

Transaction-oriented advisers often betray themselves during the early recruiting process. They are the ones who want to do everything "now," for whom there is never a reason to slow down and reflect when they "have the answer" to your needs. If there is a big enough pot of gold at the end of your rainbow they will stick around and try to close the deal, but it will always feel like a sales pitch, rather than concerned counsel.

By comparison, relationship-oriented advisers are less worried with what your business means to them now. They make the assumption that a relationship will lead to years of work and, as a result, are willing to do the little things now that help you become a lifetime business partner.

It is that attitude you need to foster in order to make your financial relationships blossom.

Let's use your banker as an example.

Banking is a business fraught with formulas. Some banks, for example, won't make auto loans on used cars that are more than five model years old. But say for a moment your car of choice is a 10-year-old Mercedes-Benz with low mileage and a lot of life left.

If you call various banks to get used car loan rates by phone, you routinely will be told that the institutions don't make loans on cars that old. In fact, however, they do—provided they understand the situation better.

If your banker knows you are a good credit risk with a solid payment history and the car is worth the money being loaned to purchase it, the deal will happen. Getting that preferential treatment without hassles and hold-ups generally involves asking for it in advance, going in and talking to your banker about financing options—the same way you should have once discussed the various features on a checking account or the trust services the bank offers.

Without a banker on the team, you will find the car first, then look for a loan, and wind up taking less favorable terms because the institution is bailing you out of a jam rather than being your partner in the purchase.

It's easy to envision similar circumstances with almost every type of financial arrangement in which you are involved.

One of the biggest reasons to have a team assembled is purely for counseling reasons—to get advice when a situation arises. But the reason you can get that sound advice in a pinch from your personal stable of advisers is that all of the players know you, your risk tolerance and your goals.

Lacking that comfort zone—and the time it takes to develop—even the best advisers can blunder and err.

Recruiting advisers early also establishes your management style before big issues hit home, ensuring that advisory relationships will be on your terms when life enters financial crunch-time.

Don't be one of the millions of people who spends more time shopping for or repairing television sets than seeking financial services. Recognize that the advisers you choose have a huge impact on the financial well-being of you and your entire family.

Consumers who hire advisers in a pinch wind up dismissing them later on, moving from one stop-gap helper to the next. They lose faith in their helpers whenever the market turns or when they see something that looks just a little bit better; they chase inferior alternatives and throw away financial plans that can achieve their goals. They are more likely, on average, to get stuck with a fraud or charlatan.

The idea in seeking financial assistance is to make your counselors partners in your success, capable of giving you good advice for years to come.

Don't settle for Mark Twain's banker. Instead, get to know your advisers and take the time to let them know you; it's the only way you can feel comfortable that you will be protected even in the worst of storms.

4   *Overcoming the sins of commission*

There's an old country song in which the singer tells his loved one: "Don't pay the ransom, honey, I've escaped."

When it comes to managing your money, paying for help can feel like paying a ransom. You want to get the object of your payoff—financial security—but can't be sure it will arrive safe and sound and that you won't just lose your money to some thief.

At the same time, escape is a real possibility. You can always do this stuff on your own.

Therein lies the quandary.

On the one hand, that escape is difficult, truly impossible for many.

On the other, no one likes being taken hostage or paying ransom for their safety, and yet they can feel like a prisoner when looking at commissions, management fees and retainers.

The result is that people focus on the payment structure, rather than on the process and results. They go to great lengths to avoid commissions.

I'm all in favor of getting things cheaply and paying no more than you have to for financial counsel, but many people who brag about not paying for advice can't be quite so boastful about performance. They rely on hearsay, cocktail party gossip or luck to make and manage their money; all are sources of information sure to be disappointing at one point or another.

Or, in the alternative, they avoid the fee they don't want to pay— usually an upfront commission—and wind up paying more on the back end. For example, mutual fund C-class shares carry no upfront sales charges, which often make them more popular than shares that have a sales load paid to the selling agent. Yet these shares carry higher costs—with the additional burden being money that compensates the adviser—that are almost certain to be more costly in terms of dollars paid over the life of the investment. In short, you may avoid the sales charge but pay more to the agent if you own the fund long enough.

When it comes to financial assistance, the idea is not necessarily to get everything at low or no cost. You simply should want to get what you pay for and to pay appropriately for what you get.

Somewhere between managing money on the cheap and paying through the nose lies the ideal payment structure for the average consumer.

There are several ways to pay for financial help. Bankers typically are not paid directly for their efforts but have their pay built into loans and other basic services. Bank advisers, however, may work on a commission basis if they are dispensing more sophisticated advice. Tax preparers, by comparison, work almost entirely on a fee-for-service basis, getting paid either for time spent preparing a return or by-the-form, by which each completed piece of paperwork is worth a set price.

Most real estate agents work entirely on commission, while brokers, financial planners and insurance agents can be paid in several ways, from commissions to a fee based on a percentage of the money involved in the transaction to a flat hourly fee. Some hybrid payment structures, such as "fee offset," combine flat payments with commissions.

The big reason people hate commissions is that it seems impossible to get a fair deal. Here is someone pushing a product that is supposedly for your benefit, yet the only way he can make money on the deal is if you buy. That removes a lot of the seller's incentive to watch out for you; in some cases, the adviser's profit motive may run exactly opposite to your best interests.

Because so many people find commission sales disarming, the financial services industry has been moving toward flat fees. These are pitched as safe, no-conflict ways to do business.

Wrong.

The most important thing to remember about paying for advice is: *No matter the fee structure, there are potential conflicts of interest in virtually every type of advisory relationship.*

While the vast majority of advisers are honest and will put your best interest first, you must always be on guard against conflicts of interest.

In an hourly rate relationship, the conflict is obvious: it is in the best interest of the adviser to rack up the hours. Even if the number is limited, it may seem like a lot to you. ("Could it really take two hours of a lawyer's time to prepare a no-frills, simple will?")

In the piece-of-the-deal or contingency arrangement, the adviser's desire to maximize his cut sometimes runs counter to your best interests. (As a home seller, for example, your adviser might turn down reasonable offers hoping for something better that may not come; likewise, a lawyer might gamble for a better judgment and end up losing a quick-but-less-lucrative settlement.)

And in the assets-under-management scenario, conflicts are easy to envision, since the adviser wants to maximize the assets he manages. (Say you inherit money and are torn between investing the money and paying off your mortgage. It is in the adviser's best interest to get that money under management—where it increases the adviser's fee— which might create a bias against conservative options such as paying off the mortgage. And some fee-only advisers have justified their ongoing fees by encouraging unnecessary portfolio moves rather than sticking to a buy-and-hold posture that might tend to be more lucrative in the end.)

In other words, no matter the payment structure, an adviser may have a reason to want to do something untrustworthy.

Accepting responsibility for that vigilance means giving up any embarrassment you might feel asking about compensation, the fear of the snooty "If you have to ask, you can't afford me" routine. Instead, compensation talk is a required part of your interviews. Any financial adviser who is not forthcoming about disclosing both the ways he gets paid and the actual dollars involved is not worth trusting.

Armed with cost information and having interviewed a few practitioners, you can make sensible decisions. You may have found a tax preparer who is cheap, for example, but you might prefer the experience and education level of an accountant who costs a bit more. Conversely, you might look at an accountant and an enrolled agent—another form of tax preparer—and decide you do not need to pay a premium to have a super-expert handle your ordinary, plain vanilla tax return.

Once you break financial help down to its costs—no matter whether the payout is in the form of fees or commissions—you will see that these services are not unlike many everyday tasks that you currently choose to pay for help with.

What's more, you will see that the form of payment is not necessarily tied to performance. Many people want to invest only in no-load mutual funds, because paying an upfront sales charge cuts into performance; but if you go to a fee-only adviser who invests in no-load funds but who takes a chunk of your assets as payment, you have the exact same net outcome. As a result, it's not the load or lack of a load that determines performance, but the skill of the money manager combined with the cost structure of the fund and any advice.

Let's compare financial services to another business that affects almost everyone, namely automotive repair.

For a moment, let's pretend magazines such as *Money* and *Kiplinger's Personal Finance* actually are *Auto Mechanic* and *Car and Driver*. Instead of stories on mutual funds and certificates of deposit, articles focus on assembling the proper roadside emergency kit or five ways to a faster and neater oil change; the ads are for sparkplugs and fuel injectors.

Now we add in the mindset of many people who frown on hiring an adviser. In this case, they become folks who hate paying a mechanic. (I compare the work of most financial advisers to that of most auto mechanics, in spite of the angry letters I get from the financial services community.)

What we are left with is the atmosphere surrounding financial services today, except that the currency is cars instead of dollars.

In the end, there would be a group of people who really know what they are talking about, a group of people trying to get along with inadequate knowledge—discernable by cars that run but make a lot of noise and break down a little too frequently—and a group of people who pay for help to fix their cars and have few or no car troubles as a result. (This last group might still wash its own cars but would leave the big stuff to the pros.)

In that kind of circumstance, your should hope to wind up either in the first or last group, knowledgeable enough to really take advantage of available resources or smart enough to know your shortcomings and pay for help before messing things up on your own.

One more key point: For most people, a car is only their third- or fourth-biggest investment in life, behind a home and a retirement/college savings portfolio at the very least.

So now consider the real-life logic in someone who has no trouble paying an auto mechanic but who can't stomach the thought of paying a financial counselor to watch his investment vehicles.

Assuming he needs help to fix his portfolio, his decision makes no sense.

Neither does picking or avoiding any type of financial adviser solely on the basis of cost or method of payment. Once you have identified your need, the object is to find counselors who will take care of it.

Cost is an object, but it's not THE object.

Instead, look at what you are getting for the money and determine a reasonable balance. If someone wants a big fat fee for selling you a mutual fund without developing an asset allocation plan or providing other advisory services, then you are paying a lot of money for something you could accomplish just as easily with a $19 piece of software, a $40 magazine subscription or maybe a free posting on a computer bulletin board.

But if an adviser completes a needs analysis, determines a plan of action that will get you from where you are now to your financial goals, he deserves some level of compensation.

Getting back to that auto-mechanic analogy, you may decide you like one mechanic better than another because he speaks in plain English and you believe his repairs are of a superior quality. You will pay a premium for that level of service, even though you might know in your heart you could be satisfied with lower-grade service at a discounted price.

When it comes to hiring financial help, the issue is not price, but rather a combination of service, quality and cost. By comparison-shopping for advisers, you can get past the cost issue and look at the bigger picture. You're not going to like paying for advice any more—it may still feel like ransom—but you will have a better idea that the "goods" will be delivered when you pay your bill.

5   *Do you want your mother's decorator?*
A guide to referrals

Shortly after I began writing this book, my wife and I started asking friends for the names of contractors who had done work on their hardwood floors.

Quickly, we had a short list of four names.

We took notes as our friends bragged about their contractor's best attributes.

One was cheap. (Okay, "reasonable" might be a better word.)

One was happy to work on the weekends to get the job done more quickly.

One was "the guy who everyone in town uses."

One "took extra time to do the job right," and didn't charge more when the work took longer than expected.

Presumably, if you were looking at the same kind of refinishing job we were considering, one of those attributes would stand out. Someone would jump to the top of your list, whether it is the guy who costs less—in our home, some of those refinished floors are almost entirely covered by rugs, so cheap is good—or the floor man with the status to get jobs from all of the right people in the community, a kind of blanket endorsement from the town we love.

What was interesting about the list was that it came from close friends, all of whom have a lot in common with one another. They all care enough about the appearance of their home to want quality craftsmanship, they all have lives similar to ours in which refinishing floors is a disruption to be minimized, and they all have limited funds available for this kind of work.

Given that background—and having seen the handiwork of these craftsmen in their homes—there is a good chance any of the contractors could meet our basic needs, albeit some a little bit better than others.

Yet each of our friends made their referral by citing the one thing that stuck out about the contractor.

And that referral, in many ways, was an attempt to justify their own decision, to say they had picked the right floor man because he was hard-working, successful, diligent or reasonable. Our choosing the same floor man—especially if we liked him—would validate their opinion.

Therein lies one of the inherent problems with referrals, the potential for conflict of interest. With referrals, you always have to wonder whether the advice—even when you go out of your way to seek it—really is in your best interest.

With professional referrals—when, say, a banker recommends an accountant—there is reason to question the motives of the advisers involved. There can be referral fees or other incentives involved, either monetary or in the form of returned favors. (This almost always is the case in full-service firms, in which a financial planner wants to keep you in the house when you need, say, an insurance agent.)

Many trade groups are happy to provide you with the names and numbers of counselors in your area. Those groups tend to have a bias toward their own memberships, which means anyone who is not a member or who has not achieved a certain credential won't be included. Your state society of certified public accountants, for instance, will not give you referrals to enrolled agents, a different status of tax preparer that may be better suited—and less expensive—to the tax-preparation needs of many individuals.

And many advisers actually pay for a spot in a referral service, meaning their names go out only if they pony up some dough; there is no qualitative standard applied to these referrals, only a monetary one. What's more, the fact that an adviser needs to pay the freight to advertise on a service for more clients is not necessarily an endorsement for the adviser's business.

Referrals from friends can carry the same judgment-coloring factors, from rewards—advisers who offer gifts or financial incentives for bringing in new customers—to the need to validate personal decisions.

And even if the referral is honest and true, it still may not deliver the right person for you. Think of it in terms of interior decorators. Your mother may have a lovely home, but it might not be your style and taste; when she refers you to her decorator, it's entirely possible that you wind up with someone who does lovely work, as long as it's for your mother.

When it comes to financial advisers, a referral should be a starting point, not a selling point.

My favorite referral story involves a prominent stockbroker in Allentown, Pa., a city where I was once business editor of the local newspaper, *The Morning Call.*

I wanted to dispel the fallacy that great monetary advice is available only in big money-center areas by holding a public stock-picking contest between some prominent local brokers. One of the people who agreed to participate—much to the surprise of almost everyone in the local investment community, I found out later—was a guy I'm going to call Jim. (I'd use his real name, but given how much he wants this episode to go away, I fear the wrath of his lawyers.)

Jim was THE broker in town, the one who handled the local money elite, the name routinely kicked around as the biggest big shot in the neighborhood. He was efficacious and personable, handsome and well-connected. He had the highest minimum in the area for establishing an account and the highest-profile clientele. When I went searching for players in the game, I sought out the recommendations of regional executives, and three of every four referrals were to Jim. I began to question whether any other area brokers were doing significant business.

But we found a few other good stock-pickers and started the year-long process of investing and managing imaginary portfolios for the benefit of our readers. The contest had rules that were a bit stilted—most money managers do not shoot for big short-term results and we were running a competition to see who could achieve the most growth in 12 months—but all of the brokers understood the situation, the same way you would hope they would understand the special needs of an individual client.

When the year was gone, so were a lot of Jim's clients.

Three of the brokers' portfolios had gained more than 40 percent, a fourth more than 20 percent.

Jim had lost nearly 40 percent.

Worse yet, he had done it with the exact same strategy he used for his real-life clients, a particularly dumb move since the vagaries of a one-year competition are a lot different than the long-term investment concerns of a wide-ranging clientele. Those customers started to realize over the course of the year that Jim pigeon-holed all of his customers into the same investments, regardless of their specific needs.

Investment choices that were inappropriate for the imaginary client in our contest were mistakes for some of his real clients, too. His one-strategy-fits-all style had never been apparent to customers until it was in the paper and, by then, Jim couldn't sweet-talk his clients into walking around wearing his poorly fitted portfolio.

Jim's performance was so wretched that his firm—one of the national giants—no longer allows its brokers to take part in such contests without written consent from headquarters.

When the whole episode was finished, Jim told me his greatest mistake was not his strategy so much as participating in the first place. As he put it: "A whale only gets harpooned when it comes to the surface."

But what stuck with me was not just that line or Jim's lack of performance, but rather a comment made to me over breakfast by a prominent local executive, one of the clients who left Jim about nine months into the game. "What the game made me realize," the executive said, "is that he's been losing my money with a smile on his face for a long, long time."

The last time I checked, Jim was selling a lot of insurance and annuity products, mostly to the long-time customers who at least left some of their money with him.

Jim had the best word-of-mouth in town but, as it turned out, everyone who kicked around Jim's name was, essentially, justifying his own decision. By making the recommendation, people got to raise his good points, re-convince themselves that their decision was a good one, and brag that they had the supposed "best choice in town." His business had survived for years more on his ability to generate referrals than on his ability to generate profits.

"Some people re-sell themselves when they give a referral," explained the late Dr. Harry Clarke Noyes, a psychologist who examined consumer behavior and who chatted with me about why someone like Jim would be so popular despite mediocre results. "They list the attributes of someone to you, and they are also re-examining the decision on their own. They may want you to choose the same person because it confirms their decision and because if you choose someone else it could raise more doubt in their mind.

"It's not that everyone who makes a referral does this, but it certainly happens."

All of this doesn't mean that referrals should be taken with a grain of salt. Getting counsel from someone else remains the single best way of starting with a short list of specialists, be it insurance agents or contractors who restore hardwood floors.

But referrals need to be fleshed out.

Most people make virtually no distinction between a "referral"—you ask for the name of someone to turn to—and a "reference," someone you grill on his experience working with the adviser.

In practice, however, there is one major difference. Referrals are taken at face value, while references undergo questioning to ascertain their level of satisfaction. (In both cases, there is the presumed conflict of interest that one reason to vouch for the adviser is to justify their own benefit. There may be other benefits such as discounted services, gifts and other incentives for helping to bring clients into the fold; all potential conflicts should be asked after.)

Getting a name from someone who answers the question "Who is your insurance agent?" is not enough. You want to know why he recommended that agent, if that agent is especially suited for your needs (something a paid adviser making a professional referral should be able to answer) and more. There is more in Chapter 11 on questioning a reference.

With the potential for conflict of interest—especially when one adviser is passing your business to another—you might wonder whether it is smart to discount referrals altogether.

Clearly, the answer is no.

My last car purchase came from an establishment where every time you refer someone who buys a car, you get $100 off your next purchase or repair job. The incentive is there for me to make the referral, but I wouldn't do it if I expected someone to be dissatisfied with the dealer. Such disappointment could, potentially, erode a friendship.

And so while my friends who recommended hardwood floor specialists may have had their own conflicts of interest, chances are they would have told me to avoid anyone with whom they had a bad experience.

Referrals put you squarely in the middle, somewhere between a friend or adviser wanting you to be satisfied and wanting to justify his own selections.

When it comes to referrals and your financial team, therefore, you must guard against the "instant trust" factor, by which you impart so much faith in someone else that you let your guard down. It is too easy to use a referral as the sole basis for hiring a financial adviser.

You trust your friend, who got a big fat tax refund check, so you believe he must have a good tax preparer. Or you get a referral from your financial planner for a tax preparer. You trust the planner (or already should have dumped him), creating instant trust in the referral.

That trust may be well-founded and the referral may be perfect, but the basic rule holds true: No one gets a position on your financial team until you have checked him out and feel comfortable that he belongs.

Referrals are a great way to make a short list of candidates for any position on your team. Asking your financial planner and banker for the names of estate-planning attorneys can yield you very good choices (particularly if they name the same person), and the word of a trustworthy friend should generate your confidence in an adviser. But the crucial thing is to compile a short list and not stray from the process of selecting a financial helper just because one candidate was built up by friends and colleagues as the "right" choice.

Remember, too, that you may not take the same approach to financial relationships as your friends or need the same kind of assistance. Your neighbor may drive a fancy car and be a "wealthy doctor," but that may also make him self-employed and dealing with a completely different kind of retirement-savings situation than you have working for a big, public company.

Your other neighbor might be satisfied getting an update on his portfolio every six months, while you want a report every time the market hiccups.

Given those possible differences in personality, you will need to examine the relationship your friend has with their hired help and be certain that something similar can work for you. What is the tenor of the relationship? How often are account updates provided? Does the adviser return calls promptly? How does he or she react when proffered advice is not taken? Just what makes this adviser so great?

Like your mother's decorator, the adviser you have been referred to may be competent and skilled but not your style.

In essence, once you have the referral, you need to treat your friend like a reference so that you can make your own decision.

Gather a series of referrals, decide which candidates sound the most promising to interview, and then make your selection. And if someone who makes a referral is offended that you went your own way and found someone without his help, that's not your problem. You'll be prepared to justify your decisions, if need be, and he will get over it.

Remember, it's a referral, not a sales pitch. There may be a lot of advisers who can satisfy your needs—just as my wife and I had the pick of experts for our floors—but no one knows your criteria for a financial relationship better than you. More importantly, no one else has to live with the consequences of your selection.

6   *Friends don't let friends become clients, most of the time*

Years ago, my wife was convinced by a friend that we needed some financial planning help.

The friend just happened to be a new financial adviser and she wanted to be the one to advise us.

I didn't think we needed any help, but Susan sold me on the idea that her friend Sandra could help us find better financing options for our first new car. Sandra also could provide a second opinion to my judgment on mutual funds and asset allocation.

Best of all, and Sandra gave us this in writing, it was a money-back deal. If we weren't satisfied or Sandra did not provide us with ideas and information we didn't have on our own, we could get our money back.

And so I signed the contract.

As you can easily figure out this far into the book—even before we get to specifics on how to pick advisers—the selection process was all wrong. I did not contact references, interview other planners, do a complete background check on the firm and perform all of the other tasks necessary for a good hiring decision.

Worse yet, Sandra did not deliver.

Her fund selections were mediocre at best; I had done significantly better on my own, so I would not pay a commission to buy her suggestions. Beyond that, her advice consisted largely of trying to help us improve our cash flow so we could purchase insurance products that, at the time, we had no need for and no real way to afford. Sandra's advice on the car boiled down to suggesting we pursue a great loan deal that I had found all by myself.

Which brings us to the money-back part.

I'm still waiting.

Susan couldn't bring herself to push for it; she didn't want to lose a friend or have me come off looking like a jerk. Sandra ran in the small circle of friends we had at the time; although talking to friends about our professional relationship would have been a breach of ethics, we feared that kind of gossip. In short, we were young and didn't put up much of a fight.

Despite telling Sandra that I was disappointed, I never got, nor did I pursue, my money back.

The lessons to take from this experience are several:

1. Hire advisers the right way. If you have a friend or relative who can pass muster and with whom you still feel the most comfortable after interviewing several candidates, so be it.

2. When possible, don't do business with friends or relatives. It's a good way to lose both.

A 1999 national survey by the American Society of Chartered Life Underwriters & Chartered Financial Consultants found that 40 percent of all people take financial advice from friends, family and business associates. While the remaining populace relies on some type of financial adviser, the study did not say how many of those advisory relationships had some sort of friendship or family tie.

But people feel comfortable relying on loved ones for financial advice, which makes it a tough call when a relative is selling financial services.

In fact, if a friend or family member goes into the financial services arena, you can expect a phone call about becoming a client. Every new financial adviser, no matter whether in banking, real estate, accounting or selling stocks and bonds, must start by building a client base. To get their businesses off the ground, most people contact friends and relatives.

Clearly, some of these situations turn into wonderful financial relationships. The initial clientele for most new mutual funds is the family and acquaintances of the manager, and surely somebody knew each mutual fund management genius before the media discovered him.

But remember, for every guru, there are countless advisers who don't make the grade; if you aren't one of the truly lucky—related by some freak of nature to a person who is a real freak of nature and, therefore, a world-class money manager at a young age—you are almost guaranteed to be disappointed in more ways than one.

In our case, with the financial relationship going nowhere, Susan and Sandra grew distant; both women surely must have known that family get-togethers would eventually lead to shop talk.

So we lost a friend and about $200. Over the years, I've come to be bothered much more by the lost money than the lost friendship, because I realized Sandra valued our friendship differently than I did or she never would have jeopardized it with a business proposition.

Indeed, one of the key considerations of doing business with a friend is whether the offer of financial help is being made out of altruism—"I see your plight and can help"—or from the need to get clients.

"F&R selling"—sales-speak for selling to friends and relatives—is a crutch for the person making the sale. Think of it like someone selling Girl Scout cookies. A girl may start sales at home, then with neighbors, then people in her parents' offices—but generating lucrative returns requires selling to strangers.

If someone you know is already established in business and is just now getting around to making a sales pitch to you, be skeptical; good advisers—and good salesmen—don't have to rely on the friends-and-family crutch for too long.

Shortly after we moved to Massachusetts, a friend in our new hometown pitched financial services to Susan. Susan explained that I have a strict no-business-with-friends policy, yet she still feared offending this man and his wife. As far as I'm concerned, "friendship" shouldn't be that fragile; had he taken offense at our refusing to do business, this man would have been showing little respect for our judgment and character. That would mean we didn't have much of a friendship.

(The man didn't stop pitching us, by the way, until he left both his wife and the financial planning business and moved away.)

For most people, doing business with a friend or family member spells trouble for one big reason: You let your guard down.

There is an assumption that friends and family get special treatment, a little extra hand-holding, an insider's edge on hot information or some extra level of dependability. In addition, the crucial element of trust—the cornerstone of your search for any adviser—tends to be in place with both your kin and your playmates. Clearly, unless they are a complete fraud, you can assume your friend or family member wants both the personal and professional relationships to prosper.

But good intentions don't always deliver the goods. The nephew with the ink still fresh on a real estate license, for example, may not have enough experience to get you the best deal on the sale of your home. Compounding the problem is a reluctance to question advice—or terminate the relationship if it's going poorly—because it could lead to family/friendship problems.

Unless you are willing to sacrifice that best deal for the sake of the relationship, you don't want to do business with relatives.

But even if you plan to separate business from friendships, the offers for help may still come and be tempting. No matter how much you try to avoid mixing business and pleasure, the comfort level you have with relations and friends always is alluring.

The important thing to remember about doing business with friends is that it can be emotional on all sides. If you ask your best childhood friend to provide a written history of his business experience and credentials, he may take offense.

That reaction is one more reason why it is hard to mix business and personal relationships. If your friend blanches when you want an interview and ask about dispute resolution or want something in writing, how will he treat you if you ever decide not to follow his advice?

If anything but a where-do-I-sign-up answer will be treated as an affront, either the friendship is guaranteed to be strained or you are surrendering control of your decision-making powers.

If you are considering a business relationship with a relative, stick to the selection process you would use with a complete stranger. It will increase your odds for success.

If, for example, you interview several prospective insurance agents and come away feeling your brother-in-law is not a good adviser, you avoid the unpleasantness of having to sever the business relationship later when it falls short of your expectations. On the other hand, if he truly is the best option, you will never second-guess whether the relationship colored your selection.

As you put a friend or relative through the adviser-selection process, put particular stress on the following five elements.

▪ **Doing a complete background check.** Even if your friend or relative is on the up-and-up, his firm may not be. Plenty of people starting out in financial services work for boiler-room operations, firms with poor reputations and worse.

Again, intentions often differ from reality. I have heard any number of newly minted brokers extoll the virtues of penny stocks—believing this stuff in their hearts—right up to the day their firms were shut down by lawmakers for illegal doings by higher-ups.

Then there are those advisers who have burned clients and now need new ones. If a friend or relation has been in business for 10 years, but only recently thought to call you up and offer his services, find out if there is a regulatory reason for the sudden interest.

Checking backgrounds requires little more than one phone call or Internet inquiry (how to do it is in the chapters on picking individual advisers) and your friend or relative will be none the wiser for your efforts, so it won't hurt any feelings.

▪ **Asking "Why do you want me as a client?"** One key to a successful financial relationship is finding someone who wants to "hire" you. When it comes to friends and family members, try to find out their motive in seeking you out.

Just as you might worry about some relative constantly calling to hit you up for money, so should you be concerned about someone who sees the value of your friendship as a meal ticket. The answer you want to hear is one based on demographics, on what the adviser has learned about people in your financial situation, of how he can fulfill your financial needs.

Be sure your situation is one with which he is familiar, and that you are a good match with his typical client. You do not want to be anybody's maiden effort into complex financial waters.

If you do not resemble that average client and he does not have a good reason for wanting to hire you—beyond the paycheck you provide him—then consider whether this is a relationship in which the benefits would be a bit one-sided.

▪ **Getting it in writing.** If he truly thinks well of you, he won't mind setting down the terms of the relationship in writing, even if such a contract is not required by law. You want specifics on how the relationship will work, what you are getting for your money, the name of a supervisor (when applicable) and how you will get your money back if you are not satisfied.

If you ever are so unhappy as to ask for your money back, there's a good chance the friendship will be ruined. In that circumstance, you will want better recourse than having to tell a judge or arbitrator that you thought this friend would take care of you.

▪ **Seeking out references.** You may have held your nephew since he was in the cradle, but that doesn't mean you have any idea whether he is any good at his job. Ask for the name of a customer (or a few customers) whose situation is similar to yours so you can hear from an impartial observer.

Again, a friend or relative may be offended that you would ask; that's a sign he does not have enough respect for you as a client to meet your requirements for making a business relationship work.

▪ **Drawing the lines between business and pleasure.** Try to make it clear that you do not want the business side of your relationship to spill over into the personal side, and determine what the two of you can do to keep that from happening.

My stockbroker, for example, is a former lacrosse teammate with whom I started working before I made my personal prohibition on mixing friends and finances. The reason the relationship works is that it is clearly defined; Tommy knows that the day he calls with a hot stock tip—something I do not want from my broker because I do my own investment research—is the day our business relationship ends. He offers suggestions and guidance when I ask, executes the trades I want to make and stays clearly within the bounds of what I want from a broker.

When we're done with business, we swap stories about our families.

Express what you want from the financial relationship and discuss how the two of you can set up limits that keep any shortfalls from spilling over and hurting the personal relationship. Tell the adviser under what circumstances you would cut and run from the relationship. Lay out your expectations too, as they go a long way to helping your buddy determine whether he really can meet your needs. By talking about this in advance, the two of you may decide that any financial relationship would jeopardize the personal side of things and not be worth it.

Remember, there is more than money at stake when you do business with friends and family. While you are going through the adviser selection process, include the extra value of your friendship in your decision-making. You stand to lose a lot more than your cash if a financial relationship with a friend or relative turns sour.

7   *Defining a match made in heaven*

Defining an ideal financial relationship is a bit like describing love.

Words may escape us, but we know when we are in it.

When it comes to financial relationships, ideal is an individual concept.

I have one friend who insists his stockbroker call whenever the market drops 200 points to talk strategy (and calm his nervous stomach). By comparison, I wouldn't expect to hear from my broker if the Dow Jones Industrial Average lost 3,000 points—unless I called him first.

Both relationships are ideal, however, because the broker acts in accordance with the client's wishes, and both clients are pleased with the level of service they receive.

In order to have an ideal relationship with an adviser, you must first decide what you want, and then express it to the adviser upfront so you both have appropriate expectations.

That's a bit tricky; you are paying for someone to advise you and, in that capacity, he is the one who is supposed to help you determine what's going to work.

So you can't create your ideal in a vacuum. You must enter the interview process with a framework you consider "right" and then see how the adviser's ideal fits in with that.

Regardless of whether you are choosing a lawyer, a broker, a banker or any member of the team, there are a few things involved in ideal financial relationships.

Personal service

Service in financial relationships is kind of like the involvement a college student has with professors, particularly at a big college at which it is easy to remain anonymous.

You can sit in the back of the class, do your assignments and go largely unnoticed, or you can work with the professor, visit during office hours and develop a relationship.

You can be well served by either type of relationship, but the important thing is to get the education you are paying for and have the relationship you want to receive for your money.

Throughout the financial services business, specialists break down into two basic categories—"relationship-oriented" and "transaction-oriented."

The transaction-oriented providers want to rack up the deals. It is the bank that charges you a fee for using a teller—don't laugh, it's probably coming to your neighborhood soon—or where there is no one in your branch who has basic decision-making powers. Or it is the stockbroker who wants to sell you the stock and has to rush off to the next customer, rather than discuss with you how the purchase fits in with your overall portfolio and strategy. It is the insurance agent who is pushing new products he wants you to sign up for before you have a full understanding of how the coverage works. Or it is the lawyer who signs you up, brings you "into the firm" and then passes all responsibility to a subordinate who will really represent you. It is the grind-it-out tax preparation services, or the real estate agent with too many current listings to recall without a printout.

Some firms are transaction-oriented for cost reasons. Obviously, most online advice relies on some form of black-box formula; even when customized to your numbers and expectations, it may feel impersonal. (See Chapter 12 for more on online advice.)

For example, you can save money buying life insurance direct from a provider rather than through an agent, but the savings results in a lower level of service, advice and hand-holding. Similarly, you can save money buy using a discount or online broker, but that's a wise idea only if you don't want or need the "full service" part of working with a full-service broker.

Even when cost is not the big issue in choosing an adviser, there is nothing necessarily wrong with using transaction-driven providers, especially if you have some do-it-yourself initiative with your finances. For example, plenty of people—I would wager a majority—don't know the names of the people who serve them at the bank but are not unhappy with that. So long as they don't want an interest-only mortgage, to get a loan on a classic car or do anything out of the ordinary, the do-it-by-machine or drive-thru bank customer can be completely satisfied.

But for most people—especially those who bought this book to improve their fortunes by managing a team of helpers—financial counsel requires more than an interface with a machine.

That being the case, the first thing you need to do is determine the level of personal service you want and what the adviser is willing to provide.

It sounds obvious, but you want to know who will actually deal with you—will it be the broker or an assistant, for example—and under what conditions will you hear from him. (There are times when it is perfectly acceptable to deal with an adviser's assistant or with a firm's specialist in the area of a particular need, but you should know who you will be working on your account and whether you will be getting the service you expect from the counselor you want.) You want to know what will prompt the adviser to call you—new opportunities or products, changes in the status of your situation, changes in the law that could affect you, the periodic need for review—and how he will respond when you call.

In a time of crisis, for example, you may want your insurance agent to walk you through a claim, rather than dealing on an impersonal basis with an insurance company adjuster to whom you are just another case number. Your agent may tell you that he or she just processes policies and leaves the claims to the adjusters; you may prefer to have someone who has a track record, borne out by references, of pushing the insurer for prompt settlements.

"The easiest way to be let down by your adviser is to not spell out your expectations in advance," says financial planner Ross Levin of Accredited Investors in Minneapolis. "That is especially true in service, because what works well for an adviser—the way they deal with all of their clients—may not be what you are looking for. Maybe they like to deal by telephone, you want to meet face-to-face.

"Find out how someone likes to do business—how do they typically interact with the customer—and decide if that is something you can live with."

Consultation

There is a slight difference between the personal service you receive and the ability to consult with your advisers. The difference might be clear this way: Sometimes you need to use your adviser's services, other times you just want to talk.

If your lawyer or financial planner recommends a particular tax strategy, for example, you might want to run it past your tax preparer for a second opinion. If you are having your advisers act like a team (an approach I advocate and cover in Chapter 21), you may want the two advisers to discuss the situation before you make your decision.

Consultations—whether they are a quick tax question for your accountant or a major sit-down to have a financial planner retitle assets to follow an estate plan—are sometimes necessary, but they aren't always free.

Advisers sometimes squirm at the thought of free time, but if the commodity involved in advisory relationships is trust, then having the meter running on every conversation discourages interaction. At the same time, you should not abuse your adviser's time, or expect him to donate a few hours to answer a complex question for you.

Define the terms of the quick-opinion/knowledgeable-resource portion of your relationship. Unless you are working with someone who charges based on a percentage of the assets involved (or who is being paid on a contingency), you should expect a bill if you need repeated, lengthy consultations. But you also want an adviser to whom you will be meaningful enough that the periodic "What does this mean for me?" phone call does not generate a bill.

Willingness to work with other financial specialists

To get different specialists to function as one unit, you need team players. Yes, your broker or financial adviser should be the lead expert on investments, but that does not mean he should be unwilling to discuss your investment situation with an accountant, banker or lawyer.

Not every one of these discussions is adversarial, pitting one player against the other. If, for example, you are considering establishing trusts or are involved in estate planning, having your lawyer and financial adviser talk to each other makes good financial sense. Aside from bouncing ideas around to determine, say, what type of trust is best for you, they need to coordinate your plan. The best estate plan can be rendered useless if you do not retitle assets to follow it.

Some advisers like to wear more than one hat, acting as an accountant and financial planner, or money manager and lawyer, but you may use them for just one particular skill. If they must consult with your hired gun in their second area of expertise, you need to make sure they will not be upset because they don't have that slice of your business. (Chapter 22 deals with what I call the "utility infielders" of the financial world.)

Every adviser you consider should know who your other counselors are, particularly if there could be circumstances under which you would want them to interact.

"No one wants to think they are going to fight with your other advisers," says Dick Wagner, a partner in the Denver advisory firm of Sharkey, Howes, Wagner & Javer, "but they aren't really providing you the kind of service you need if they won't even talk to your other advisers. If they fight the idea that they may have to deal with your accountant—or argue that they can do everything themselves or within their firm—then you have to wonder if they will be able to handle direction and hard questions, whether it comes from another adviser or from you."

Understanding

No good adviser wants you to buy something you don't understand.

It is hard to tell from an initial interview spent feeling each other out, rather than talking heavy-duty finances, whether an adviser can explain things to you clearly. (If the first meeting is over your head or includes a heavy-handed sales pitch, it's a rush job—which is an instant turn-off).

But in an ideal advisory relationship, decisions are made only after you have complete understanding and agreement. Every key decision—whether it is why you should purchase a tax-free investment or why you should price your home at a certain level—should be explained until you are comfortable with it.

If you never grasp the whys and hows, the adviser should be willing to change tactics—without getting frustrated or angry with you—as opposed to trying to convince you he is the expert and knows so much about the situation that you should trust him.

Tolerance for "stupid" questions and "excessive" requests

If you intend to actively manage your finances, you will have a lot of questions. They may be as simple as "can you tell me how municipal bonds work?" or they might involve complex issues based on your desire to understand something such as how the government taxes mutual funds.

Assume you will be a high-maintenance client because you intend to manage the managers. Some advisers hate that; despite saying they want to build long-term relationships, their dislike appears when you start asking questions and making them really work on your behalf.

Clear, and clearly followed, instructions

A financial adviser I met in Pennsylvania used to argue with me that the "planner-as-a-doctor" analogy was a good one.

"You go to a doctor, explain what is bothering you and then wait for a diagnosis," he said. "The doctor then takes the steps needed to make you feel better or to give you the cure."

I granted him that situation was possible, especially that the doctor does the work without explaining his or her assessment/recommendation.

What worries me, however, is that a lot of people go to financial "doctors" complaining about a headache, only to have the doctor skip that portion of the body and examine the patient's feet.

One of the biggest problems individuals have with advisers involves instructions.

You may recall the story in Chapter 5 about "Jim," the stockbroker who lost the investment contest and a lot of his business in the process. The scenario for the competition was an investor who had a sum of money that, for personal reasons, needed to be withdrawn after one year. There was a time deadline, and a reason to invest and trade the account aggressively.

Clearly, that is not a common scenario; most people looking at a short time horizon are very conservative with their money, fearful of downturns from which they have no time to recover.

A long-term investor might buy more of a stock when it declines, provided that he believes the long-term prospects of the company will prompt a rebound. A short-term investor unloads losers and looks for faster horses.

Jim kept buying more of his losers—and his losers were plentiful. When his initial results were not good, he stopped listening to the imaginary client and didn't even attempt a short-term strategy, investing instead with a longer-term outlook. If the game had been a five-year contest, and the investments had time to rebound, Jim might have done just fine; for the contest, his decisions meant losses in a year during which the market was up.

An adviser should be comfortable with the relationship you set up. If that means you don't want to hear about "hot" investments, then you should never get a sales pitch on the latest tip or fad. If it means a short-term time frame, then the decisions should fit into that context.

Experts assume they know more than you. They might know more about investments but not about when you have a tuition bill due, how your spending habits have changed or how your financial situation disrupts your sleeping habits.

Mutual understanding over the roads not taken

One key mantra for managing your financial help is "I'm the boss." If your advisers do their jobs and lay out everything in a way you understand, you should have easy-to-explain reasons why you do or do not follow their suggestions. But no matter how good their logic, or poor your reason for balking, it is still your move to make.

If an adviser waves his or her expertise in your face—"I do this every day and you don't, and yet you trust your judgment over mine"—run away as fast as you can.

Ideal financial counseling has no hard sells, no "be grateful to work with me" guilt trips, no threats of "maybe you should work with my associate in the future." A trusted adviser should not have to pitch you hard and should recognize when and why you are reluctant to make a move.

If the adviser understands what you want from the relationship, he should ask questions about why you rejected his advice and what made you uncomfortable, and he should try to determine why the two of you did not connect. With that kind of discourse, the relationship evolves, and the adviser's future ideas probably will be more in line with your own.

No underlings, unless previously approved

You are going through a rigorous selection process to pick an adviser, someone you trust, to help with your finances. If you subsequently find out that your affairs will be handled by someone else in the firm, you had better either meet that person or take your money elsewhere.

If you go to a broker who then passes you along to a junior associate, you are suddenly dealing with an entirely new entity. The background checks, the references or referrals, the initial interview and all of the rest of your work is out the window.

In all various realms of personal finance, there are advisers who farm out some of the work or summon subordinates or peers to handle specific problems. You need to know of that possibility before it takes place.

Unless you approve of the people you will be working with, there are no substitutions or exchanges. A good adviser knows this and will not take on so much work that he can not devote the proper amount of time to you.

Approval of your spouse, partner, heirs or executor

In the event something happens to you, your adviser needs to be prepared to work with the folks who will manage your estate. He should not be condescending or demeaning—even if he is used to dealing only with you.

You want someone who can work comfortably with you and your heirs, even if there is a radical difference in your levels of financial sophistication. If an adviser wants to work exclusively with the knowledgeable partner in a relationship, then the less-savvy person could be headed for trouble if he or she ever needs to manage household affairs or the estate.

If your relationship with an adviser does not meet those basic criteria, chances are that it will come up short down the road, leaving you disappointed with the service (or lack thereof) or the person.

Remember, too, that almost every adviser will jump through hoops and promise the moon to get you in the door as a client. Determining whether he can craft the kind of relationship you want and need will be a big part of your hiring decision; knowing what you want from the relationship will go a long way toward helping you find that ideal.

8 *Your first meeting with an adviser*

A colleague of mine once complained about a financial planner he was working with, someone he had been "meticulous" in choosing. My friend was disappointed with the planner's level of service, responsiveness and fee structure.

"If you were so meticulous in picking this planner, why didn't you know what to expect?" I asked. "Hadn't you discussed fees, what you would get and how fast she would respond to you?"

"Well," my friend said sheepishly, "we never really got to that."

It seems my friend let the planner take charge of the initial interview. Instead of a wide-ranging feel-each-other-out chat, the planner asked a raft of questions, all designed to determine how much money was involved and my friend's goals and objectives. Then the adviser asked if she should go ahead and prepare a basic financial plan.

She seemed excited to do the work—more so than the other two planners my colleague interviewed—and he liked her energy, so he gave the go-ahead.

He was told the plan would be ready in three weeks.

The planner then dismissed my friend to get to work. Interview over.

Not quite a month later, my friend received by mail exactly what had been promised, an action plan for how to reach his goals. The plan was devoid of investment selections, advice on allocating 401(k) retirement plan savings and specific suggestions on how and where to cut spending to improve cash flow and reduce debt.

Lacking as it was, the plan was more costly than expected.

The planner in this situation—considered one of the nation's elite advisers, by the way—clearly thought she was being hired to do a one-time periodic review; my friend, just as plainly, thought he was going to receive much more specific advice.

The miscommunication—cleared up to everyone's satisfaction after I prodded him to request a second meeting to express both his displeasure and what he expected from the relationship—occurred because the interview went from being a how-do-you-do? to a "You're on the job."

It should never happen that way.

Your initial meeting with any adviser is a physical and mental handshake, an exercise in sizing someone up. It is a working session only in the sense that the adviser presumably is working to earn your business, you are struggling to pick the best adviser and everyone involved wants the first interview to be the cornerstone of a long and rewarding financial relationship.

But it should never be a foregone conclusion that your first meeting will lead to working together, particularly since you will interview more than one candidate before making a decision.

Unless you simply need someone to facilitate a transaction, plan to interview between two and five advisers. The reason you need to do so many interviews is that you have to find the right balance between art and science.

The science part of any financial relationship is how well someone does with "procedures." Just about any lawyer can draft a will, and you will seldom meet a tax preparer or accountant who would back down from a challenging tax return. Presumably, he is qualified to do the work and make the necessary arrangements for your affairs to be in order.

What distinguishes one adviser from the pack is how he or she finesses the science and blends it with art. It's how he goes from simply producing a will to knowing all the right steps to take to craft a protective legal document, or how he minimizes your tax liability without increasing the likelihood of an audit. And it's how he makes you feel during the process, which should be comfortable and in control.

The first adviser you talk with is always going to sound good; he will be able to answer your questions—the very questions that drove you to hire financial help rather than trying to do it yourself—and you are very likely to spend the most time with him because the discussion will be new territory for you.

Most advisers I talk with say, that to the best of their knowledge, the bulk of their clients never did multiple interviews. They were hired by the end of the get-acquainted meeting and assume they have gotten the brush-off when a prospective client has to "think it over." All have had the occasional client wash-out, when either the adviser or the consumer did not do enough work to make a good match and the relationship dissolved down the road.

No matter what kind of financial adviser you are looking for, the search and initial meeting should follow a similar pattern. In the chapters discussing how to select each type of counselor you will find specific questions to ask during an initial interview, covering the unique circumstances of each specialty.

Here, however, are the elements that are crucial to every adviser meeting—regardless of what kind of specialist you are hiring—and to the interview process itself.

Do some advance work by telephone

You don't want to waste an adviser's time—or your own—so try to ensure that you and the adviser make a good match before scheduling a get-acquainted meeting.

For example, you will want to ask about costs upfront; it makes no sense to talk to a lawyer who charges $200 an hour when you are looking to pay $100 per hour. Similarly, many advisers have account minimums; it's silly to interview a financial planner with a $500,000 account minimum when you have $50,000 in assets.

This is also when you get the basics on whether you fit with the profile of the adviser's average client. If you are scheduling meetings with financial planners to work on estate-planning issues, for example, make sure prospective advisers actually work on those matters regularly. Many financial planners specialize in money management and may not be focused on the need that has driven you to seek assistance.

Whenever possible, talk directly with the adviser, rather than an assistant. While most advisers will not turn away potential business unless they are too busy to handle new accounts, what you hear in their voices will go a long way toward helping make your decision. Obviously, as you lay out the basics of what you are looking for—and the size and scope of the job—you should be listening for interest and energy.

Schedule your meeting at least 10 days in advance

Once you are certain you want to meet with an adviser, set up an appointment but leave yourself time to do the necessary background checks. It may take a few days to properly check on an adviser's background; unless you have checked on his regulatory history before ever calling to chat, you will want to have that work done before you get acquainted. (You will find the information needed to make background checks in the chapters on hiring each type of adviser.)

In addition, many advisers will want to send you material to streamline the interview process. Leave enough time to read everything, complete any paperwork they send and gather necessary documents and records.

If you are married, your spouse should look everything over, even if he or she is not the primary decision-maker on these matters. Remember you are purchasing trust, so you want to make sure your partner knows what is going on and has faith and confidence in the adviser.

When you schedule the initial interview, find out whether you will be charged for it. Some advisers are on the clock, even for a first-time sit-down, while others waive the initial consultation fee if you become a client. Charging for a how-do-you-do is a privilege advisers earn when they are successful; time is their currency, precious enough that they don't want to waste it on unproductive interviews. (Still, my experience is that the majority of advisers do not charge for an initial get-together.)

The problem when someone charges for an interview is that it puts pressure on you to choose that adviser because you don't want to waste your money. That said, try to avoid initial consultation fees when possible, and never pay a consultation fee to someone who stands to make big money from you on contingency (if he sells your home, wins your court case, etc.).

And while it is important to value and respect an adviser's time, don't throw money into a first interview until sufficiently checking out those candidates who do not charge for a first sit-down. There are many qualified advisers out there, and there will always be someone—perhaps with less of a track record, but not necessarily with less expertise—for you to choose from.

Do your background checks

Everyone has his own tolerance level, and you need to make sure an adviser falls within yours before the first meeting.

Over time, many financial counselors have disagreements with clients, often no more than simple misunderstandings. In today's litigious society, that means there are a lot of good advisers out there with one or two black marks in their pasts.

Before your first sit-down, you want to arm yourself with information about those incidents. You can do this either when you are first sorting out advisers—doing the work on your short list of candidates before the initial interviews—or immediately after your phone conversation, when you have decided to set up an interview.

If the adviser is sending you any paperwork to prepare you for the meeting, ask him to include any regulatory or background information, such as a Form ADV for financial planners. (You'll get more on these types of forms in the chapters on picking advisers.)

You want the background data in hand before your initial interview so you can ask about any black marks or red flags and get an explanation of what happened and how problems were resolved. Clients may have had unrealistic expectations; the adviser may have created that kind of problem. Whatever it is, you want the adviser's side of the story—and you don't want to see too many of these problems in his past.

Again, this comes under the heading of trust, which is the first thing you must establish in a financial relationship. If an adviser won't talk about what you have found on his record, or if the story sounds implausible or just plain sloppy, look elsewhere.

In addition, any adviser whose file comes back with several black marks on it already may have exceeded your tolerance level. In that case, cancel the interview.

Do your homework

Before an initial sit-down, prepare a written statement of what you want from this relationship. In addition, complete whatever materials the adviser sends you.

Again, couples must read the materials and prepare the statement together. A good adviser will want to hear from both of you; if one partner sits in the room silently, a high-quality counselor will try to draw him or her out. Equally important, you will want your partner to concur on your written statement and to have given thought as to the household's financial goals.

Bring everyone involved to the meeting

A *Boston Globe* retiree once came to me with questions about his adviser. The big thing he wanted to know was how to get his wife to like the guy. Apparently, she didn't "like the looks of him," not to mention the fact that he talked over her head, using financial jargon that all sounded like Latin to her. (To be honest, the husband didn't understand everything the adviser was saying either, but that's another story.)

I told him it was time to get a new adviser.

He objected, saying he liked the guy.

Your work with an adviser affects the entire family, not just you. For that reason, you want both partners—or parents or children if they are involved—at the initial meeting.

If you or your partner dislikes the adviser's clothing, dress, manner or whatever, find a different adviser. It may seem silly to get rid of a potential financial helper because you don't like, say, his haircut, but it is valid if it makes you uncomfortable. (Truth be told, an adviser's gender, age, personality and the convenient location of their office always have a lot to do with the selection process, no matter how much detail and science we apply to choosing helpers. All are acceptable factors in differentiating one potential adviser from the next.)

In the case of the retiree, his wife no longer wanted to go to planning meetings with him because of her feelings toward the adviser. If he didn't honor his wife's wishes, and later died before her, she would be stuck during her time of grief dealing with someone she hated.

Yes, she could get another adviser at that time, but as this book is proving to you, selecting financial help is neither fast nor easy.

If an adviser is working on behalf of the entire household, he must have the trust of everyone. Both partners must be comfortable with any adviser chosen and have veto power if, for any reason, the chemistry just doesn't seem right.

Come out from under the covers

If you can't trust someone enough to open up to him, he has no business advising you on financial matters.

You must disclose all relevant information so your advisers can make informed decisions; no adviser can meet your expectations and help you reach your goals without a complete and truthful picture of your situation. (For example, some people meeting with a financial planner for the first time fudge their debt amount because it embarrasses them.)

Be honest about yourself, the kind of person you are—if you intend to call every week, he should know that upfront, for example—and your needs. Be honest about your assets, too. Understand that every house has faults, for example, and that the real estate agent will want to hear them from you; similarly, an insurance agent or financial planner is in the best position to help you if he has a true picture of your earnings, assets and liabilities.

Reveal any unusual life circumstances that might affect the adviser's work. A gay individual or a couple in a non-traditional relationship may be reluctant to share this information right away. Yet there are special rules and strategies that come into play in these situations, and you will want to be sure the adviser has the technical expertise to help you.

In short, make sure the adviser gets the same information you had while you were doing things on your own.

Lastly, be sure to tell the adviser why you are in the office—what brought you to the point of hiring help. It might be that you have a specific need, are nervous about what you have done on your own or are unhappy with the services of your current adviser. That disclosure will push the discussion over ground you absolutely must cover in order to make a good selection.

Don't try to show how smart you are

Just as you would not talk to your doctors using words such as "subdural hematoma" instead of a bruise, don't try to be flashy with what you know when meeting an adviser for the first time.

This does not apply just to what you say, but also to what you hear. If the adviser is talking over your head and you fake your level of understanding, the adviser might believe you. That's how people wind up with arbitration or court cases.

If an adviser uses jargon or moves too fast thinking you understand, make him slow down and explain things at your level. If he can't do that in the initial meeting—when things should be pretty simple— then you undoubtedly will want to hire someone else.

Decide on the services you need, and what they cost

Remember my colleague whose initial interview led to overpriced planning-by-mail? Find out specifically what the adviser intends to do for you and how (and how much) he will be compensated for his services.

Yes, you asked questions like these during your initial phone contact, but the face-to-face meeting may have brought out new circumstances and changed things. Leave the meeting with a clear understanding of what you will get if you sign up as a client, and what it will cost you.

Never expect something for nothing

If you think an adviser will solve all your problems in the initial meeting (and at no charge), you will be disappointed. You may get some free counsel—most advisers can't help themselves—but you shouldn't expect fast, free help.

Just because the initial meeting does not leave you with any solutions is no reason to take an adviser off your prospect list. You may unnecessarily eliminate the best candidate for the job.

If you have reservations, spill your guts

Be fair to the adviser and yourself; if something has been said—or not said—that needs to be addressed (or covered again), ask.

It might be that you want clarification about how you could get your money back if you are not satisfied. It might be the discussion of the red flags raised during a background check or anything that makes you nervous at all, but try to get a better explanation before leaving the office. It could be that you are dissatisfied with your current adviser and haven't heard enough to convince you that the new relationship will be different.

If the adviser can not adequately address your concerns, hire someone else.

Many times, the adviser dominates the interview. He needs to get information from you and, since he has these meetings all the time, knows the directions in which this session needs to go.

Still, you can't afford to be bashful.

If you don't ask about your concerns, you have a big problem. In general, there will be no way for you to answer these nagging questions on your own; since you can't resolve them, your search for financial help will drag on and you will have a tough time making a good decision because of your reservations. Or, worse yet, you wind up hiring someone who you are nervous about.

Make sure the adviser wants to hire you as a client

This has already been said several times in this book, always applying to your behavior, the type of person and financial situation you represent. In this case, however, it talks about your conduct in the get-acquainted meeting.

If you ignore the previous steps outlined in this chapter, you run the risk of having an adviser label you as a potential problem or a high-maintenance client. Good advisers run away from that kind of trouble—they don't want their next client to become that rare black mark on their record and are not desperate to add new customers—so make sure that you do your part.

Ask for references

Some advisers consider "I have to go home and think about it" to be the brush-off. (You can show them this book and tell them you are using it to help in the selection process if you feel compelled to reassure them of your sincerity.) You want and need that time, not only to do other interviews but to check references.

There is a potential problem here, in that some firms do not provide references or give out only the names of people to whom they give referrals, such as a financial planner using the lawyer to whom he refers estate work as a reference.

Explain, as politely as possible, that references will allow you to ask about the character of a relationship. You expect a reference to be sweet on the adviser; what you want to know is the tone and tenor of the relationship. How does this adviser work with you, how does he respond when you have questions? How did the reference come to choose this adviser? (Dealing with references is covered in Chapter 11.)

If your adviser is unwilling to give you the names of references (especially clients, rather than professionals, with whom there might be a business or monetary tie coloring the reference), he may not be worth keeping on your short list.

That's a tough call. References are an additional check-and-balance, but an adviser who uses confidentiality and convenience as an excuse to withhold names has not necessarily killed the deal, particularly if the adviser has addressed your reservations and if you found him through a referral from a friend or other financial counselor.

Having completed a detailed interview, armed with references (or with the knowledge that you are okay not getting them), you can leave the office, go home and mull over the adviser. Having repeated the interview process with at least one other adviser, you should be comfortable making a decision and receiving advice down the line.

9   *Swimming through alphabet soup*

H.D. Vest must like initials.

The founder of a nationwide financial services firm that bears his name, Vest not only goes by his initials, but he drops a lot of other letters, too. On the cover of one of his books, for example, he lists 18 different professional credentials, sometimes two different designations from the same group.

I am not making this up.

According to his latest book, Vest is—try to say this in one breath— an MS, MSFS, MSM, DIBA, CEBS, CFA, CFP, CFS, ChFC, CLU, CMA, CPA/PFS, FLMI/I, AMC, EPTC, PECC.

Wow.

I assume his parents simply gave him the H.D. and that he didn't have to take a class somewhere to get it.

Credentials make an adviser look impressive—and perhaps a bit more intimidating on those occasions when you question his advice— but they don't necessarily make the advice any better.

Truth be told, I ran Vest's credentials past some of the nation's leading financial advisers, and they couldn't identify all of the designations. Neither could I.

Nor should you care if someone has that many professional designations.

Credentials are misleading. Even if you know what a CFP, or Certified Financial Planner, is, chances are you do not know what goes into achieving that designation. And CFP is a common credential, unlike a lot of the business card alphabet soup out there.

What credentials generally prove is that an adviser is furthering his education, knowledge that is crucial since the rules regarding all areas of finance seem to change almost every day.

But all of those credentials don't make someone worthy of being your adviser.

I come to that conclusion from personal experience.

In June 1995, I was one of five journalists who took the two-day, 10-hour exam to become a Certified Financial Planner. It was a media play by the folks who administer the CFP standard; even if we had passed the test, we would not have qualified as CFPs.

I did not study for the test and did not expect to pass it—nor did I want to, because I would have lost all respect for both the test and the group if I could ace it without formal training.

None of the journalists passed.

But what I learned was not how tough the test was, but rather that the mark of CFP—a standard I have tremendous respect for—does not make someone a great financial planner. It proves his technical proficiency, his ability to analyze your portfolio and make appropriate suggestions, but has no bearing on his "relationship" skills.

An adviser could pass the CFP exam largely by boning up on some basic formulas and rules, but could be lacking the basic human skills necessary to build a comfortable relationship. Since the entire concept of hiring a financial helper hinges on developing this working partnership, credentials alone are not enough to make someone worthy.

Don't get me wrong. Technical expertise is critical, especially when it comes to the legal, insurance and tax arenas in which a mistake could have severe costs.

But I do not know of a single financial planner—and I have asked hundreds of them in the years since I took the test—who ever had a client come in and ask for the calculation of the Sharpe Index of Performance on a mutual fund. In fact, only one or two of the planners I've queried could actually calculate the Sharpe Index without the formula in front of them. (The Sharpe is so esoteric that most mainstream financial dictionaries ignore it, most planners can't adequately explain it and I'm not even going to attempt it here.)

Yet the Sharpe Index is on the CFP exam.

Meanwhile, subjective decision-making about how someone can cut spending to improve savings or reduce debt is not anywhere on the

CFP exam. And all of the same planners who have earned the CFP and have never been asked by clients to calculate a Sharpe Index have dozens of clients who need help changing their spending habits.

Taking the test answered one of my most troubling questions for the financial services business. Until I saw what the test measured, I never understood how the CFP Board of Standards had bestowed its precious mark on some of the very best and very worst planners I know; the answer is that the exam is an incomplete gauge of an adviser's skills.

That's why credentials are a starting point and not the Good House-keeping Seal of Approval.

One key thing to remember in hiring financial help is that, with the exception of lawyers, none of the rest of the members of your financial team truly is a professional.

Most dictionaries define the word "profession" as a vocation or occupation that requires advanced training either in sciences or the liberal arts. You do not need an advanced degree to practice as a banker, insurance agent, real estate agent, stockbroker, financial planner or accountant.

The standards vary for each role, with state or federal law dictating whether practitioners must even be registered. Most states, for example, require that financial planners be registered, but they have no standards for education or experience to back that up; anyone can become a planner, as long as he registers. You don't need a CFP credential, let alone the Personal Financial Specialist, Chartered Mutual Fund Counselor or any other designation.

In many instances, the governing bodies that designate the criteria for a particular standard are warring with competing organizations touting a different standard. (For example, there are Chartered Mutual Fund Counselors and Certified Fund Specialists. Two different groups award a "CFS," one for mutual fund experts, the other for "certified factoring specialists.")

It makes evaluating credentials difficult, even if you are dealing with someone such as H.D. Vest and his amazing wall of certificates.

Indeed, there are some credentials for which you must have a minimum amount of experience or the ability to pass a test, and others that can be acquired for the cost of a membership or the work of a mediocre correspondence course. Some designations require continuing education, others simply encourage it.

It is against this paucity of standards and uniformity in credentials that you must arm yourself. You must also be wary of frauds—people who simply appropriate nice-sounding designations without doing a shred of the required work.

Later in this book, as it explores the way to choose each specialist, there will be a breakdown of professional designations you might run across and the qualifications that are supposed to come with the fancy letters on the business card. (This book will stick to what I consider meaningful and/or common credentials, so don't expect to find all 18 of Vest's affiliations back there.)

In the meantime, however, there are four questions to ask when you interview an adviser who greets you with professional credentials:

1. What did it take to earn your stripes and why did you consider it important to achieve this distinction?

Some credentials require experience, knowledge and the ability to pass a test, others grandfather in old-time practitioners and others are simply membership organizations.

That's why you want to know specifically how someone earned a designation. When verifying credentials, you may want to double-check the various steps an adviser must take to earn the designation and keep it current.

In addition, you want to find out why the adviser went to the trouble of getting the credential. Hopefully, it was for more than mere first impressions.

If a financial planner did the work to earn a "Chartered Financial Analyst" designation, he would presumably want to tell you how that will help him manage your money. (CFAs are held primarily by stock analysts and institutional money managers, and a planner who earns one would likely tell you it makes him a better stock/mutual fund picker.) Conversely, a "registered investment adviser" has paid a modest fee, met some minimum standards and submitted certain filings to the Securities & Exchange Commission; their "credential" is not likely to help you, the client, one whit. Worse yet is the F-O credential used by some financial planners; it signifies "fee-only," and is given by the National Association of Personal Financial Advisors not for any expertise but simply because the adviser charges exclusively on a fee schedule rather than commissions.

2. Are there continuing education credits? If so, describe what you have been doing to meet them.

Ask about the courses your prospective adviser has taken to stay current on the credential, and ask how that education might help him in his work with you. Continuing education courses run the gamut from nuts-and-bolts practice-management classes to specific ideas for helping clients get more from their money.

You want an adviser who is building expertise as it relates to you (rather than learning how to get more profits from each client, which some organizations consider suitable continuing education). Rules and laws governing money management change so quickly that anyone who stays out of the loop for over a year may never be able to get back in.

3. Can you get the number for the sanctioning body?

No adviser should be afraid of you calling the group that issues the credentials to make sure everything is on the up-and-up.

Because most consumers don't do their homework and make appropriate background checks, crooks who pretend to have credentials they never earned stay in business. In addition, most sanctioning groups will kick out members who run afoul of by-laws or codes of ethics, so someone who has a credential up on his office wall may not necessarily be entitled to continue using it.

If he works with the sanctioning group (and the addresses and phone numbers for those groups appear later in this book) he should have the phone number and should not fear you calling it.

If the adviser acts insulted that you are planning a background check or can't come up with a valid telephone number, get nervous. If he gives you the phone number, call it. If credentials play any role in your decision-making process, it pays to make sure everything is in order.

4. Does the designation mean anything unique in the service?

With tax preparers, for example, an enrolled agent can represent you in an audit; the return-preparer at the corner fast-food tax joint can't.

An accountant who also has a law degree, meanwhile, may be adept at trust and estate planning work. The same could be said for a financial planner with a law degree.

In every specialty, there are credentials that have meaning and can be helpful, and there are others that are self-serving and worthy of being ignored.

One person who read the first edition of this book wrote to ask if I had ever heard of a financial planner with a "CPhD," a pompous sounding designation that was new to me (and to every regulator I asked about it). It turned out to mean the planner was "certified in philanthropic development" by a national philanthropy group, something which might have been terrific if the reader had been looking for estate planning, but which had no real bearing on the basic financial planning that was being sought.

One thing you can assume about credentials is that the letters after an adviser's name mean something in terms of the price, as in "the more credentials, the bigger the bill." If that turns out to be true—and it usually does—then be sure you need and get what you are paying for.

You don't want to pay for expertise you don't need. You may decide you don't need a certified public accountant to do an ordinary tax return, for example. At the same time, you might prefer hiring a lawyer who has taken specialized classes in elder law. And you probably won't care if your financial planner has a CPhD.

By making the adviser spell out the benefits you get from his expertise, you go a long way toward defining what you expect to get from the relationship.

Once you have answered those basic questions about an adviser's credentials—and that could take hours if you are interviewing H.D. Vest himself—you can go about the rest of the interview process with an eye toward whether the person is good at what he does or merely proficient in doing what it takes to add some initials to a business card.

10 *They're smarter than I am; how do I keep control?*

In talking about troubled relationships between advisers and clients, I always worry about overstating the case.

After all, I know countless financial advisers of all stripes, and only one or two of them have had so much as a serious arbitration dispute over the last 15 years. The lists of disciplinary actions taken against members of the financial planning or brokerage communities, for example, are tiny compared to the number of practitioners.

Clearly, the rogues and scoundrels out there are in the distinct minority.

But there are plenty of honest advisers out there who simply aren't very good at what they do, who couldn't manage their way out of a paper sack if you showed them where the opening was.

For you to have successful relationships with your financial helpers, you need to avoid the buffoons at least as much as the bad guys.

Yet bad counsel is hard to discern; an adviser dresses well and talks in a language that is all at once confusing, mysterious and alluring. It is very easy to give an adviser, even a bad one, the proverbial keys and let them drive the relationship.

To protect yourself, you must be in control of the relationship from the very beginning. That starts with the first interview, and gets tricky right off the bat.

You want to choose counselors who want to "hire" you every bit as much as you want to hire them. If they do not value your business, you will not get the level of service you desire.

But in proving your worth to an adviser, it is absolutely essential you maintain control and do not simply fall in as a member of the adviser's flock. (Remember, the person who follows the herd steps in a lot of cow pies; you need to follow a path that is correct for you.)

The person across the desk from you is the hired gun, the expert whose help and guidance you are seeking. He may or may not talk in terms that are over your head—in which case some people mistakenly play along as if they understand every word—but the typical emphasis is on getting information out of a client or potential customer, and then making business decisions.

You need to provide him the information he needs to make judgments and give you options and then rein him in so that the relationship moves at your pace.

If you are assembling a financial team of experts—and you will over the course of your lifetime—you must start by repeating the following mantra until you are ready to live it:

"It's my money."

Your advisers are partners in your financial success, but you have the most at stake and, therefore, run the show.

As such, you are entitled from the very beginning of the relationship to ask about anything you want, from why a recommendation was made to why something cost more than you expected. Just as important, you are to be treated like "the boss." Some advisers treat customers shabbily if the client does not follow proffered advice; this kind of reaction should function as an instant warning sign that the adviser respects his own position more than yours—and has put his own interests (and possibly his wallet) ahead of yours.

It does not matter who is smarter or who knows more; your financial advisers are being hired in order to help YOU make the best decisions possible for managing your affairs.

As you go about managing your advisers, there are a few things to remember:

Never sacrifice control

Sign away control of your assets to someone else only in the event you are incapacitated.

We've all heard stories of the sports legend or movie star who turned a large fortune into a small one by letting an agent or financial planner "handle the money." They let someone else do the investing and money management and never used their own judgment as an appropriate balance, and they got wiped out for their naivete.

It doesn't have to be someone who is out there trying to rip customers off. He simply needs to exercise bad judgment.

Take S. Jay Goldinger, for example, a nationally recognized expert in bonds, syndicated columnist and all-around big wheel in the 1980s and early 1990s. His trading practices backfired and virtually wiped out his own firm—taking client money in the process. By all indications, Goldinger didn't get rich while the ship was sinking; instead, he went down with the ship.

That doesn't make it any better for the investors who were lost at sea with him.

There are advisers who do very well with total control, who do not "churn" accounts—a practice of trading heavily to generate commissions—and who have earned their customers' trust. But as far as I am concerned, surrendering control of your investments is an invitation to trouble. You want an adviser to believe he must do a reasonable job of representing your interests in order to remain on the team; if he knows that decisions must be run by you—and that he may have to justify choices—he is less likely to take actions that could jeopardize the relationship.

Never abdicate your responsibility

It sounds like a semantic difference from "never lose control," but it's more than that. Just because you haven't signed control over to someone else does not mean you have lived up to your role in running your affairs.

No matter who you hire to do any number of your financial chores, you retain a basic responsibility, whether that is reviewing statements, reading a mutual fund prospectus, asking for alternative investment selections, etc.

Delegating authority is great, surrendering it isn't.

A successful manager or coach offers adequate supervision, tells the players what is expected of them and reviews the progress and asks questions before being satisfied with the results. This is your job in overseeing your financial helpers.

You can't just pick experts and expect the rest of your financial life to run itself.

In the late 1980s, for example, a conservative investor who told his adviser to select top-performing bond funds with good star ratings might have wound up with a junk bond fund.

This has to do with the complicated risk-versus-reward measuring system the popular ratings agency Morningstar employs; there are times when that system favors one type of hot investment, when asking for a four- or five-star fund puts you into one asset class, such as junk bonds among bond funds in the late 1980s.

If the adviser offers you a high-yield fund with a good star rating, it hardly sounds like junk. What's more, the adviser may believe in the fund manager and the Morningstar seal of approval (junk bonds are a very good investment for some people); the question is whether you recognize what you are being sold.

A quick read of the prospectus would provide enough information to avoid this kind of mistake. Even if you don't understand the Martian language fund companies tend to use in their documents, you probably could get enough clues to question your adviser.

Similarly, just because you pay a tax preparer to put together your return doesn't mean you shouldn't read it before signing. If the preparer messes up—either in your favor or against—you are swearing to the information and making yourself liable, an action that demands a few minutes of your attention.

One very simple example of how this plays out comes in brokerage confirmation statements. If you work with a full-service broker, trading confirmation sheets—the tickets that describe the transaction you have made and detail any monies owed—show you whether the brokerage firm is a "market-maker" in a stock. Market-makers, in a nutshell, maintain an inventory in specific issues—which typically mean more profits for the firm. Firms routinely plug stocks they make a market in, and may give brokers additional compensation for trading in those shares.

If your broker continually recommends stocks in which the firm is a market-maker—to the exclusion of outside selections—it is fair to wonder whether the broker is receiving incentives for selling issues from the company's hot list. Without either asking the question or reviewing the confirmation slips, however, you might never know.

Acknowledge your smarts and your shortcomings; make advisers talk to your level of sophistication and tell them when and why you have reservations and why the feeling in your gut tells you not to follow their suggestions. If an adviser does not respect those things and your judgment, you may need to reconsider the relationship.

Never do anything you don't understand

The job of an adviser is to be your expert and convince you to follow the plan of action he devises. A good expert can explain financial situations down to the level of a novice and doesn't lose patience when asked basic questions.

Your adviser should want—and be able—to provide simple answers.

The moment you agree to a financial decision you do not understand, you surrender control to the adviser. You are at his mercy, in that you will only understand what he explains to you—and a lot of unscrupulous advisers can really put the shine on the sewage and make a bad investment sound like a good one right up to the moment you are out of money.

Make sure you ask all of your questions. No adviser should make you feel like this is a bother. You need sufficient information to feel comfortable, and if that forces the adviser to work a bit harder explaining things to you, so be it.

Do not feign knowledge; if an adviser spews out a bunch of statistics and jargon and you nod your head knowingly, he may assume you know more than you really do. This will only encourage him to speed up the discussions, let more terms go unexplained and—through very little fault of his own—confuse you further.

Always be forthcoming with information

You do not control advisers by giving them only a smattering of information. They need to know everything relative to their specialty in order to advise you successfully.

By making sure they know as much about your situation as you do, they become an extension of you.

Some people don't want to tell an adviser about their financial embarrassments or figure that the adviser needs to know only about the very specific situation he is working on, so a stockbroker, for example, may not be told about retirement savings through an employer that will never become part of the brokerage account.

What the adviser doesn't know CAN hurt you, as he can't accurately plan for your needs and your future if he doesn't have the complete picture.

Worse yet, you can't adequately judge an adviser's work when you haven't supplied enough information to allow for good decision-making. The best advisory relationships occur only when the counselor and client are on the same wavelength and reviewing the same information.

Set the ground rules up front. Make sure your adviser knows his or her role

Before engaging an adviser—no matter the specialty—you should know what to expect.

By spelling out your expectations up front and repeating them at crucial times—"I thought we agreed we would go over the plan together rather than by phone"—you keep the relationship on your terms. This is particularly important when you pursue a big-name adviser, because many of the top players in each specialty are so busy that clients sometimes get short shrift. It may be great to sign up a marquis name for your team—a planner featured regularly in your local paper, an accountant who heads the local CPA group or the lawyer who has done estate plans for the biggest families in your town—but only if you can get him on your terms.

Just as important is that you let each adviser know his role on the team. There are plenty of insurance agents who double as financial planners—and vice versa—or accountants who are qualified attorneys, or bankers who now offer financial advice. Define the role you want for each player—the banker handles your borrowing needs, for example, but should leave the financial planning to another adviser on the team—and make sure he feels comfortable with you as a client on those terms.

You may want to have an adviser play dual roles—such as an accountant whose tax knowledge and legal degree make him appropriate to set up an estate plan—but you should qualify him separately for each job before giving him two hats to wear. (You'll read more about that in the chapter on "utility infielders.")

Never do anything with an adviser whom you can't meet face-to-face

You may do the bulk of your business by phone, fax, Internet, e-mail and the U.S. Postal Service, but the ability to have a face-to-face sit-down is very reassuring.

It is perfectly acceptable to have an investment adviser, tax preparer or any other type of adviser be thousands of miles away (so long as he is licensed or registered to do business in the state in which you live), or to interact with an adviser who manages customer accounts online, so long as you can come down and see the operation and visit the adviser whenever you want.

Anyone who would not be comfortable accepting your check—or discussing your situation—in person is not worth trusting.

Consult with other experts and advisers

I hate radio talk-show advice, when someone calls into a station, gives a two-minute snippet of information and is told by an expert that his adviser has led him astray.

The radio host has an incomplete picture of his finances and little information to go on.

The same goes for most online chat rooms and other places the average person can turn to for a second opinion.

But if your adviser has made a suggestion that makes you nervous, you may want to consult with someone. It may be other financial advisers—your accountant or tax preparer knows your finances well and may know enough about financial planning to comment on whether you are getting sound advice. If you have multiple advisers where areas of expertise will overlap, you should always consult your lead expert on any particular subject.

I've heard countless horror stories of investors who went to redeem bank certificates of deposit and whose banker sold them mutual funds or other investments that were inappropriate or simply a bad choice. On the one hand, the investor trusted his adviser, the banker in this case; on the other, he did not consult with his financial planner, his primary adviser on investment selection.

Make sure you take enough time to get this consultation; it's not that every tidbit of advice heard on the radio or sprayed across the Internet is inappropriate, but rather that you want to make sure the person providing your second opinion knows enough about you and your finances to make a qualified judgment.

In addition to experts, consider huddling with friends or family, even if those people are not the most knowledgeable about financial matters. This forces you to explain—in plain language—what is going on. If you hear yourself talking and it sounds like a sales pitch you would be embarrassed to make to this friend or family member, then you can be pretty sure it is not right for you.

Do not avoid confrontations

Repeat after me: "It's my money."

If your broker or planner is dragging his or her feet issuing statements, processing your redemptions or simply in meeting your expectations, demand satisfaction now. You are the boss.

These situations do not get better on their own; do not let the problem fester or you will have a mess that almost certainly can't be solved without replacing a key member of your advisory board—or, worse yet, without hiring a lawyer and filing suit.

Always let an adviser know when he has let you down, when something has happened—whatever it is—that is out of line with your expectations.

Many advisers will let a relationship start on your terms, and then move it to their own—because they are comfortable dealing with all clients in a cookie-cutter fashion. Don't let this happen—or prepare to make a change if the tenor of the relationship is changing and you can not get it back on your terms.

By making it clear that you will stand up for your rights and demand that your expectations be met, you are much less likely to be taken advantage of. If something doesn't seem right, get an explanation immediately; if a satisfactory one is not forthcoming, get ready to move on.

In the end, you can always retain control of advisory relationships by making decisions with your feet.

11 *Getting blood from a stone; how to get good answers from references*

There's a men's store in the Northeast that uses the slogan "a satisfied customer is our best advertising."

Management is encouraging customers who don't believe the prices or the quality of the clothes to get some references before shopping.

And that's for a suit, something worth from one to three hours worth of time with most high-quality lawyers, accountants or financial planners.

But in financial services, references are tricky business. Plenty of advisers will volunteer names when asked, but others put up a stone wall to keep you from getting to their customers.

First off, they cite confidentiality issues, protecting the privacy of their clients. That's a good excuse for not giving a reference, and one that will put off many customers.

It's also lame.

The vast majority of satisfied customers would be happy, if asked, to vouch for their advisers. Some volunteer their praise, but even those who don't raise their hands to accept this chore will acquiesce if the adviser places a phone call. When an adviser refuses to work with you on something as simple as a consumer reference—as opposed to a reference from another type of adviser with whom they work—you should question whether you will ever be able to get the relationship onto your terms.

When you ask for references, don't expect to be given the names of the last five clients who walked through the door—a measure that might provide some objectivity—but rather the names of good customers or volunteer praise-singers.

If you are given professional references—other advisers with whom he works and who can speak somewhat knowledgeably about the business—be concerned by the business connection. Most likely, the reference will be someone to whom your prospective adviser makes referrals when affairs go beyond the scope of his or her knowledge. That person won't want to give a bad reference because doing so could stop the gravy train.

Regardless of the reference, assume you are getting the names of people who are strongly on the side of the adviser.

Some advisers include that assumption in their reasons for not offering references. They argue that a prospective client doesn't have much to gain, while their existing client loses both confidentiality and time. Since they expect your conversation with a reference to be nothing more than an endorsement, they may even have letters of recommendation; otherwise, they may simply try to pooh-pooh the whole process, pointing out that you already have *de facto* references, namely the people who gave you a referral in the first place.

(As the chapter on dealing with referrals noted, you will want to question those people the way you would a reference provided by the adviser. Remember, too, that many referral services are paid listings, which is pure advertising as opposed to a qualified referral.)

So be prepared that an adviser might not want to give you references and may even tell you it is his policy not to provide names, citing the confidentiality and inconvenience issues. He may say he doesn't ask customers to act as references so he has no names to give you; you can simply ask him for yesterday's luncheon appointment or any of the last three people in the office or for five minutes of time from the person who is in the waiting room.

Politely explain to the counselor that, despite the inherent biases, there are questions that a reference can answer that an adviser can't, notably dealing with the tenor and tone of the advisory relationship. The counselor can say how he intends to work with you, but only another client can give you an idea of how he actually does that work.

The trick is for you to be able to draw those comments out from a reference, and to listen carefully to what is being said. Then you can picture yourself walking the proverbial mile in the other client's shoes and deciding how they fit.

If necessary, show the adviser this book and explain that it will help you ask the right questions (although I do not recommend sharing the questions with the adviser, because it might color his choice of which clients to offer you). Note that professional references really don't work because one adviser cannot shed light on the way another one works with clients and makes customers feel; only a customer can do that.

In addition, explain that you intend to call references only as a final check, as the last piece in your decision-making process, so that you will not bother the references of an adviser until you are close to making your selection. What's more, point out that you will not be asking the reference "How much money do you have with this adviser?" or "How much money has he made you?," as those things are none of your business and not relevant to your personal situation.

If the adviser still will not give you the names of customers—rather than other professionals—you will have to decide whether to keep him in the selection process.

"In choosing someone to work with, I would want to talk to a customer and I would be suspicious or nervous if someone just flatly refused to provide me with a client contact," says Robert N. Veres of Morningstar Advisor. "I understand why people wouldn't want to have their clients bothered and I understand the confidentiality issue. I still want the contact.

"While there is nothing unethical about someone not giving you the names of referrals—and not just professional referrals because those aren't worth much—I might prefer to go to the next person. It's going to be hard to get very comfortable with a person who won't do something this basic for you."

In the chapters on hiring each type of adviser, there are questions that may be specific to a particular specialty. But no matter which kind of adviser you are hiring—and whether the reference's name was given willingly or through cajoling—here are the general questions you will want to ask references.

How did you come to work with the adviser? How long have you been working together?

Just because you picked up this book and learned to pick an adviser the right way doesn't mean the adviser's other clients did. Get the story on how this person found out about the adviser and what kind of work he put into qualifying the person before hiring, as it will go a long way to coloring the rest of what you hear from this person and whether he is someone who is detail-oriented or leaves things to chance.

The more you determine about the reference's background, the more easily you can evaluate whether his standard of a good relationship measures up to yours.

Obviously, you want to know how long the reference and adviser have worked together and whether the relationship is ongoing. (Many references for real estate agents and lawyers are people who have no continuing tie to the adviser because they do not have a current need for services.) If there is no current relationship, find out how long ago the person worked with the adviser; you would prefer a recent client to one from years ago, when the practice presumably was smaller.

How often do you hear from the adviser? Who initiates contact and what are most of those calls about?

A big part of every successful advisory relationship is communication. That doesn't necessarily mean a phone call every week, but it does mean an adviser should show appropriate concern.

For an insurance agent, for example, it may be when policies are up for renewal. In the case of real estate agents and lawyers working on a case, it may be at regular weekly intervals or whenever there is any action you need to know about. For brokers and financial planners, the amount of contact will vary depending on the scope of the relationship.

The rule of thumb is that the bigger percentage of your assets you entrust with someone, the more often you want to hear from him.

If the adviser initiates all contact, but the calls are made only when there is a sale to be made—a hot stock tip, a change in the recommended mutual fund portfolio or a new insurance product that might generate a commission—that would be a sign the adviser is more interested in doing transactions than building a relationship, even if his happy client/reference hasn't figured it out yet.

Does the adviser always return your calls promptly? Does he or she give you the time necessary to answer questions?

You can never overemphasize communication. While you can't expect an adviser to take an hour in the middle of his day to take an unsolicited phone call that rambles over various points of your financial situation (and maybe on to how the kids are doing, etc.), you have a right to expect that each phone call will be taken seriously.

Find out, too, how the adviser reacts to what might be considered dumb questions. Even if you never ask one, you want to feel like you can without being made to feel stupid.

(There are no dumb questions, only things that people would be embarrassed to ask; you should never be embarrassed if you have a good working relationship with your adviser.)

Does the adviser include your spouse—or parents or children—in discussions and meetings?

Every good adviser gets to know the family, at least in the beginning. After that, however, many deal exclusively with the decision-maker.

There's nothing terrible about that. In my household, for example, my broker, insurance agent and tax preparer all deal with me. Susan is included in important meetings and has enough of a relationship with each adviser to feel comfortable if anything should happen to me.

But if you and your partner make all decisions jointly, you want to make sure the adviser is happy explaining things to you as a couple and has the patience to do that rather than pressing for instant decisions.

How does the adviser react when you raise questions or come in with suggestions?

Many advisers try to make all clients fit into the same basic circle of reference. Accountants, for example, decide which types of deductions they like to pursue and may focus on those; insurance agents and financial planners have their favorite products.

If you ask questions, rather than immediately accepting the advice as gospel, or if you bring suggestions to the table ("I read about a tax deduction for this situation and think I might be eligible . . ."), you want to make sure the adviser won't give you the brush-off.

Have you ever decided not to take your counselor's advice? If so, how did he react?

Just because the reference is happy with the adviser's service does not mean he has taken all advice blindly. You want to find out what suggestions the adviser may have made that the client didn't like—why did the client decide they were not appropriate?—and how the adviser responded when their recommended course of action was not taken.

Have you ever had any pricing/billing problems? (If so, how were they resolved?)

You always ask an adviser about how he charges for his work. You should ask the reference to make sure there never have been any problems with the adviser's charges.

If there have been billing problems, you will want to know how things were settled (and you may want to rehash billing procedures with the adviser before making your hiring decision).

Has anything about the relationship surprised you?

This is a good way to find out if the relationship has lived up to, or exceeded, expectations.

Has the adviser's service ever disappointed you and, if so, what did you do about it?

Many times, a client working with an adviser does not recognize problems or disappointments until he is asked to think about them. Problems then may come into sharper focus.

A reference's disappointments may not bother you—perhaps he wanted more face-to-face contact and you don't care about that issue—but it's important to ask about shortcomings.

Have you ever worked with other advisers? If so, why did you make a change—and what does this adviser do better than the last one?

In Chapter 1, Robert Clark of Morningstar noted that many people bounce from one adviser to the next, rather than picking one adviser with whom they can work comfortably for a lifetime.

If the reference has worked with other advisers, his experience may be valuable. Presumably, the old relationship was lacking in some way, and the new one doesn't have the same problem.

Again, this helps qualify what the reference wants from the relationship—and how it compares with your desires—as well as how well those needs are being met.

What do you think this adviser does the best?

Hopefully, what an adviser does best is something you value as a prospective client.

Remember Jim, the stockbroker in Chapter 5 who was supposed to be the best broker in town but wound up losing the stock-picking contest by using the same miserable advice he was giving clients? What he did best, apparently, was schmooze customers and make them feel important.

No one knows better than you what you want out of an advisory relationship, whether it is hand-holding, financial acumen, the emotional discipline to stay the course or whatever. You are looking for an adviser whose strong points fit your needs.

Is there any area in which you wish the adviser would give you even more attention?

This is a logical follow-up to the previous question. Again, it helps you determine whether your expectations for the relationship are in line with the reference's and helps you decide if the adviser can meet your specific needs.

How long do you anticipate working with the adviser? (Or, if the adviser is hired on a need-now basis, such as a real estate agent: Do you anticipate working with the adviser again?)

You are looking for financial relationships that can last a lifetime, or close to it.

Yes, a reference is going to be biased and say nice things. But if he can't see working with that adviser for a lifetime (or again), then you need to know why he might hire someone else. Indeed, you might want to hire someone else, too.

12 *Can my computer replace traditional advisers?*

When the first edition of this book went to the publisher in 1997, there were no significant Internet sites offering "customized" financial planning.

You could find financial advice on the web, of course, but much of it came from chat rooms and other places where smart consumers questioned the validity of the opinions, not to mention the expertise of the people providing it. Most of the early personal finance web sites were designed to teach you to do your own financial planning, rather than to offer fee-for-service advice.

By the time the first edition came off the printing press in 1998, that had changed.

Today, it seems every week there is another site offering customized personal finance advice. From DirectAdvice.com, MyMoneyPro.com, MyCFO.com to financialengines.com, 1-800-MUTUALS (which started as a telephone contest service before providing financial advice online) and all the way down to ihatefinancialplanning.com, you can find countless web sites offering some measure of personalized financial advice. There are even web sites such as TheRightAdvisor.com that are designed not to give you financial guidance online, but help you find a financial planner you can work with in person.

Theoretically, all of these services, plus online brokerages and the online services offered by traditional brokerage, mutual fund, accounting and other firms, could make most forms of financial guidance obsolete.

And that's without even considering the thousands of personal finance sites that can help you educate yourself so that you don't need a financial adviser at all. While some of those sites have severe limitations—most notably the expertise (or lack thereof) of the people proffering counsel—there are plenty of name-brand sites including CBSMarketwatch.com or CNNfn.com, as well as investment-company-sponsored sites such as Vanguard.com, where you can get educational material and knowledgeable commentary.

With all of that in mind, traditional forms of financial guidance really could become obsolete if you count yourself as being Internet savvy and willing to do much of the work on your own time and with limited guidance.

But if you bought this book because you want to hire an adviser who can marshal you through life's major monetary responsibilities, online financial services probably will not cut it. (The obvious exception being an online broker, hired exclusively because he gives you Internet access to the market.)

In each chapter on hiring a specific type of adviser, one key question to ask is whether you can perform this service on your own, without help. The answer almost always is "Yes, I can do this on my own," provided you are willing to invest the time and energy into learning the necessary elements. Many web sites can help you on that score.

But if you have opted to hire help, then you should look at fee-for-advice sites as similar to hiring an adviser who you meet in person, with the exception of the method by which you interact with the adviser and receive the majority of your guidance.

You will check out an online adviser the same way you would any other, with an additional focus on the means by which you will interact with the company and receive what you pay for.

Do not confuse free-advice, chat-room communities designed to educate and entertain you with a fee-for-advice service.

In the end, you are likely to find that paid-advice web sites fall short of your expectations because much of what you truly desire in an advisory relationship *is the relationship rather than the advice*. It's the emotional discipline to define a strategy and develop the faith to stick to it. Even the best financial advisers will tell you that you need to back up your decisions with a certain measure of conviction, and that level of confidence is hard to develop when the adviser is a faceless entity on a computer screen.

Chapter 7 of this book talked extensively about "transaction-oriented advisers" versus "relationship-oriented advisers." Obviously, any service that provides its advice online falls into the former category.

Essentially, what most online financial planning sites do is allow you to enter personal data, usually as a precursor to some form of free report or forecast. Your information goes into what the financial services industry calls "a black box," a computer program that slices and dices it and then sees where you fall short of its programmed norms.

This is not all bad. The Financial Engines web site, for example, was built using formulas and forecasting models developed by Nobel Prize-winning economist William Sharpe. It is worth viewing—and if you have a financial adviser and question the advice you get, it makes for one heck of a second opinion—but that doesn't necessarily make the paid advice portion of the site worth the cost.

So the crucial element in online financial advice services is determining whether you are paying for something that can not only deliver the results you desire, but also a level of service and personal interaction that will meet your expectations. It makes no sense to pay for guidance online today only to dump that adviser in favor of a "real person" a few months or years down the road. You will be wasting not only money, but time, which is one of the most important commodities in long-term financial planning.

With that in mind, here are the questions to have answered before entering into a relationship with an Internet-based financial consulting service. Many of these items are easy to find, in "frequently asked question" (FAQ) sections on the web sites. Not all of them appear there, however, and the tougher ones to answer are the most important ones.

Before entering into an agreement with a web-based financial service—and in addition to asking the questions shown in the chapters on hiring each type of adviser—make sure the informational contact person or webmaster has answered all of the following questions:

How does this service differ from traditional advice?
This is the first question to answer, because it determines everything else about how you deal with the service provider.

If the answer is "These are traditional services adapted so you can use them on the Internet," then you will ask not only the questions in this chapter, but also all of the questions that apply to the specific type of adviser you are hiring. If the site offers something not available elsewhere (and I have yet to see such a thing, but I acknowledge the possibility), you will need to decide if the service is so good and important to alter the traditional interview process.

Do not let different packaging make you drop your guard or be less diligent in your shopping habits. If you are certain that you would prefer to deal with an online adviser rather than a traditional one, change your interview process so that you sample three or four web sites, instead of interviewing three or more advisers.

Web-based advice services tend to be cheaper than traditional counselors, and they offer you tremendous convenience, in that you can take your active role in managing the situation while in your pajamas at 2 A.M. They also offer interactivity and, in most cases, the ability to view what is happening to your portfolio on a real-time basis.

Still, you will want to know what, besides convenience, these firms bring to the table, as many traditional advisory firms now offer interactive web sites that let you review your situation online at your leisure while still offering you the face-to-face contacts when you want them.

How and how much are you paid for your services?

This is a key question in any advisory relationship but particularly important with web sites, where it sometimes looks and feels like you are getting something for nothing. If the counseling comes free or for a minimal fee, the advice may be steering you to investments or other services on which the people behind the web site truly make their money.

One of my father-in-law's friends, for example, called me up after having had an initial consultation with the folks at 1-800-MUTUALS. In the end, the advice he was being offered boiled down to little more than "Your asset allocation is pretty good, but you could do better in *these* funds."

Those funds all carried sales charges. Implementing the plan was going to cost thousands of dollars in sales fees and taxes. That might be palatable had the advice radically changed the investor's portfolio and steered him to something that would help him avoid a shortfall. That was not the case; this was essentially a replacement portfolio in which any benefits from marginal improvements in fund selection would have been swallowed by sales charges paid to the adviser.

Once you know how the adviser is paid—and in the online world, it can vary from flat-rate charges to asset-management fees, commissions, or payments from the companies that get the ultimate benefit of your actions (essentially referral fees that the web site gets from the investment firm that gets your business)—you can start looking at what you get for your dollars.

How many clients do you have and who is your average client?
This is particularly important for Internet-driven advice because it gives you an idea of just how personal your service is going to be.

Web sites may say that the advice you get is personalized, but if the site has more than a few hundred customers, you can be certain that human review of your situation is minimal. Instead, you program your inputs and the web site runs them through its black box program to come up with the right "solutions" for you.

Depending on your personality and how technical those inputs, this might be perfectly acceptable. If you truly want advice tailored for you—something that understands, say, your ultra-conservative nature—you are probably looking for a site that thinks outside the box.

The more customers the web site has, the more it wants to keep everyone contained in that box.

Likewise, you want to know the average clientele because it will give you a good idea whether this service has been working for people whose financial situation looks like yours. Just as you would not hire any adviser who was not used to dealing with a situation like yours, so should you be wary of any web site for which your financial situation varies from the norm.

The reason for this is straightforward: Black-box solutions tend to be based on certain assumptions about how people will act and react to the markets. Over time, these assumptions and measures are refined, typically as the webmasters learn more about their customers.

Don't be some web site's test pilot. If it doesn't have a track record handling people like you, get your help elsewhere.

What biases or possible conflicts of interest do I need to be aware of?
We've already discussed the compensation bias. Be aware of any other place where the research or forecast automatically brings you to the conclusion that you need help.

I have referred many people to the free forecasting tools at the Financial Engines web site, for example, yet I do not know of a single person (myself included) who has had his forecast come back saying he was virtually certain to reach his financial goals.

It could be that these people all were not saving enough, or that they didn't input everything correctly. Or it could be that some measure of uncertainty is good for business, so that the free forecast inspires people to want to take the paid service.

I do not know that to be the case, but Financial Engines is far from the only web site where no one's portfolio appears good enough to succeed without the paid advice offered by the site.

Beyond those types of conflicts, find out if the web site has business ties to any other financial services firm. Some web sites have ties to specific businesses. Insurance sites may work with only a short list of companies, so you may have to shop several in order to get a good idea of what's available. Some financial planning sites have ties to certain fund companies and tend to recommend funds from those families to everyone.

Be aware of these kinds of traps. The conflicts of interest rife in all kinds of financial counseling are present on the Internet, too.

How will I interact with the company? What happens when I have questions or problems?

Forms that take your information and e-mail correspondence are fine, up to a point. The day something goes kaflooey you may want to talk to a real person and have some idea of who that person is and how you will reach him.

Some of these sites have star advisers or money managers as investment strategists, and these big names are the ones that may draw you in. But when the stock market is tumbling rapidly, or when you have a question about your insurance policy in the wake of a claim or have a problem in any of the specialties for which you could substitute an online service for face-to-face contact with a person, you need to know the fallback position and how things will work at crunch time.

Learn how the web site handles both the routine and the extreme before signing up.

Is there one person assigned to work with you as a customer?

Different sites have different policies, so find out if you are working with a team of advisers or one person. If you have a specialist assigned to you, learn that person's background. Just as you might not want to hire the junior underling of some big-name adviser, make sure you are comfortable with the person who will be handling your account online.

If you are not assigned a specialist, ask yourself if you want to be dealing with a faceless, nameless adviser. It might work fine for purchasing investments or insurance or for doing your taxes, but it may not feel so good when a stock blows up, you face a liability claim or the IRS sends you an audit notice.

Can I see samples of what I am paying for?

Most web sites offer samples, for which you click to see what the reports, documents or advice prepared for you is going to look like.

Insist on seeing the finished product, and if you don't get a good sense of what, specifically, you will receive for your money, ask the firm to send you a sample plan so you can review it on paper and at your leisure, showing it to your spouse or partner and anyone else who might weigh in on whether the service will be sufficient.

Can I have a copy of all applicable regulatory paperwork?

You will learn in the chapters on hiring specific advisers that registration and other documents are essential for helping you establish whether the adviser really is qualified to help you and has avoided disciplinary problems.

The fact that the adviser works in the online medium should not change the paperwork and registrations needed to do business, most notably a Form ADV for financial planning. Hopefully, these documents are posted on the web site—although you still will want to make sure that what is shown is legit (see the chapters on each advice specialty for instructions)—but don't be shy about asking.

Can I get the names of a few clients to act as references?

You are taking advice, in general, from an expert you can not see. You are trying to determine the tenor and substance of a relationship that may have had no interpersonal contact aside from an e-mail or instant message.

The least you can expect before turning over your money is an available reference. Treat this person as you would any other reference (see Chapter 11).

Try to get names, addresses and phone numbers for references, not just e-mail addresses, as it will give you a better chance of having some way to make sure the reference is legitimate and not just the adviser in disguise.

How do I terminate this relationship if I am not satisfied?

Never enter any financial agreement without knowing your responsibilities in the deal and how you can terminate the relationship if and when you are dissatisfied with the service.

On some advice sites, an e-mail is not enough to cancel a contract and get your funds returned to you. There may be a requirement forcing you to produce a notarized letter or signature guarantee, which is something you are going to want to know in the event you feel compelled to change advisers in a hurry.

13 *Hiring a financial planner*

People hire financial planners because they need service; they fire them because they don't like the investment returns.

That's the right way to hire a helper, but not the right expectation.

Don't hire an investment manager to "beat the market."

Hire a financial planner to provide you with security and make sure you can reach long-term goals regardless of what the market does.

Remember, the stock market does not know when your next mortgage or tuition payment is due, nor does it understand your current financial needs.

Advisers should aim to beat the market only if that is what your personal circumstances call for. Otherwise, their efforts should be focused on your long-term goals.

If the idea of managing your money is to never run out and live out your life comfortably, then that is the benchmark you should shoot for. Everything else is noise.

Financial planning is a wide-ranging topic, and it can be hard to find the right match of skill and service to meet your needs. But if you enter the relationship with the right expectations—that you want someone to offer you service, as opposed to merely picking winners—you are likely to come away with an adviser you can trust for a lifetime.

Here are the questions you will want to answer as you go about selecting and working with a financial planner.

Can I do this myself?

As Dwight D. Eisenhower once noted, "Plans are nothing, planning is everything."

So it goes with your financial situation. Everyone has plans for what they want their money to achieve, but not many people are reaching their goals comfortably.

No one actually needs to hire a financial planner or investment counselor, unless all they have on their own is a plan.

The average individual investor can manage a lifetime of savings and investment in no-load mutual funds and no-commission Treasury bonds. He can get advice from newspapers, magazines, friends and web sites.

A financial planner provides "emotional discipline." It is the planner's job to make sure plans are acted upon, not just drawn up in your mind. He provides guidance, reassurance, support and stability to help you set and stay the course toward long-term financial goals.

You need a planner if you don't have the knowledge or time to tackle your finances on your own. Even if you have that understanding, however, you need the discipline to invest regularly—aggressively enough to reach your goals but without excessive risk—and/or the confidence to pursue your goals in all market conditions. Lacking any of those things, chances are you can't do your financial planning successfully, without at least a modicum of financial assistance.

What is a planner's role and responsibility to me?

You define this during the interview process. You may want just a fiscal physical, a snapshot of where you stand now and what you must do to reach your long-term goals, or you may want to hire a money manager to plot a specific investment course for your money.

Whether you are seeking periodic check-ups—plenty of planning clients see their advisers once every two years after an initial consultation sets them on the course toward their goals—or an active day-to-day manager of your affairs, the planner should be able to play a role as adviser to you and to any other financial helpers you have hired.

Legally, planners have a responsibility to provide counsel that is suitable for each individual client. "Unsuitable advice" is inappropriately risky, such as a super-aggressive small-company stock funds for a post-retirement age, low-income investor. It may also have hidden costs or charges the adviser could have avoided by making more savvy choices.

Picking investments that do not grow is not automatically considered inappropriate counsel. Suitability has less to do with performance than with the process that led to making an investment in the first place.

Selecting investments should be a small part of a planner's role; if the only reason you want to hire an adviser is to get the names of good mutual funds, chances are you are paying too much money for a service that will let you down the first time any fund pick fails to pan out.

Worse yet, an adviser whose role is defined as picking investments can be made obsolete at little or no charge by any number of web sites, magazines or computer software programs.

Am I better off having my insurance agent or accountant or stockbroker function as my overall financial planner?

You may already have an adviser with financial planning credentials and a background in advising customers. (You will see in Chapter 22 reasons to limit each of your advisers to one job.) Because a planner most likely will function as quarterback of your financial team, the job is too important simply to hand over, even to an adviser with whom you already have a relationship.

That being the case, if an adviser says he can handle your planning needs, run him through the complete interview process. If he isn't as good or better than every other adviser you talk to, he should get no consideration toward playing two positions on your advisory team.

How are planners paid?

The entire financial planning community has been moving away from traditional methods of payment over the last few years.

Instead of traditional commission-based sales, a growing number of advisers are paid either on a flat hourly rate or as a percentage of assets under management.

Fee-only advocates would have you believe there is one of their brethren for every potential customer; but that's just not true. It is hard for low-net-worth individuals or couples to find a fee-only adviser; instead, they most often wind up working on a commission basis that essentially allows them to pay for the specific services they need when they need them.

Despite the fee-only trend, or perhaps because of it, it is more important than ever not to assume how a counselor exacts his fee. Be sure to find out if costs are associated with products or with overall services, and be careful when those lines are blurry.

For example, some advisers claim to be fee-only, but the moniker applies only to their investment products. The minute they sell you insurance, they are back on commission.

Likewise, advisers may get a piece of the action for helping to keep you in certain mutual funds. A "12b-1 fee," for example, is a marketing charge that some funds apply to accounts every year. Essentially, the fund takes as much as 1 percent of your account balance to pay for "marketing and distribution costs," and then pays a portion of the fee to your broker. This charge is in addition to the ongoing management fees charged by the fund itself.

Payment options boil down to fee-only, commission only, "fee-offset"—in which commissions reduce a fee for planning, so that a client knows the maximum amount he can pay for advice in a year—and fee-plus-commission.

If you move your account from one adviser to another, make sure any applicable marketing fees or "trailing commissions" get credited to the new adviser. This encourages your new helper to retain those holdings that are appropriate, rather than gutting the entire portfolio (a move you are likely willing to make if you have switched advisers) for entirely new choices.

Lastly, your planner may offer you an investment management account with something called a "wrap fee," which combines management and brokerage fees. These fees can run as high as 3 percent of the assets under management, which is steep. Something closer to 1.5 percent or 2 percent is about average for a stock wrap account; 1.0 to 1.5 percent is the norm with mutual fund wraps.

A wrap fee lets you know in advance what you will pay a money manager, but it will be worthwhile only if the manager trades actively and if you have a significant amount of cash—at least $25,000 and preferably $100,000 or above—to commit to the program; if you and the manager employ a buy-and-hold strategy, run the numbers to make sure you aren't better off with straight commission.

What credentials are important?

More than any other advisory role, financial planners are going to trot out their credentials, only some of which are truly meaningful.

It is important to know that financial advisers typically have to register with the state in which they work, but they do not need any credentials or designations to practice. In most states, registration requires little more than filling out some paperwork and paying a small fee.

That said, you will probably want to hire an adviser who has some type of advanced credential. Here are the ones you are most likely to run across.

The **Certified Financial Planner (CFP)** mark has become the backbone of many searches for a financial adviser and is considered by many experts to be the minimum credential needed to make a planner worth considering. Essentially, the CFP program is a self-study course—although many advisers now earn their designation taking classes at regional colleges and universities that have developed programs in financial planning. Advisers must have a minimum of three years of practice experience, plus the course work, and must successfully complete a two-day exam covering everything from insurance to investments to estate planning to employee benefits, taxes and more.

In addition, the Certified Financial Planner Board of Standards, which maintains the licensing requirements, expects licensees to adhere to a strict code of ethical conduct.

Advisers who concentrate on investment selection may have a **Chartered Financial Analyst** (CFA) designation, one of the most prestigious of all financial services credentials, awarded by the Association for Investment Management and Research (AIMR). The CFA mark requires several years of work experience, as well as passing a study course and exams in securities analysis, portfolio management, financial accounting, economics and ethics. The designation is common among institutional money managers and Wall Street analysts; it is an ideal credential to look for if you have a lot of money for which you want a planner to help allocate and choose investments.

If an agent comes to financial planning from the life insurance specialty, he may hold a **Chartered Financial Consultant (ChFC)** designation. Like its sister designation, the **Chartered Life Underwriter (CLU)**, the ChFC is awarded by the American College in Bryn Mawr,

Pa., and requires extensive educational training. Members of the Society of Financial Professionals (the trade group for CLUs and ChFCs) specialize in insurance issues. If you prefer to leave your insurance planning to an insurance agent, this credential may be less of a selling point than some of the others.

The *Personal Financial Specialist (PFS)* label goes to certified public accountants (CPAs) who concentrate on financial planning issues and meet rigorous educational requirements. Keeping this credential means retaining membership status in the American Institute of Certified Public Accountants, completing course work and undergoing periodic peer reviews.

In looking for an adviser to captain a financial team, experts who are particularly good at mixing investment knowledge with tax expertise often prove to be the best candidates, but that does not limit you to the relatively small world of the CPA/PFS. There are many CPAs and enrolled agents who also have their CFP credential; those particular dual-designations (CPA/CFP or EA/CFP) strike me as an even stronger combination for a team leader.

Beyond those designations, there are a number of credentials a financial planner might trot out to you. In alphabetical order, they include *Accredited Asset Management Specialist (AAMS)*, which is awarded to investment advisers who have completed the Asset Management Program offered by the National Endowment for Financial Education; *Accredited Estate Planners (AEP)*, who pass a test and meet minimum continuing education requirements set by the National Association of Estate Planners and Councils; *Certified Divorce Planner (CDP)*, a relatively new credential that signals that the adviser has passed a study course on the financial issues surrounding a marital break-up; *Certified Employee Benefit Specialist (CEBS)*, offered by the International Foundation of Employee Benefit Plans for a 10-course, 10-exam program covering all areas of planning and administration related to benefit plans; *Certified Fund Specialist (CFS)*, given to advisers who pass a course and exam on mutual fund selection and portfolio management; *Certified Investment Management Consultant (CIMC)*, awarded by the Institute for Investment Management Consultants for passing its study course; *Chartered Mutual Fund Consultant (CMFC)*, which is the National Endowment for Financial Education's version of the Certified Fund Specialist designation (as someone who writes a weekly column about mutual funds, I find neither of these designations particularly crucial to a financial adviser, but would prefer the CMFC if I had to pick one for an adviser to toss into his personal alphabet soup); **Certified Trust and Financial Advisers (CTFA)** work for a bank or trust company and have passed the Institute of Certified Bankers' course covering taxation, investments, personal finance and fiduciary duty; and **Registered Financial Consultants (RFC),** who have at least four years of practical experience, a degree in business, economics or law, and a CFP, ChFC, CPA or more to boot.

Even with all of those credentials, there are a few other initials an adviser might toss onto a resume or business card. One is membership in the **National Association of Personal Financial Advisors (NAPFA),** a group of fee-only planners that is almost militant in the way it views advisers who work on commission. The group has stepped up its membership requirements in terms of education and practice knowledge, but the basic standard remains that the adviser charges clients on a fee-only basis. It also awards the F-O credential—which stands for fee only—to any adviser (including non-members) who works strictly on a fee-only pay scale.

The **Licensed Independent Network of CPA Financial Planners** (LINC) is a membership group of fee-only planners who also are licensed as CPAs. No exam is required for membership.

All told, credentials are a sign that someone is proficient in the nuts-and-bolts, number-crunching side of financial planning. But as discussed in Chapter 9, an adviser's service and manner (and not his abilities with a scientific calculator) generally make the difference in a successful relationship; virtually none of the class/exam time involved in earning any of these designations is spent on the human side of a financial planning relationship.

Where do I start my search?

With all of the credentials out there, it can be hard to determine a starting point for a search. Obviously, friends and relatives can give you referrals, but that can be a particularly tough fit with financial planners, because your personal circumstances can be so much different than those of your loved ones, and planners tend to work best with a clientele that is similar in needs.

Beyond word of mouth, you might go to the referral lines offered by the credential and membership groups themselves.

You are going to interview several candidates before making your selection. I suggest at least one of your candidates be someone who was not a word-of-mouth referral; this allows you to have something of a "control group," to see whether your judgment is colored by the advice of a friend. Many people who have tried this at my suggestion have found that the adviser with whom they had no connection came off as most knowledgeable and helpful; a big reason for the difference is that their loved one picked a financial planner by serendipity, rather than science.

Here are several organizations that can supply names of financial planners in your area:

▪ The Financial Planning Association will give you a list of planners with the CFP credential in your area, along with materials to guide you through the selection process. Call 1-800-282-7526 for information (hearing impaired call 1-800-438-9968), or check out the planner search portion of the group's web site at www.fpanet.org.

▪ The National Association of Personal Financial Advisors, whose members must be fee-only planners, will give you a list of members from around the state, along with a financial planner interview form and a disclosure form to help you illustrate how and how much the planner and planning firm will be paid if you sign on. Call 1-888-FEE-ONLY or go to www.napfa.org.

▪ The American Institute of Certified Public Accountants provides the names of members who have earned its Personal Financial Specialist (PFS) designation. Call 1-800-862-4272 to ask for CPA/PFS referrals in your area.

▪ The Investment Counsel Association of America provides its membership directory free of charge to interested investors. The directory lists firms and provides details about the size and type of investment practice, along with account minimums. Although you will find some of the member firms accepting accounts of as little as $100,000, the majority of these firms work only with investors whose assets exceed $500,000. Call 202-293-4222 or go to www.icaa.org.

How do I check them out?

Check all brokers out in at least two places, starting with your state securities regulator (whose number is listed in Appendix 1) and including the groups that have awarded any credentials important to your decision. (The phone numbers typically are the same ones called to get referrals; if the adviser uses a different credential to sell you on his services, ask him to provide the organization's name and phone number so you can do a background check.)

Most states register financial advisers and will be able to share with you an adviser's Form ADV, which includes disciplinary history. The adviser should give you this information, too, but make the phone call to be sure you are aware of any current complaints and actions; many advisers have been known to hand out old registration paperwork, figuring it would keep a potential customer from checking with the state.

In addition to checking out the adviser, run the firm's name past the securities office, too. You do not want to be dealing with the most reputable character at a disreputable firm.

Still being developed as this book went to press was a web site that would allow you to view these forms and disciplinary records. The site is being developed by the NASD Regulation (an arm of the National Association of Securities Dealers); when the service is available, it either will be located at www.nasdr.com or you will be able to link to it from there.

If the financial planner is also a registered representative licensed to sell securities, you will want to get his Central Registration Depository (CRD) number and make sure he has no problems on that side of his practice. (If he sold securities in the past, get his CRD number so you can make sure disciplinary problems did not lead to the career change.).

Likewise, if you intend to use a planner for your insurance needs, make sure he is licensed with the state—you will need to call the insurance commissioner's office (phone numbers are listed in Appendix 2)—to make sure he has a clean bill of health all around.

What should I ask during an interview?

The late Charles Wilson, one-time chairman of General Motors Corp. and a former U.S. Secretary of Defense, once said in a speech, "No one can prevent a stupid person from doing the wrong thing in the wrong place at the wrong time—but a good plan should keep a concentration from forming."

Your job in selecting an adviser is not to be stupid about it, so that you can build a plan and never worry about making bad moves at the worst possible times.

To do that, you will want to cover all your bases and make sure your financial planning relationship lives up to your expectations from both an interpersonal and financial standpoint.

Here is the ground you will want to cover with a planner before making a selection:

What is your educational and professional background?

Look at a planner's background to see if he has a stable employment history. You want an adviser who will be there for you in the years ahead, as well as one who has not bounced from job to job because his work did not satisfy previous employers.

If an adviser has had more than two jobs in the last three years or has a regular pattern of job-switching, find out what's going on. While a planner may switch firms to get better career opportunities or to specialize in a personal field of interest, he also might move after having disciplinary or other troubles. If necessary, call the previous employer for a reference check.

A planner's educational and pre-financial planning background also is interesting to know. Many planners come to the field as a second career. Their first interest may have been teaching or money management or art. You can often learn a lot about an adviser—and get a feel for the human skills he brings to the job—by learning what he did before becoming a planner.

What continuing education classes have you taken?
What certifications, if any, do you have?

The section on credentials already established why you want this information. An adviser who gives you the name of a credential should also be willing to tell you how to make sure he really has it. Ask him to give you the group's phone number, if only so you can call to get a better explanation of what the credential means and what kinds of financial specialists earn it.

Can I have a copy of your form ADV, both Part I and II?

As far as I'm concerned, this is a deal-breaker, so ask early and pay close attention to the response.

Form ADV is an advisor's registration form. By rule, the adviser must give the form to all new clients. BUT, by the same rule, the adviser is required to give you only Part II of the form.

The problem is that Part I is where all disciplinary actions are listed.

The adviser knows you can get this information from the state securities office. Despite this, most firms give out only Part II unless you specifically ask for both sections of the form.

If a financial planner will not give you both parts of Form ADV—and cites the rules in doing so—the interview is over. Just walk away.

A planner who knows you intend to do a background check but refuses to give you information you can get on your own certainly is acting as if he has something to hide. Don't risk it.

If a planner says he does not have a Form ADV, find out how he achieved some exception to the registration rules. It may be that he is a bank trust officer, for example, for whom an ADV is not necessary, or he might be a broker and have different registration forms.

In any case, tread carefully with any adviser who does not have an ADV; unless you want an adviser for whom providing investment advice is NOT a key component of the service, an unregistered planner probably is someone to stay away from.

Who is your typical client?

If the average client looks like you and has concerns like yours, chances are the adviser has already dealt with whatever situation your personal finances can dish up. In addition, planners put the bulk of their educational time toward figuring out how to better serve their client base, which means learning about things that will benefit their average client.

Make sure the planner's answer doesn't focus solely on age, income and size of portfolio. If you are a union worker with a particular type of pension plan, you want someone who understands the workings of those plans, as opposed to a consultant whose clients are largely self-employed and setting up their own retirement plans.

If you resemble an adviser's average client, there is a good chance he will want you as a customer because you fall comfortably within his circle of confidence.

How—and how much—do you get paid?

You might recall the movie "Jerry Maguire," in which a sports star tells his agent to "Show me the money!" Make your prospective adviser do the same in terms of costs for his services.

Remember, straight commission sales are not always worse for the client than a management fee; it will depend on your needs and the amount of buying or selling you do. Make an adviser discuss all payment options and show you the math.

The adviser also discloses how he is compensated in Part II of the ADV, so make sure the paperwork and the in-person explanation are in sync. Many advisers claim the fee-only label, but then charge commissions on insurance products; you want to know that before purchasing a policy that way.

Remember, too, that there are thousands of financial planners out there; if you can't afford the services of one, there will be others who you can hire without breaking your bank.

What service will I get?

You might recall from Chapter 8, which dealt with your first meeting with an adviser, how one of my colleagues once met and hired a financial planner in the same day, only to be disappointed when he received—by mail—an action plan that was full of strategy but devoid of investment selections and specific suggestions on how to make financial moves to improve cash-flow and cut debt, along with a bill that was for more than he anticipated having to pay.

This question tries to avert that kind of situation.

You have just asked how the planner will get paid, now find out specifically what you will get for your money.

You want to know if an adviser will provide advice on any or all of the following: cash management and budgeting, tax planning, investment review and planning, estate planning, insurance needs and retirement planning. You want to make sure that you get a written review of your goals and a written analysis of your situation and what steps you should take next.

In addition, you will want to know if the adviser offers ongoing counsel, periodic reviews or both, and which he would recommend for you.

How often will I hear from you, and what will prompt your calls?

This question covers both phone calls and statements. You should find out how often you will get a statement of your account, as well as when you might expect a phone call from the planner.

Some financial planners do a lot of hand-holding, stroking clients to preserve the emotional discipline necessary for long-term investing. Others call only when there is a need or an investment recommendation to make. Good planners talk about many things besides immediate sales.

How many active clients do you work with at one time?

There are only so many hours in the work week. If a client promises regular attention, but then tells you he has 200 clients, something doesn't add up. Either he palms off a lot of work on subordinates, or he doesn't live up to his promises.

Many of the top financial planners in the country work with no more than 60 clients at any one time. When their calendars are full, they simply stop taking new customers.

An adviser is not necessarily doing you a favor by squeezing you into his datebook, particularly if you aren't going to be satisfied with the attention he can offer you.

Why do you want to hire me as a client? What kinds of people do you NOT want as clients?

Presumably, the answer to this question gets back to the fact that you are within the adviser's target client range, with a situation he finds appealing. But if an adviser tells you what kinds of people he turns away, and he is describing you—but doesn't know it because this is a first interview—you will be better off going elsewhere for your financial help.

Do you have an area in which you specialize?

Some planners are generalists; others are highly focused.

Obviously, educational credentials go a long way toward showing you someone's expertise, but you still want to find out how much time the adviser spends working on situations like yours. It is always best to work within the adviser's specialty.

Do you give financial advice only, or do you execute the transactions?

Anyone who executes the trades may have a conflict of interest, but, in any event, you will want to know how you will go about implementing the strategy you are paying so much money for.

What is your investment philosophy?

What criteria do you use before deciding what to buy?

Under what conditions do you sell?

Sure, you are hiring an expert, but the logic behind his investment choices must be something you agree with. If he tells you astrology plays a key role in his decisions for example—and I know a few brokers and planners who use star charts—you may decide to hit the road.

Find out how a planner selects investments, because that criteria will be the basis for all recommendations made to you. If it doesn't sound good now, imagine how nervous it will make you when there is money on the line.

Can I review sample plans and statements?

You are paying to get a report on your finances and advice on where to go next.

Having reviewed literally hundreds of financial plans, I can tell you that some of the world's most respected financial advisers can't put a plan into plain English. They may be among the brightest minds in the field, but they can't communicate that knowledge to anyone but the most knowledgeable clients.

Conversely, I have seen plans that talked down to even the most clueless of customers.

Advisers can black out or alter the names and addresses of clients to show you samples of their work. I know several big firms that will give you real plans for which the names and occupations have been fictionalized to everything from Prince Charming to Zeus.

As for a sample statement, go over the form with the adviser to make sure you understand everything. It will be your responsibility to monitor these forms, so you want to make sure you understand the statements before you become a customer.

Can I get the names of a few clients to act as references?

Just because you have seen work samples doesn't mean you don't want to check with real people. Ask clients about the character of their advisory relationship and try to determine if the planner works with customers in a manner with which you will be comfortable.

Do you take possession of, or have access to, my assets?

Do you have discretion to change my investments without my approval?

Generally, the answer to these questions is "No."

If a financial planner wants you to sign a discretionary account agreement giving him the right to manage your money in accordance with your wishes (but without direct approval of each maneuver), you should balk. This is a form of abdicating control; if you have picked a rogue planner (or just a stupid one), giving him discretion over your money could be a costly mistake.

There are rare circumstances under which an adviser might hold assets—or be able to access them at will—but these are extremely rare. Some financial advisers ask for "limited discretionary powers," especially if they are managing money in accounts at mutual fund supermarkets, such as those offered by Fidelity or Charles Schwab; make sure you understand the limits you are agreeing to.

The rule of thumb in these situations is to walk away from any financial adviser who pressures you for too much control over your assets.

Will anyone else be working with me?

Financial planning firms come in all shapes and sizes. I know of one prominent planner who functions largely as a rainmaker, bringing clients into the firm and then passing them on to subordinates; the big guy does the initial meeting and dispenses the advice, but he is little more than a puppet for the back-room personnel that does the grass-roots work of strategizing.

If you are told that someone besides the planner you meet will work on your account, find out why. Then find out who; arrange to meet that person and examine both parts of his ADV.

If an adviser promises to work with you but consistently lets you deal with an assistant, the relationship is in trouble.

Do you personally research the products you recommend?

If an adviser relies entirely on someone else's research, that should make you nervous. It means he is simply selling product, rather than necessarily believing in it himself.

Good advisers know how to analyze financial products and which investment analysts they trust, and they make decisions based on their own experience and intuition, rather than on something they got in the firm's sales manual or a recommendation from a service they subscribe to.

If an adviser does not do his own research, ask whether he puts his own money into the products he recommends.

How will we resolve complaints if I am dissatisfied?

Chances are you will sign an agreement to try arbitration before turning to the courts; some arbitration agreements—the good ones—do not take away your right to pursue action in court, they merely attempt to settle things using lower-cost, faster-working arbitration.

Before you get to that, however, you want to know how the adviser would handle a problem in your account—whether it is a technical glitch or a transaction you don't recall making.

Many planners try to reassure you that this stuff never happens. Make them guide you through the complaint process anyway.

And if the planner works for a large firm, get an introduction to either the office manager or the firm's compliance officer, the first people you are likely to deal with if there is a problem. Get business cards from these people and keep their numbers handy.

All of these actions tell the planner that you will not stand for any shenanigans; a diligent customer is the best deterrent to fraud.

How can I terminate this relationship if I am not satisfied?

An advisory agreement should favor you, not the planner. That means it should come equipped with some sort of ejector seat. Most advisory contracts can be terminated with a month's notice—with fees prorated—at any time.

Still, be sure you know how to open the escape hatch before you climb into the cockpit.

Have you ever had complaints filed against you by customers? How have those complaints been resolved?

The planner knows you are going to check his record with the state; this is when he gets a chance to come clean and explain what, if anything, you will find in Part I of his ADV.

You want the adviser's side of the story, whether the complaint was the result of miscommunication or unrealistic expectations or whatever.

If the planner tells you he has never had these kinds of problems and the state tells you something different, the game is over and you should turn elsewhere for financial help. If a planner tries trickery when he knows you are looking, what will he do when you have an established relationship and your guard is down?

Keep in mind that even the best advisers sometimes run into bad relationships—people who believe they were entitled to investments that only increased in value or whose demands were simply unrealistic. You want to know why these problems happened so you can ask:

How do we make sure that I will not have similar problems?

If the adviser has learned anything from his troubled clients, it is that he doesn't want those hassles again. Find out what he intends to do to make sure you do not become his next problem client.

Describe your nightmare client, the worst one you ever have had.

This is an old hiring technique, in which you ask the job applicant to describe his worst day on the job. More than once, when I was a boss, an applicant describing his worst days was actually talking about an average afternoon in my shop.

While you have asked the adviser about who he does not want as clients, this takes the question further. If he talks about his nightmare and is describing you—or if you even think the worst client's feelings and actions were justified—you may want to go elsewhere.

What should I ask before making any individual transactions?

How much commission will you and your firm earn on this trade?

You should always find out what a transaction will cost you; remember, even fee-only advisers sometimes charge commissions on certain transactions (and may accept 12b-1 fees and other investment-related charges in addition to their proscribed fee).

What is your rationale for picking this specific product?

How does it suit my needs and risk tolerances?

What standard will we set for performance and how will we monitor progress?

A planner should be able to justify decisions and mesh his advice into your personal circumstances. If he can't, you are getting off-the-rack counsel, even though you thought you were paying for a custom tailor.

After all fees are paid, how much must this investment gain in value before I break even?

Again, this looks at the cost of making an investment, showing you in dramatic fashion whether a trade puts you at a financial disadvantage. If costs are high, an investment may have to outperform the averages to generate the returns you want. With above-average performance potential comes above-average risk; make sure that's something you want to get involved in.

Will this sale help you win any prizes or sales contests?
Financial advisers often have incentives to sell you something, even if it doesn't show up in their compensation. I have friends in the planning business who have won trips all over the world, literally, as a result of being a top producer.

If the financial product meets your needs, there is nothing wrong with that—although I want the conflict of interest disclosed. More often, however, contests lead advisers to produce cookie-cutter plans, putting all of their clients into one basket because it delivers the incentive, and yet passing the service off as being individualized.

How long do you expect me to hold this investment? Why?
Most financial planners pursue a buy-and-hold strategy.

Unless someone can successfully time the market over a long period of time—and the vast majority of Wall Street's top experts get it wrong, so there is no reason to believe your planner has been touched by genius—constant portfolio turnover is likely to reduce returns.

Make a written record of how long a planner suggests you will hold a security. There's nothing wrong with holding on longer, but if he comes back and suggest selling in a few months—unless there is a significant change in the investment's status that warrants a move—you can give him a wake-up call that he is straying from his original plan.

If he consistently sells more quickly than anticipated, it could be a sign he is mostly interested in the commissions your account can make him, or in proving to you that your portfolio requires active management and that his fee is justified.

Can I get out of this investment quickly?
This is not a strange question, even in light of the last query about expected holding times.

No financial planner should sell you something without saying if it is hard or costly to unload. There may not be many buyers for an individual municipal bond, for example.

Other investments, such as annuities or mutual funds, may be easy to get out of, but could carry steep penalties, surrender charges, exit fees or back-end sales charges.

You've said what it costs to buy this investment; how much would I get if I were to sell it today?

This is about "spread," which you may face if you use a planner to buy stocks and bonds.

Think of it like a new car, for which you pay the sticker price but could not sell it back to the dealer at the same price the second after you drive it off the lot.

What is the worst-case outcome for this investment?

Before buying any investment or following any financial strategy, find out what the worst possible outcome for your investment could be.

What should I NEVER do in working with a planner?

- If you are buying an investment, never make the check out to the representative.

The money goes to the firm (or the company offering a particular investment product, such as a variable annuity) and is to be invested in your account. The firm will pay the commission and use the rest in accordance with your instructions; if you make a check payable to the planner, you just might find that he has left with your money.

- Never send money to any address other than that of the firm or of an operation designated in the prospectus (such as a transfer agent).

Again, this stops a rogue planner from diverting money into his own pocket.

- Never allow transaction confirmations and account statements to be sent to your adviser instead of you.

These are your record of what is happening in the account; without them, you don't have the paper trail necessary to build a strong case when things go wrong. If an adviser wants confirmations and statements, he can help you arrange for duplicates.

How can I develop and build the relationship?

Whether an adviser is a regular partner in your financial decisions or just someone you turn to for a check-up and fine-tuning of your own strategy, you will want to build a relationship.

This means calling with questions and concerns, arranging the occasional lunch when there is no business to transact and integrating his services into your own financial planning agenda. In addition, involving a planner when you work with your other financial advisers is a wise idea (although you will always want to know whether you are being charged for any of these phone calls or ancillary meetings).

At the same time, busy planners don't have a lot of time for chit-chat. Spend a few minutes planning your call to a financial adviser so you can be efficient and get the information you want without tying him up. Not only will he appreciate that approach, but he will be happy to take and return your calls.

What are the danger signs that the relationship is not working?

Other signs of trouble include:

- Paperwork you don't understand.

If you are ever asked to sign any agreement that does not make sense to you or does not seem in keeping with what you and the planner have arranged for, get nervous. Some planners pass discretionary agreements in front of customers as a matter of course; the authorizations make it much easier for the broker to mismanage your money, so don't sign unless you agree to.

- Statements that don't arrive on time, or no statements at all from anyone but the adviser.

You should receive regular statements from the investment or insurance companies with whom your planner works. If all you get is a statement from the planner, something is amiss.

Be prepared to follow up directly with the company if something is wrong with your statement; if an adviser is mismanaging your money, you almost certainly will have to go around him or her and go directly to the investment company to get copies of your statements that show how much of your investments have actually made it to where they were supposed to go.

- "It's just a computer error."

Glitches are extremely rare; when they happen, they should be corrected in a snap.

Do not tolerate this excuse if something shows up on your statement that does not belong there. If it is not corrected immediately, you have a problem.

- The only products being offered are run by the house.

This is a bad sign for two different reasons. First, planners sometimes get more compensation for selling products developed by their firms. Just as important, however, is that you want a free thinker—someone who does not give you formulaic, one-size-fits-all planning.

- Significant declines in investment value for which you were not prepared.

There should never be any surprises in your investment portfolio. Products may decline in value or be hard to liquidate, but you should be aware of all that.

If you aren't, it's a sign of poor communication. There may be nothing illegal going on, but no adviser worth his salt would let a client get bushwhacked by bad news.

- The planner does not return your calls promptly.

To be an active partner in your financial life, a planner has to be interested in you and your case. When he doesn't return calls promptly or answer your questions at his first convenience, he has lost interest in you.

Once you sense that lack of interest, start the search for someone who can serve you better.

What if my adviser changes firms?

There are many legitimate reasons why a planner would switch firms. Find out the reasons for the change and do a background check on the new employer.

If you decide to follow the planner, find out if he or she gets a bonus for bringing over new customers. Also find out who pays any transfer fees involved, or whether you might incur taxes because you'd be forced to sell some investments to follow along (which could happen if you have to sell out of the "house funds" run by the adviser's old firm).

If you choose not to follow your adviser, you will have to start the interview and background-check process over again, starting with a new adviser who works for the old firm who will serve as an interim replacement. You can then decide whether this planner merits consideration as a permanent replacement, or you can start shopping for an adviser all over again.

How do I complain or seek restitution if there is a problem?

The complaint process always starts with the individual planner, but it can escalate quickly.

Your advisory contract most likely will put disputes into arbitration or mediation before allowing you to go to court; make sure you do not waive your rights to seek restitution through the legal system.

If the problem is operational—such as failure to deliver securities or checks due to you—and the planner is not helping to solve the situation, put your complaint in writing and seek a higher-up. If the planner is a sole practitioner, you should go immediately to the state securities office.

At the same time you are making this case in arbitration or court—and it generally takes between eight and 12 months from an arbitration case to go from your filing to a hearing—pursue the matter with state and federal securities regulators. They generally do not have the power to get your money back, but they can lean on an adviser—who knows what a black mark on his record might do to future business—and may be able to help speed a settlement.

In addition, your complaint will dissuade others from repeating your mistakes.

Don't let a complaint sit around unfiled; the statute of limitations on these issues varies, but the general rule is to file the paperwork as soon as you recognize there is a problem that is not being solved amicably.

14 *Hiring a broker*

Oscar Wilde, the playwright and novelist, once noted that "with an evening coat and white tie, anybody—even a stockbroker—can gain a reputation for being civilized."

Brokers gained a reputation for being less-than-civilized because, for decades, the stock market was a mysterious place that most individuals didn't understand. It was the Wild West, where the good guys and bad guys were hard to tell apart but impossible to avoid because they were the only ones with access to both information and the markets themselves.

In addition, those brokers were, until recent years, always paid on a commission basis, meaning many encouraged selling and trading in order to generate their own income at the customer's expense.

Actions like that caused people to think the reason someone is called a "broker" is because that's what you are after dealing with one.

These days, however, brokers are reinventing themselves, offering more services, acting more like financial planners than mere sellers of investments and charging for their services in different ways.

The reasons for this evolution have to do with changes in the rest of the financial services industry, but they boil down to an effort to survive amid the financial planners who offered complete service and the ability of the do-it-yourself crowd to buy stocks and funds without help from anyone.

While the changes in the brokerage business were designed to make things easier and more straightforward for consumers, they really have made things more complex. Today, a consumer shopping for a broker has more options that sound good and more confusion about how to get the best representation.

As with all financial advisers, the key to finding a good broker is having a good idea of what you want and knowing how to look for it.

Here are the questions to consider in selecting and developing a relationship with a broker.

Can I do this myself?

No one actually "needs" a broker. The average individual investor can take care of a lifetime's worth of investment needs by purchasing no-load mutual funds and stocks. The number of stocks that are being made available to the public on a commission-free, no-broker basis has grown to the point that you can assemble a nice portfolio that way; online brokerage firms let you function as your own broker from the comfort of home. Treasury bonds, too, are available on a no-commission basis, direct from the government.

Likewise, anyone working with a financial planner, investment adviser, money manager or the trust department of a bank could find a broker's services redundant and unnecessary.

But if you intend to invest in municipal or corporate bonds or want stocks beyond the universe of the few hundred that currently sell shares directly to the public, you will need a broker in there somewhere, either the full-service variety or a discount broker (read the next chapter to see how to pick an online broker).

In fact, you may want to work with several brokers, each one specializing in meeting a specific need or handling a particular type of transaction. With that in mind, you will want to know:

What are the different types of brokers?

The traditional broker is a "full-service broker." As the name implies, this is someone who can handle all types of transactions and provide advice and information to guide your investment choices. Today, full-service brokers often go by other titles, notably "investment consultants" or "asset managers," but, no matter what you call them, their job is the same: they identify investment opportunities and put investors together with appropriate choices.

Unfortunately, millions of customers pay the full-service rate without getting full service.

Linked to various news services and agencies that track every conceivable bit of data about public companies and bond issuers, a relationship with a full-service broker should be part-guidance, part-research and part-execution. In an ideal relationship, the broker gathers information, passes it to you, outlines each prospect and supports it with analyst recommendations, research reports and other data. Once you have made your decision, the broker makes the trade.

Discount brokers, by comparison, generally offer a stripped-down version of that service (which is why a full-service client should get what he pays for). Typically, a discount broker will not offer the investment guidance or its own research reports, but will pony up the research of others and make the trade. Most online discount brokerages make reams of information available.

Still, as much as the name implies that they are cheaper than their full-service counterparts, there is a lot to watch out for. Sometimes those research reports come at an additional cost. Other times, there are costly account fees.

And unless you plan to trade regularly, you may not work with anyone at a discount brokerage firm on a regular basis. Instead, you will get the broker who is available to process your trade, a far cry from the comfort and assurance you can get from a long-term relationship with a full-service broker.

So-called "deep-discount brokers" offer no-frills, ultra-cheap service for anyone strictly looking to execute trades. Some do all of their business online or by telephone. As with ordinary discount brokers, be careful of fees and expenses. Otherwise, you could wind up paying for the firm to mail you annual reports and other shareholder materials from the companies in which you invest.

If you are a buy-and-hold investor, price is less important than getting the service you want. You should do business where you feel comfortable and where the staff takes the time to service your account properly, not necessarily where you get the biggest trading discount.

Two other points to consider regarding full-service brokers: 1) Many will discount their commissions, particularly for good customers or on big-dollar trades, so don't be bashful about asking; 2) on very small trades, generally those under $2,000, the flat-fee charged by a discounter may actually wind up being more than the percentage commission taken by a full-service firm. Be sure to do the math.

Many people use more than one broker, hiring a full-service broker for advice and research, but using a discounter when they come up with ideas on their own. Some people use a full-service firm to buy but redeem their shares at a discount firm.

Some brokers (and financial planners, for that matter) actually work as "money managers." Effectively, they function like the manager of a mutual fund, buying and selling stocks and bonds to meet a particular investment objective, except with a personal touch.

Managers often take a fee of as much as 3 percent of the money they manage each year (the average mutual fund takes 1 to 1.5 percent). In addition, money managers want a lot of money to manage; that may mean account minimums from $25,000 to $2.5 million.

Unlike someone functioning as your broker—unless you have given him discretion over your account—a money manager will not call you to confirm trades or request your approval, so you must have tremendous confidence in his abilities. Don't be fooled into thinking that any old broker can manage your money in this fashion, however, as giving up control of your funds is one of the easiest ways to be scammed. Typically, a financial planner or one of your other advisers will make an introduction to a money manager; the money manager does not do the routine daily chores handled by most brokers. If he talks like a money manager but looks like a broker to you, be doubly cautious.

What is a broker's role and responsibility to me?

The broker functions like a salesman but, unlike someone pushing vacuum cleaners or refrigerators, simply persuading you to write a check does not legally constitute doing his job.

Brokers have a legal responsibility to make sure each and every recommendation they make is suitable for you, your financial circumstances, goals and objectives and level of understanding. Anything less than that, whether done out of greed for a commission or mere stupidity, leaves the broker liable for resulting losses.

An "unsuitable investment" is one that is inappropriately risky, such as junk bonds for a conservative retiree. It may also be just plain inappropriate, such as a costly variable annuity with a "life insurance kicker" sold to someone with no real need for the insurance feature; if the insurance tie-in significantly erodes the client's investment—and those things can happen—then the investment is unsuitable.

What is suitable, therefore, is defined by you and not necessarily by the broker.

(Unsuitable, by the way, does not necessarily mean investments that lose money; a broker is not liable for losses that are a normal part of investment ups and downs, as long as he clearly explained in advance the possibilities and circumstances that could lead to losses.)

My father once had a broker who suggested what amounted to a high-cost, high-risk regional bank mutual fund. My father asked my opinion, and I told him the investment was inappropriate given his conservative nature, his outlook and his needs.

When my father called the broker to say he would not be investing, the broker went on the defense, asking whether my father thought that he knew more about investments than the broker did.

My father explained that the broker knew more about investments, but not enough about him. (He subsequently stopped doing business with that broker.)

While you want a broker to present you with opportunities and reasons why you should—or should not—buy or sell a stock, bond or mutual fund, the broker's job is to get to know you well enough to present you only with opportunities that meet your needs.

If the broker doesn't know you—if he has just called on the phone and never met you in person, for example—and he does not ask a number of detailed questions, you should wonder whether he has enough knowledge to adequately do his job.

Am I better off with someone from a nationally known firm?

It is more important to have a broker who is expert at what he or she does than to have someone who is affiliated with a national wirehouse such as Merrill Lynch, Morgan Stanley Dean Witter or Prudential Securities.

Yes, the big names have access to more of their own research and may sell exclusive products, but there are few other operational differences between them and the smaller, regional brokerage firms. And I have heard cases of "selling pressures"—brokers feeling management's push to reach certain sales quotas—from both types of firm, so there is no way to know whether a broker from one type of firm is more likely to face heat if he can't convince people to buy.

The additional research is important, but you want a broker who does his or her own research rather than relying solely on the firm's reports. In fact, you want a broker who is not unafraid to do things that are out-of-step with the firm, advising you to stay away from industries or companies that make him nervous even if the brokerage house analysts don't share those fears.

How are brokers paid?

Unless they charge an asset-management fee—in which they take a slice of the assets they manage each year—brokers get paid on commission.

That said, it's not always easy to figure out just how much commission a broker is getting or how he is paid for each type of product he sells.

With stocks, for example, smaller trades and low trading volume generally result in higher commissions per share. If you buy just a few shares of stock, for instance, you may pay 50 cents per share, whereas the cost can decrease to as little as pennies per share on a big-volume order placed with a discounter.

On mutual funds, brokers will be paid a "sales load" that can either be taken off the top as a front-end charge or paid in the form of higher expenses over several years of owning the fund. While front-end loads run as high as 8.5 percent, 3.0 to 5.5 percent is more common. Back-end loads—sold as Class B, C or some other letter shares of a fund—either face a heightened lifetime of expense ratios or will charge you a fee if you sell within the first few years of ownership.

When it comes to bonds, usually there is no explicit commission amount. The broker buys the bond at one price and sells to you at another; the "spread"—the difference between the two prices—represents the commission. As in stocks, the more bonds bought, the smaller the spread.

Then there are other products, ranging from limited partnerships to annuities, life insurance, new stock and bond issues and more. Commissions can get as high as 10 percent in these cases.

The rule of thumb on these types of financial products is that the more complicated and harder to sell, the bigger commission the broker will get for convincing you to buy it.

In addition to upfront commissions, brokers sometime get ongoing fees from your investments, such as a "12b-1 fee," which is a marketing charge that some mutual funds apply to accounts every year. Essentially, the fund takes as much as 1 percent of your account balance each year to pay for "marketing and distribution costs," and then pays a portion of the fee to your broker. This charge is in addition to the on-going management fees charged by the fund itself.

Annuity companies and partnerships often charge similar ongoing fees.

Because these ongoing fees are removed painlessly, as opposed to getting a bill or confirmation statement in the mail that lays out the exact cost, they are easy to forget about. Don't. If you should decide to change brokers, make sure any and all ongoing fees are transferred to the new broker; if you do not specify the change, the broker (or firm, if the broker has changed firms or left the business) will con-tinue to receive these ongoing payments in perpetuity, without pro-viding you with one shred of the ongoing service you are actually paying for.

Lastly, if your broker is functioning as a money manager—essentially developing and executing an investment strategy on your behalf—he may charge something called a "wrap fee," which combines manage-ment and brokerage fees. These fees can run as high as 3 percent of the assets under management, which is pretty steep. Something closer to 1.5 percent or 2 percent is about average for a stock wrap account; 1.0 to 1.5 percent is the norm with mutual fund wraps. A wrap fee lets you know in advance what you will pay a money manager, but it will be worthwhile only if you have a significant amount of money—at least $25,000—to commit to the program, and the manager trades actively; if you and the manager employ a buy-and-hold strategy, run the num-bers to make sure you aren't better off with straight commission.

What credentials are important?

Brokers sometimes pursue the same credentials as financial planners. Like a planner, however, no credentials are necessary. A broker, how-ever, must pass exams in order to practice, the basic tests known as "Se-ries 6" and "Series 7" exams.

Those will not necessarily be much help, since the typical licensing review course takes only two or three days. Moreover, the exams are more concerned with a broker's technical proficiency—understanding of investment issues and legal and regulatory requirements—than with developing a real-world understanding of the various forms of risk or what makes for a suitable investment.

Studies by the National Endowment for Financial Education consis-tently show that rookie brokers are trained without a significant emphasis on "understanding a client's overall financial picture and as-similating the role of individual investments within that picture."

Until recently, brokers did not even have to undergo continuing ed-ucation to retain their licenses, although it is now required at certain licensing anniversaries.

That means that you want a broker who either has some form of ad-vanced credentials or who has been in the business long enough to de-velop an understanding of what it takes to help a client (instead of one who knows only how to sell the product).

To make himself look like he has better credentials, a broker may tell you he is a *registered representative*, a *Registered Investment Adviser* (RIA) or both.

The former is a fancy way of saying someone has passed the exams needed to sell the products he represents (Series 2 or 6 for variable an-nuities or mutual funds; Series 7 for general securities). The RIA, mean-while, was aptly described by Worth magazine as "Not really a credential, it simply means an individual or a firm has submitted cer-tain filings to the [Securities and Exchange Commission] and paid a modest fee."

Brokers may work to earn their *Certified Financial Planner, Certified Fund Specialist, Chartered Mutual Fund Consultant* or other designations that are described in the preceding chapter among the credentials common to financial planners.

But if an investment adviser focuses predominately on securities analysis, he may pursue a *Chartered Financial Analyst* (CFA) desig-nation, one of the most prestigious of all credentials, awarded by the Association for Investment Management and Research (AIMR).

Earning the CFA mark requires several years of experience, a study course and exams in securities analysis, portfolio management, finan-cial accounting, economics and ethics.

The designation is common among institutional money managers and Wall Street analysts; it is held in high regard in those circles, so if you find a local stock-picker with a CFA, he may merit strong consid-eration in your selection process.

What should I ask during an interview?

With brokers, you have an initial interview and, if you should do busi-ness, regular subsequent mini-interviews each time you discuss a particular investment. The first interview should define the relationship and establish your comfort level with the broker; the other is part of ongoing maintenance and is designed not only to keep the broker honest but also to keep you informed and aware of what is happening with your account.

When you first meet a broker, start with these questions:

What is your educational and professional background?

A broker's background will provide you with clues to his competence.

If he has been jumping around from one firm to the next, there could be trouble ahead. Many firms don't fire brokers, but simply encourage them to leave before they get the axe; when that happens, a poor performer packs up and moves to the next firm.

Good brokers sometimes jump ship, too, especially if they have been lured by bonuses and improved commission schedules.

If you find someone who appears knowledgeable and experienced but who has moved several times in recent years, be prepared to call the broker's previous employer for a reference. Ask the manager of the former office whether he would hire the broker again and whether there were any discipline problems; some office managers will feel constrained by confidentiality rules not to tell you, but most will warn you away if there were real problems. (After all, if they warn you away from the adviser, they may also be able to capture your business.)

What continuing education classes have you taken? What certifications, if any, do you have?

Classes aren't a necessity, but they do show a commitment to staying on top of available products and laws. This is particularly important if you plan to have a broker advise you on more than just plain-vanilla, pick-a-stock/fund/bond issues.

What is your CRD number?

This is one of the few deal-breaker questions in all of financial services, so don't waste your time by saving it for the end of an interview.

CRD stands for Central Registration Depository, and it is the centralized clearinghouse used by regulators for filing complaints against brokers. When a broker passes the exams and gets a license to sell securities, he gets a CRD number.

Any complaints filed against him—even if he is cleared of wrongdoing—go into a file listed by his number.

In performing a background check, having the CRD number—or the broker's Social Security number as a back-up—guarantees that your state securities administrator will open the correct file. This is particularly important if the broker has a common name, as asking the state regulators or NASD Regulation to find "Michael Johnson in Massachusetts" could lead to them pulling the wrong file.

It's not that you can't do a background check without the CRD number, but having it makes the work easier and faster. It also sends a message to the broker that you plan to do your homework.

Brokers may not know their own CRD number. Chances are they have never been asked and may not have it handy. That's an honest excuse, but it can be overcome. The broker's Social Security number also is on the CRD file and ensures that you get the right adviser when you tap into the CRD for a background check.

If a broker will not give you either his CRD number or Social Security number, end the interview immediately. Just walk away.

Think of it like walking into a room and finding your children with something in their hands; when they see you, they put their hands behind their back. Presumably, they're hiding something.

When a broker knows you intend to check backgrounds and refuses to help you check his, he must have some idea of what you are going to find in his CRD file. Don't take chances.

Who is your typical client?

As with all forms of financial advisers, you want a broker whose average client looks like you and has concerns akin to yours. Typically, brokers look for good investments and then try to match those selections with good candidates from within their clientele.

If the bulk of a broker's clientele are singles and young couples, chances are he will spend the bulk of his time looking for more aggressive stocks and, possibly, high-grade zero-coupon bonds to fund education. If you are nearing retirement age, that broker is not likely to bring you a bevy of suitable options because you are out of the mainstream; he is looking largely for investments suited to someone else.

In answering this question, don't focus solely on age, income and size of portfolio issues. Look instead at what the typical client wants to buy. This will give you an idea of whether the broker has a particular specialty. Remember that just because a broker is adept at picking stocks does not make him ideal for picking corporate bonds; make sure he will be able to meet your needs or be prepared to split your business between a few different specialists.

How do you get paid?

Always ask about the money, especially because it can lead to discussions of your payment options. If the broker can act as a financial consultant and get paid a percentage of the assets you give him to manage, you may be better off than paying straight commission.

Can I get a copy of the firm's commission schedule? Is it negotiable?

Discount brokers will give you their fee schedule in a flash, because it is a major selling point that they have lower prices than a full-service shop.

Full-service brokers may not be so willing, hemming and hawing about how the schedule is not really fixed and how the commission can vary on each trade.

If at all possible, get the commission schedule, even if it means going to the office manager. With the schedule in hand, don't be afraid to negotiate for a discount; it may be a blanket price cut—brokers have discretion to lower the fees they charge—or you may negotiate price breaks on a case-by-case basis. Find out what, if anything, a broker is willing to do for you.

What service will I get for the commissions I pay?

If all you get from a broker is processing trades—with no measure of portfolio management, investment research and suitability analysis— you might as well go with a deep-discount broker.

Keep in mind that "full service" means different things to different people. To some people, it's an occasional phone call; to others it means twice-daily faxes. "Discount" varies in meaning too. Find out what these terms mean to your prospective broker and make sure his definition meshes with yours; if not, either you must let the adviser know you are raising the bar and want more attention than the average client, or you must find a broker willing to meet your needs.

Will I pay account management fees?

It would be a simple world if brokerage houses earned all of their money on commissions.

They don't.

Some will nickel-and-dime you at every turn, for everything from failing to maintain a certain balance to not generating a proscribed amount in commissions every year. Others offer "cash management accounts," which may charge you high fees for the convenience of check-writing and credit-card privileges.

You may even pay a fee for opening and closing your account.

These fees add up—especially at discount firms—so make sure you know about all potential ancillary charges before you sign up.

Are there any contests right now for signing up new clients? Do you get anything special if I decide to do business with you?

You may have gotten a cold call because you were the next name in the phone book or because a friend gave out your name; your broker might also be working to sign up new clients in order to win some sort of prize from the firm.

It's not that signing up during a contest period is necessarily bad, but make sure you believe the broker's interest in you extends beyond a potential prize for bringing you into the fold.

How often will I hear from you, and what will prompt your calls?

This is a good question because it helps set expectations for the relationship and allows you to direct the broker to the right way to work with you. If you don't want a call every week pressuring you to invest, this would be the time to speak up.

At the same time, if the broker promises to call weekly and those calls become more sporadic, you will know immediately that you have a "loss-of-interest" problem.

You want to know why the broker will call, because you may not want continual sales pitches. Good brokers call to talk about a lot of things besides immediate sales. They act as emotional disciplinarians to help clients stay the course when the markets are volatile, notify clients of changes in tax laws, and talk about how their opinions concerning certain market segments are changing. If a broker plans to call only when he believes he has something appropriate for you, eventually you will have the problem my father encountered, namely a broker who values your contact only for the commission it can generate.

How many active clients do you work with at one time?

Because the job involves finding investments that fit any number of their clients, a broker can work with a fairly large number of people on an ongoing basis. Once he finds the right investment, he may spend the whole day just culling the Rolodex looking for prospective sales.

But if you want guidance, you want someone who will give you more than a sales pitch.

Do the math. You know how often to expect the broker to call because you've asked. If the broker has a huge clientele and calls the average client once a week for five minutes, you will know quickly that he spends more than half of his time selling rather than researching.

The broker is not supposed to be just a conduit for trading, so make sure the number of his clients allows him the time to adequately research and come to conclusions about investments and how they fit with your needs.

The broker who was upset when my father didn't buy on a particular suggestion, for example, was pushing a product rather than making sure he had a good fit for his clients.

What criteria do you use before deciding what to buy? What makes something a sell?

It's time to figure out how the broker puts his expertise to work. You want to know how he picks the stocks and mutual funds he recommends to customers, and how he matches different types of funds to the individual needs of each investor.

If a broker can't tell you in plain English what gets him excited about an investment, then all you are getting is a practiced sales pitch rather than the benefit of real knowledge.

You also want to know upfront why a broker buys or sells securities to make sure those conditions hold up later in the relationship. If you have been working with a broker and he or she suddenly changes stripes and starts recommending buys and sells that are out of character, you will recognize immediately that something is wrong and that the broker appears to be pushing trades—which generate commissions—that go against his own philosophy.

Can I get the names of a few clients to act as references?

You will want to check references to determine the character of the broker-client relationship and decide if the broker works with people in a way you expect to be comfortable with.

Can I review the papers you want me to sign when I open an account? Can I review and get a copy of my "new account form?"

Some brokers have clients routinely sign up for margin accounts or options agreements. Some also push discretionary agreements, giving them control over the trading activity in the account.

Don't do it.

In addition, brokers fill out new account forms whenever they get new clients. These forms include information on your net worth, income and investment objectives; they get filed away and are never seen—let alone signed—by customers.

Rogue brokers, however, fictionalize these forms, putting incorrect information in so it looks like you want commission-generating activity. (Some brokers may tell you they have a great investment that they can't sell to you unless the forms say your net worth exceeds $250,000; if you fudge the paperwork to get in on the deal, you might be killing yourself in arbitration if and when things go wrong.)

Help the broker fill out the form, coming up with a definition for your investment objectives, and get a copy of the new account form for your own records. It could come in handy if there is ever a problem with how the broker managed your account.

(Lawyers at arbitration cases put tremendous value on "pre-dispute correspondence," written instructions about goals and objectives. If the broker will not let you participate in the new account form, put your investment circumstances in writing in a letter to both your broker and the office manager. If a dispute ever arises, this letter will go a long way to helping your case.)

Who will hold the securities? Why?

Most brokerage firms prefer to hold securities "in street name," which means they keep the shares registered in their names, but in an account registered to you. This makes it easy to buy and sell and to complete trades. (Current rules provide that transactions must be closed—the money or shares turned over—within three days of the trading date; the standard will soon be dropped to one day.) They also like this because safekeeping the shares means you will likely use the firm when the time comes to sell, instead of redeeming shares through a discounter.

The majority of investment customers keep shares in street name, but make sure your broker explains the process and tells you how to get your stocks or bonds if you want them, either to move to another firm or to hold on your own. Many brokerage houses charge a fee for issuing stock certificates, a charge that is overblown—it does not cost a firm $15 to handle issuing certificates, since all it involves is pushing around some papers—but which may be unavoidable.

Make sure you understand how and why the broker explains the benefits of keeping your shares before agreeing to it. And if you prefer to hold all shares yourself, explain to the broker that this is how you do business; no broker worth his salt would let this be a deal-breaker.

How frequently will I get statements; will you go over a sample statement with me?

It's not the broker's fault if the firm's statements are hard to read; it is the broker's fault if he doesn't teach you how to read them.

Get a look at the firm's statements, find out whether you will get them at regular intervals or only after there is activity in your account and make sure you understand how to read them.

Will anyone else be working with me?

Some brokers have so many clients that they need sales assistants. These people call you on the broker's behalf. Very often, assistants get the clients who are less likely to make a trade. (In my father's case, when he decided to think for himself and not take the broker's tip, the broker threatened him with having to work with an assistant in the future.)

Sales assistants generally have a sales license but don't always have the full expertise or knowledge concerning your situation. That could make it tougher for them to answer your questions.

If you will ever field calls from someone in the firm besides your broker, find out why. Then find out who; arrange to meet that person and, at the very least, get his CRD number.

If a broker promises to work with you but consistently has you deal with the sales assistant, chances are you have a transaction-oriented salesman who is more interested in generating commissions than in developing a good long-term relationship.

Who will control the decision-making in my account?

If you sign a "discretionary agreement," you are giving up control of your investments. For your own financial safety, this is a bad idea.

Make sure trades will not be made in your account without your approval. As obvious as it seems, make sure the broker acknowledges that this is your wish, and that he promises to contact you and get your authorization before moving your money.

How will we resolve complaints if I am dissatisfied?

The firm probably will have you sign an agreement to try arbitration before turning to the courts; you would prefer not to lose your right to pursue action in court, keeping arbitration as a lower-cost, faster-working means to an end.

Before you get to that, however, you want to know what would happen if there is a problem in your account and how the broker would handle it—whether it is a technical glitch or a trade that you don't recall authorizing.

The broker may laugh off the likelihood of this happening. Make him humor you and walk you through the complaint resolution process anyway.

In addition, make the broker introduce you to the office manager or the firm's compliance officer, the first people you are likely to be dealing with if there is a problem. Get business cards from these people and keep their numbers handy.

All of these actions serve notice to the broker that you won't tolerate trouble with the account.

How can I terminate this relationship if I am not satisfied?

Never enter any financial arrangement without knowing how to get out of it.

Have you ever had complaints filed against you by customers?
How have those complaints been resolved?

The broker knows you are going to check his record in the Central Registration Depository. This is fess-up time. Complaints that require outside help in order to be settled—even if they clear the broker of wrong-doing—will be in the CRD file.

Essentially, you are asking the broker for his or her side of the story regarding whatever you are likely to find in the CRD (although don't describe it this way, because you wouldn't mind hearing about troubles that were resolved before hitting the file).

If the broker tells you he has never had these kinds of problems and the CRD report shows something different, call it off. Learning from past mistakes is important stuff, and if a broker tries to slip one past you when he knows you are looking, what will he do when you have an established relationship and your guard is down?

Over time, even the best brokers run into a customer who sues over the loss of principal, even though he understood that his stock portfolio might decline in value. What you want to hear is why these problems happened so you can ask:

How do we make sure that
I will not have similar problems?

The broker does not want you to become his next problem client. If he has learned from what went wrong the first time, he will explain what happened and what he would do differently to make sure the problems would not occur again.

You will want this remedy—which may boil down to something as simple as improved communication—to be a part of your relationship with the broker.

Is your firm a member of the
Securities Investor Protection Corp. (SIPC)?

SIPC provides limited protection to customers if a brokerage firm becomes insolvent or tries to shut down in the face of its financial responsibilities. SIPC does not insure against losses created by a decline in the market value of your securities.

In addition to SIPC protection, ask whether the firm has other insurance that carries over beyond the SIPC limits. Most good firms do provide this extra insurance; chances are you will never need it, but it's a comfort if you are the type of investor who worries that your brokerage firm will disappear overnight.

(For further information, you can contact the Securities Investor Protection Corp. at 805 15th Street N.W., Suite 800, Washington, DC 20005-2207, or call 202-371-8300.)

If a brokerage firm is not a SIPC member, don't do business with it—no matter what excuses or additional coverage you are presented with. It's simply not worth the risk.

What should I ask before making any individual transactions?

How much commission will you and your firm earn on this trade?

Yes, you asked about commissions and for the fee schedule during the initial interview, but you still need to check it out again with each and every trade.

At most firms, a broker can get extra commissions for selling stock that the firm wants to get out of inventory. The firm may also offer extra money whenever it is a "market maker" in a stock, meaning that it buys and sells a certain issue out of its own inventory.

Your confirmation slip should tell you whenever the firm is a market maker, but by then it is too late; you already have paid the commission.

Similarly, brokers may get a commission boost when they sell the house mutual funds.

By asking, you get a chance to maybe get some of that commission back, in the form of a discount. In general, brokers have the authority to cut commissions from 20 to 60 percent, although your chances of getting that discount probably depend on just how good a customer you are.

Just as important as getting a discount is asking a related question: "Would your recommendation be the same if you weren't being paid more?" If you question the sincerity of the broker's answer to that one, make him justify the decision by comparing the investment to similar choices on which the commission would be lower.

After all fees are paid, how much must this investment gain in value before I break even?

This is another way of getting at the costs involved in the trade, but it helps you see in dramatic fashion just how big a hurdle trading costs are. If trading costs are a big nut to crack, it will make it harder for an investment to deliver real, after-expenses returns that meet your expectations.

Will this sale help you win any prizes or sales contests?

Yes, you asked something similar during the initial interview, but that was a bit different. Contests to sign up new clients aren't bad, because there is no inherent conflict; if you need brokerage services, there is no real conflict between your interests and those of the broker.

But if the broker is being paid to sell you an investment—whether he receives a health club membership, a fancy dinner or some bigger incentive—that's a problem. If the broker is selling all of his clients the same product to win a prize, he does not have his clients' needs at heart.

The National Association of Securities Dealers has cracked down on contests and wiped out the worst abuses, but you should still find out whether the broker is involved in a sales contest. If the broker's advice doesn't feel like it's a great fit and you then find out there is a contest involved, you probably can develop enough of a gut feeling to decide whether or not to do the trade; without the knowledge of the contest, you might shrug off your uneasiness and assume the broker knows better than you do.

How long do you expect me to hold this investment? Why?

Most investors are better off pursuing a buy-and-hold strategy, but commission-based sales make a broker want to trade. Unless a security shoots up in value, short-term profits may be swallowed by the costs of the trade.

Make a written record—which you may want to confirm with the broker—of how long he suggests you will hold a security. That way, if he comes back and suggests selling in a few months—unless there is a significant change in the company's status that warrants a move—you can give him a wake-up call that he is straying from his original plan.

If that doesn't work, you may be making a wake-up call to the office manager (and your written record could come in handy).

Can I get out of this investment quickly?

This may seem a strange request given the previous question, but there is a difference.

The broker should tell you, before you invest, whether a product is hard or costly to unload. There may not be many buyers for an individual municipal bond, for example.

Other investments, such as annuities or mutual funds with a back-end load, are easy to get out of but carry steep penalties. Make sure you know about these charges in advance, too.

Are there other available share classes or any cheaper ways to pay for this?

Sometimes the broker has payment options, such as Class A, B, or C shares for mutual funds, each of which charges a different load/fee structure. Make sure the broker does the math and shows you how the costs vary over the life of the investment. One share type will be less expensive in the short run, another over 10 years, so mesh the answer to this question with the answer to how long the broker expects to hold the security.

You've told me what it costs to buy this stock (or bond or mutual fund); how much would I get if I were to sell it today?

This is not just a commission issue, but one of "spread" and market value. Think of it like a new car, where you buy the car for the sticker price but could not sell it back to the dealer at the same price, even if you had not driven it off the lot.

If the spread is too big here, you should get an explanation why, and you may decide the investment is not worth it.

What is the worst-case outcome for this investment?

Not every investment makes money or hits its target. Before purchasing any security, you need to understand the most dire circumstances you could face.

If a broker "guarantees" something, make sure he is offering your money back—and that you know how to get it and have it in writing—and he is not just using an expression that shows he is confident a security will make money.

Is this in keeping with my investment strategy?

This question applies only in those cases when the broker is providing investment counsel or portfolio management services. A full-service adviser should always be able to explain how an investment choice fits into the overall scheme of your portfolio. If he can't answer this question, chances are you have not done enough work together for him to know exactly what is a suitable investment for you.

You will want to be aware of a broker whose selections represent a drastic shift in your portfolio, such as the regional bank mutual fund that was an oddball choice for my father's investment portfolio. If the investment raises a red flag, be sure to know what the broker is basing his or her selection on.

What should I NEVER do in working with a broker?

- Never send money based entirely on a telephone sales pitch.

You can work with a deep discounter over the telephone—although many people are not comfortable with the idea—because you will be the one initiating those contacts; the broker will not be trying to sell anything, but merely processing trades.

Convincing you to buy over the phone is a different matter altogether. If you can't go to the broker's office and meet him in person—after checking out a license—forget about it.

- Never make a check out to the representative.

The money goes to the firm to be invested in your account. The firm will pay the commission and use the rest in accordance with your instructions; if you make a check payable to the broker, the broker just might cash it and leave you high and dry.

- Never send money to any address but that of the firm or of an operation designated in the prospectus (such as a transfer agent).

Again, this avoids schemes by which an unscrupulous broker diverts money from a brokerage account into his own pocket.

- Never allow transaction confirmations and account statements to be sent to your broker instead of you.

These are your record of what is happening in the account; without them, you don't have the paper trail necessary to build a strong case when things go wrong.

If a broker asks you to do any of these four things, contact the firm's office manager or compliance officer immediately. Chances are you will want to end a relationship in these circumstances, because any broker who asks for these things—even if he has not taken any of your money yet—is playing fast-and-loose with the rules.

You're asking for trouble if you stay with a broker who asks for these concessions from you.

Where do I start my search?

Brokerage services tend to be a word-of-mouth business. Whether you meet a broker as the result of a cold call or on a tip from a friend, however, the important thing is that you gauge his skill and practice knowledge.

All of the best brokers once started out making cold calls; it's a fact of life in the business. So you need not shy away from cold calls if you happen to be looking for a broker, but you will want to mix that selection with advice from friends.

In addition, many brokers hold local seminars, designed to educate consumers and draw them in as clients. Don't be bashful about attending these seminars, which usually are free. Just remember that the fact that someone can fill an auditorium or a fancy restaurant does not make him the right broker for you.

How do I check them out?

Check out all brokers in at least two places, starting with NASD Regulation and extending to include your state securities regulator.

Armed with the broker's CRD number, these checks will be easy (the phone numbers and web sites for the agencies are included in Appendix 1).

In addition, check with any agency from which the broker claims to have credentials or professional designations. (The numbers for these agencies also are listed in the appendix.)

How can I develop and build the relationship?

There's an old saying that the best way to get good market information is to "take a broker to lunch." It's not far from the truth.

The best way to develop a relationship with a broker is to be able to talk about money and investing when there is no commission on the line and no sale to be made. The more you learn about your broker and his or her attitudes towards money and the markets, the better your working relationship is going to be.

These meetings don't have to be regular, just often enough to get a feel for how the broker operates and give the broker a better understanding of who you are and how you tick. It takes more than an initial interview and subsequent phone calls to do that.

At the same time, a busy broker doesn't have all day to schmooze. When you have questions, spend a few minutes planning your call to the broker so that—if he has other business—you can be efficient and get the information you want without tying him up. Not only will he appreciate that approach, but he will be happy to take and return your calls.

What are the danger signs to a bad trade? What are warnings that something is amiss in my dealings with a broker?

It's not important whether a stockbroker wins or loses; it's where he places the blame.

That's not just a play on words of a famous maxim, it's a true statement.

When things go wrong, listen carefully to the explanation, as it will speak volumes about whether the relationship is in trouble.

Beyond pushing on you the things you should never do with a broker, there are other signs of trouble, such as:

- "Happiness letters." That sounds pretty innocuous, which is the problem. These really are "activity letters," when the brokerage firm has spotted a lot of trading in your account. You get a letter from the office manager, sounding like an introduction, recognizing your trading activity and wanting to make sure you are "happy" with the firm, offering you the chance to sit down and discuss more opportunities there.

If the trading continues, you may get another one.

This is a hint that perhaps your trading pattern is not normal. The firm is trying to alert you without making you unduly alarmed.

At the same time, this letter is designed to give the brokerage firm proof that it warned you of the abnormal activity in your account.

If you get a happiness letter, review your account statements immediately.

The second or third happiness letter may ask for you to sign the document and return it to the firm; the broker may even tell you that he needs you to sign it or he could get in trouble.

Don't do it, at least not until you have finished reviewing your records and made sure everything is in order. You may even want to get another opinion.

If you sign a happiness letter and later have problems with the account, your signature will be the first thing trotted out before the arbitration panel. Remember, too, that a broker can not make you sign these acknowledgements; the worst that can happen is that failing to sign one may force the firm to refuse further activity in your account, which might not be such a bad thing.

- Paperwork you don't understand.

Just because the broker says you will have control of investment choices doesn't mean he won't pass a discretionary agreement or a form to allow him to trade in options in front of you. Some ask all clients to sign these agreements as a matter of course, but the authorizations make it much easier for the broker to mismanage your money.

- "It's just a computer error."

If there is an unauthorized trade in your account and the broker tells you not to worry because it's just a computer glitch, you should get very nervous. As time goes by and the error is not corrected, it will become harder and harder to get it straightened out.

Technology is so advanced now that there are virtually no computer errors in brokerage statements. It is the proverbial needle in a haystack.

If there is a problem in your account and it's a "computer error," see the office manager. He should be able to get it straightened out immediately.

- Inside information, allegedly confidential stuff, an upcoming research report, merger rumors or "dynamic new products."

Hot trades like this tend to have bigger commissions. They also may be excessively risky, and you may not have a good shot at capturing the kinds of profits that attract you in the first place. Hot new-issue stocks are distributed to big favored brokers and customers, and your broker most likely will not be among the lucky few. That's why a deal that sounds too good to be true probably is.

- Being treated like "quota bait." Generally, this means the broker is trying to increase a monthly paycheck or reach sales goals, all about five days ahead of the end of a billing cycle. That would be around the 19th of the month.

If that is the only time you hear from your broker—and all he does is talk sales and not strategy—you should question whether he is interested in you as a client or merely as a commission.

- "The deal is done," "It's too late," or "You have no choice" on a trade you did not authorize or understand completely.

Just because the broker says something is a done deal does not make it so. Sometimes, there are errors and trade disputes, and the broker knows that anything you do to set things straight is going to cost him some money.

If there is a problem and your broker throws this line at you, see the office manager.

- The only products being offered are run by the house or are stocks in which the firm is a market maker.

This is a bad sign for two different reasons. As mentioned previously, the broker tends to make more money in these trades.

But just as important, you want a broker who is a free thinker, who makes his own evaluations and does not rely entirely on the firm's research. Brokers know which analysts in the firm are the most on-target and whose judgment they trust the most, and they should be able to sort out the firm's recommendations for what to sell all customers from what is right to sell you.

Remember, you are paying for expertise, and not just for executing you a trade or bringing you the brokerage firm's latest tip.

- Significant declines in investment value for which you were not prepared.

The new generation of brokers has not lived through any significant, lengthy market declines.

There may be nothing illegal going on here, but the truth is that—short of a market crash that brings everyone down—no broker who respects a client would let him be ambushed by a huge decline in portfolio value. There should be no surprises in your relationship with a broker.

"Many of today's brokers have no idea markets can decline," says Mary Calhoun, a former broker who is now a securities arbitration consultant in Watertown, Mass. ""They believe it is only a question of how long before something goes up.

"It's a broker's job to explain the possible downside of your investment. It's not that losses are the broker's fault, it's that you should never be shocked by what happens in your account."

What if my broker changes firms?

As discussed previously, there are many legitimate reasons a broker would switch firms. Make sure your broker has one of those reasons when he makes a change.

I once met a couple whose broker was changing firms for the second time in three years, moving from a national firm to a regional one. They worried about the small firm, but wanted to keep the broker.

Whenever a broker changes companies, do a background check on both the new firm and the broker. A broker's record can be sullied quickly, so get current details. Just because the broker was clean when you started working with him doesn't mean he's have stayed that way.

In this case, the couple had never done a background check on their broker. He explained he had left a big firm for a pay raise and less sales pressure. A background check uncovered problems, however, notably several complaints concerning the suitability of his choices for older couples. That was enough to convince the couple not to follow the broker.

If you end up following your broker, find out if he or she gets a bonus for bringing over new customers. Also find out who pays any transfer fees for the security, or whether you might incur taxes because you'd be forced to sell some investments to change firms.

If you choose not to follow the broker, you have to start the interview and background-check process over again with a new adviser at the old firm.

How do I complain or seek restitution if there is a problem?

If the problem is operational—such as failure to deliver checks promptly or correct an error—start with the broker. If he or she can not immediately rectify the problem, contact the branch manager and follow up your initial complaint with a letter.

A written record of your complaint is important, so write letters detailing your dispute and how it is not being resolved.

If the manager is not responsive, contact the state securities administrator's office.

The same path applies to misconduct on the part of the broker. Keep all records—give copies only to the office manager—and be prepared to pursue an arbitration or court case if necessary. Most brokerage agreements state that disputes will be settled in arbitration whenever possible.

At the same time you are making this case in arbitration or court—and it generally takes between eight and 12 months from an arbitration case to go from your filing to a hearing—pursue the matter with state and federal securities regulators. The complaint will eventually hit the CRD and help dissuade others from repeating your mistakes.

Don't let a complaint fester; the statute of limitations on these issues varies, but the general rule is to file the paperwork as soon as you recognize there is a problem that the broker, office manager and firm are not able to resolve to your satisfaction.

Remember, there's no limit to the promises stockbrokers can make, only to the promises they can keep.

15 *Picking an online broker*

As I worked to revise this book, one of my friends who trades frequently online ridiculed me for my idea to add a chapter on selecting an online broker.

"You don't hire an online broker, you pick a brokerage firm," he said. "You're dealing with the company, not with a person."

To me, the difference is semantic. Just as you can pick your banker—even when your primary concern is the cost of a checking account and the location of fee-free ATMs, not personal service—so can you pick an online broker.

There may not be a person involved with your account, but there is an intermediary handling your trading activity and there can be a tremendous difference dealing with one firm or another.

With those things in mind, there are key considerations to make before picking the firm (or firms) you want to work with.

Here's how choosing an online broker differs from other types of financial advisers. The first question you answer with virtually all other advisers is "Can I do this myself?" With an online broker, you either have the knowledge and confidence to do it on your own or you wouldn't consider hiring one.

That said, there are different roles an online broker can play in your financial team. Some people do all of their investing on their own, through an online firm, while others use an online broker only to handle the "fun money" they manage on their own. Some people hire full-service brokers for advice and direction, but supplement that professional knowledge with investments they make on their own (possibly following an asset allocation into sectors recommended by their hired gun).

The other considerable difference is that your "interview" with an online broker isn't really a conversation at all. Mostly, it is you having questions answered from the web site and possibly from a customer-service representative.

By the summer of 2000, more than 100 firms were functioning as online brokers, with some of the big-name, traditional full-service shops joining the party. That growth has meant a wide disparity in services and prices.

That said, there are key considerations that go a long way to determining if you are happy with the service you receive for your money and that go into determining which online firm is right for you.

Frequent traders have different needs than buy-and-hold investors; savvy investors need less hand-holding than newbies. There are many broker surveys done that enable you to match your personal style to a firm; you will find plenty of information and links to this kind of data at www.investorama.com or www.cyberinvest.com.

Before selecting an online broker, analyze the following:

Commission costs

These days, you can find online brokers who will process your transactions for any price from $30 per trade to no cost at all (though that usually has some pretty tight strings attached); the top 20 brokers averaged about $15 per trade in 2000.

Keep in mind, however, that what you see in advertisements and online may not be what you get once you sign up as a customer. That may depend on the size and frequency of the trades you make.

Consider what you expect to be the most common size for your trades. The ultra-low prices touted on television may not apply to anyone trading less than 1,000 or even 5,000 shares. If it does apply to smaller trades, it could require you to keep a minimum level of assets in your account or make a certain number of trades per month.

The vagaries of these pricing policies are a big reason one investor can love a specific firm while the next investor has a bad experience and feels he is getting ripped off.

Hidden costs

Commissions are just one part of the equation.

You could be facing fees for delivery of stock certificates, for transfers, for wired payments, for annual "account maintenance," and even for terminating your account. Some brokers even charge postage and handling fees, which are built into the commission schedule.

All of these nasty annoyances must be detailed in the firm's fee schedule, so study it carefully. Don't fall into the trap of picking the lowest-commission shop you can find, only to be nickel-and-dimed to nearly full-service, traditional brokerage costs by the tacked-on charges.

Trading capabilities

Most online firms can serve most online customers.

But you may not be most customers. You may want to trade penny stocks, options, futures contracts, bonds, mutual funds, foreign securities and more.

If that's the case, make sure the online firm can get what you want. And check the commission schedule for those more-esoteric areas; if the brokerage firm can't trade those securities electronically, you could wind up paying a much higher, full-service-like commission on your transactions.

Another capability you must worry about involves limit orders and other specialized trades. This is when you place an order to execute a trade at a specific price or within a certain amount of time.

Not every online brokerage firm offers limit orders, so be certain you will be able to not only trade what you want, but also in the way you want to trade it.

Real-time abilities

This is a big selling point for many firms (though it will be less of one as it becomes more common).

That said, it can be a bit like those ultra-low commission promises. Real-time quotes may be just for accounts of a certain size. They may not be streaming—meaning you have to search for what you want rather than have it fed to you.

If this is part of why you want a certain firm, make sure you understand its definition of real time and how it applies to you.

Quality execution of trades

An online broker is an intermediary, a middleman, just like any other type of broker. You may hit the "send" key on your order or get an electronic confirmation, but that means only that the broker has received your order.

From there, the order goes through a market-maker (on Nasdaq trades) or specialist (on New York Stock Exchange trades) to be completed.

Learn the broker's full execution process. Most send e-mail confirmations when the trade is executed, but some slow the process by having a human being review trades (how old-fashioned!). Some firms routinely sell their orders to specific market makers (which is one reason they can offer such low commissions).

Get a clear explanation of how the process works before you go through it.

Remember, too, that the quality and speed of execution may not be as important as you think. If you're a buy-and-hold investor planning to hold a stock for 25 years, a few minutes of delay getting a trade executed is not a big deal. If you are a trader who might be selling the stock again in 25 minutes, every lost second counts.

Know yourself; don't get too worked up over the minutia of execution if it's not essential to maintaining your blood pressure.

Support

Ask online traders for their biggest beef about brokerage firms and the most common answer will have to do with how the firm responds to questions and complaints.

Yet the amount of support you receive should be pretty well spelled out by the firm in advance. If you go for the ultra-low-cost trades, you can expect virtually no hand-holding whatsoever.

If you pay at the higher end of the commission scale—in the $30 per trade range—you can get 24-hour, 7-day support and hand-holding.

Make sure you know the support that comes with the basic service, and what the firm considers above-and-beyond the call.

Before you ever sign up with a firm, make sure you know who to contact if there is a problem and how disputes will be resolved. You would not let a traditional broker get away with lousy service, so be prepared to stand up for your rights as an online customer, too.

If you have to click your way through three or four layers of screens before you can find out who to complain to, you can assume the firm is not that interested in hearing what you might have to say. Avoid firms with that attitude.

Ask if you can reach a real person if the need exists (find out if there is a charge for talking to that person, too).

Send the firm an e-mail question before signing up and see how quickly it responds; if it doesn't jump through hoops before you open an account, what will happen once it has your money?

Account minimums

Some firms have no minimum investment to open and maintain an account, while others have clearly defined levels and charge fees when you fall below the specified target.

In any case, make sure you know the rules regarding what you must keep in your account—as well as when that money must arrive when you are making trades. (Consider establishing a line of credit if it keeps you from running afoul of charges in this area, although usually there are fees on credit lines, too.)

Sweeps and money-market features

Most online brokerage firms have money-market accounts, which is where new deposits—plus any dividends or money received from the sale of your stocks—sits while awaiting your next instructions.

Find out if the firm automatically sweeps idle money—such as dividend payments—into your money-market account at the end of the day. (If it waits longer, you are losing interest on that money.) Be sure you know what its money-market account pays in interest, and inquire about check-writing privileges (and any fees for writing checks off the brokerage account).

Research and other goodies

Each brokerage firm has its own resources and access to others. Some of these things are free, built into the commission price. Others come at a charge.

Find out the cost and content of a site's investment research tools (company profiles, earnings estimates, stock charts, technical analysis, analyst reports and so on).

If you need these tools, pay for them. If you trade frequently and do your own research, you may want to go with the lowest-price firm and avoid additional charges for using the brokerage firm's research tools.

Margin accounts

Some people want to borrow against the stocks in their account to buy stocks, stretching their buying power (and increasing the risk in their selections).

If buying on margin appeals to you, make sure you know the rules on margin loans. Rates vary dramatically from one firm to the next.

Perks and freebies

If frequent-flier miles, extra real-time quotes, free trades, cash bonuses and all of the other niceties now being thrown toward new online brokerage customers sound good to you, then look for firms that offer what you want.

Don't let the bonuses outweigh the basic service, but don't be shy about taking what's out there or using perks to break a tie between two firms that are running neck-and-neck for your business.

Crash protection

We're not talking stock market crash here, as there is nothing an online brokerage firm can do to help you then.

System crashes are another matter altogether. Find out what a broker will do someday when an emergency strikes. Will you be working by telephone or have a personal contact?

Know what the brokerage will do in these instances so you feel comfortable if it ever becomes your problem.

Easy navigation and your gut feeling

When the rest of this stuff is sorted out, you still need to decide where you feel most comfortable and which service you like the best.

Do the free demo trades available on virtually all brokerage sites so you are familiar with what will happen when you are a customer. Pick the firm that offers you the best combination of costs and services, but also one you feel comfortable manipulating and working with on your own.

It makes no sense to have a brokerage account with a firm that you don't actually like doing business with, so the quality of the web site and your personal preferences should never be overlooked in the selection process.

As with any other advisory relationship, the hope you should have with an online firm is that you will be a satisfied customer for life.

With online investing, however, there is no real drawback to having accounts at multiple firms. In fact, it can be an advantage in those rare times when systems crash or there are other problems. Since an online brokerage account can take a little time to set up, having two open accounts—which allows you to move seamlessly from one to the other if problems arise—can be a good form of insurance.

16 *Hiring an insurance agent*

For many people, insurance coverage is the leaky roof of financial products.

When it's raining, it's too late to fix it.

When it's sunny, it works as well as any other roof.

An insurance agent, therefore, is like a roofer, building shelter for clients by providing coverage that protects against storms that could not be weathered alone.

But in insurance, as in homes, there are a lot of ways to build or fix that roof. It can be plain asphalt shingles or fancy wooden ones, old covers can be ripped off or simply covered up and improved. It can be designed to last a few years or a lifetime.

And the quality of the craftsman building it will go a long way to determining your happiness with the product.

Enter the insurance agent, roof builder to your financial house.

The basic idea behind insurance is simple: Protect those things you can not afford to replace yourself, and cover yourself for outcomes you could not otherwise afford to pay for.

That means, for example, that you might want insurance to replace a new car, but might not carry collision protection on an old clunker. In both cases, you would carry liability insurance, so that your bill resulting from an auto accident would be limited to a manageable deductible.

There is a saying in financial services circles that insurance is always sold and never bought, meaning no one purchases protection unless he is required to or receives a convincing sales pitch. With most forms of insurance, that's not far from the truth.

You must consider your own mortality or the possibility of disaster, neither of which most people face up to without some prodding. From a financial standpoint, you must be willing to part with current disposable income to protect yourself against something that may never happen—or for which the benefits will not become obvious for many years.

The other reason insurance products are sold versus bought is that they often involve complex jargon and, in the case of life insurance, illustrations.

The combination of stomach-turning topics and mind-numbing words is a real turn-off. As one friend of mine put it: "Every time I talk to my insurance agent, I have a headache by the end of the phone call. That's why I don't talk with him as often as I probably should."

But in putting off the selection of an insurance agent, many people fall victim to the very sales process they disdain. They delay the process until the day they get a cold call or meet an agent at a party, and take the chance encounter as a sign that it's time to get protection. The agent with the lucky timing becomes the adviser and has a client who is ready to accept an active sales pitch.

The best way to avoid that problem is to tackle insurance head-on, hiring an agent early and working with him to develop, upgrade and maintain a program of financial protection that will always keep a roof over your head and your family.

To select that agent, you will want to answer the following questions:

Can I do this myself?

There are two ways to look at this question—in terms of insurance and the need for an agent.

If you have no insurance, you already **are** doing this yourself; it's called "self-insurance." If something happens tomorrow, you are liable for all costs associated with the problem.

If your home is burglarized and a television is stolen, that might not be so bad, the same way you might prefer to pay to repair a fender-bender rather than report the accident to your auto insurer.

But if you lose all of your possessions to a fire or suffer a major disability for which you have no coverage, you will find out quickly just how inadequate your resources are.

If you want insurance, but don't want an agent, you are looking at the low-load insurance market, in which an insurer sells directly to the public. This is an emerging industry with new options available every day. It's also worth shopping around quote services such as Quotesmith.com, Insweb.com and Quicken.com's insurance site, where you can quickly do some comparison shopping and get an idea of what's available at what cost. Examine closely the terms and conditions that are part of each offer; if you don't fully understand what you are being sold, you may find there is a difference between doing this on your own and doing it well.

What kind of insurance agent do I want?

There are two basic choices for agents: independent agents, and exclusive or "captive" agents.

Independent agents represent any number of companies and may change the firms whose lines they carry depending on whether they are satisfied with price and service. In theory, independent agents offer more choices because they work with more companies that are competing for your insurance dollar; in practice, they may only you only the options that bring them the most money.

Captive agents, as the name implies, work with only one insurer. The good news is that they will know the provisions of their policies better than an independent agent because they work with just one company and, over time, learn its policies inside and out. The independent agent may have too many insurers to deal with to become that well-acquainted with each product.

The rest of the good news is that exclusive agents tend to earn lower commissions than their independent counterparts; the bad news is that those commissions may still be every bit as costly as what you can get from an independent agent, and the coverage you are shown will represent the only choice offered, with no low-cost competition to speak of.

Do I need an agent, or can someone else help me?

The answer to this question depends on your circumstances, the type of insurance you are purchasing and the state in which you live.

While low-load insurers sell policies direct to the public, their service may not be available in all states, and they don't offer all types of coverage. You may be able to purchase life and auto insurance from these firms, for example, but not a disability policy.

Insurance quote services may sound like a direct-purchase choice, but they are not. The telephone and online quote services—which often promise the best available rates on simple policies such as term life—effectively are independent insurance agencies representing many companies. By doing a bulk business, they cut costs and offer basic policies at a slight discount.

Effectively, you are buying coverage through an agent, without the benefit of the service you might expect from hiring someone local. In addition, the great prices don't always turn out to be any better than you can get from an agent in town, because the quote services may offer bare-bones "teaser" policies designed to get you interested. You may not qualify for the policy—your health isn't good enough or you fall outside of certain age restrictions—or the agent does a needs analysis that shows you need coverage beyond the basics and suddenly you are looking at a higher-priced policy that is no better than what you could have gotten from your local seller.

Insurance brokers (they prefer to be called advisers) may be a better alternative to the quote hotlines. Their job is to analyze a policy on your behalf but, unlike an agent who works both for you and the company, they work only for you.

Life insurance advisers can help you obtain coverage at wholesale rates or through the direct-sellers. For their services, insurance advisers collect a flat fee, usually based on the amount of insurance you will need to purchase. One easy way to find qualified insurance advisers is to call the Life Insurance Advisers Association at 800-521-4578.

What credentials am I looking for?

Credentials are not necessary, but they are one way good agents distinguish themselves. With insurers setting prices uniformly, you won't be able to play one adviser against the next—unless the second agent can come in with a different insurer who can deliver the same product for less—so you might as well choose someone with a high degree of professional achievement, whose expertise might help you find ways to make your coverage more efficient.

The other reason to pursue a credential is for the codes of conduct that generally go along with membership in these groups. Insurance agents are dual agents, working for both you and the insurer; they are supposed to serve the best interest of both masters. Professional standards will help them accomplish that difficult goal.

For life insurance agents—and that is where you should focus your search since state insurance commissioners set acceptable premium levels for many other types of coverage—consider the Chartered Financial Consultant (ChFC) and Chartered Life Underwriter (CLU) marks. Both are awarded by the American College in Bryn Mawr, Pa., with the CLU generally considered the top credential for life insurance agent and the ChFC a financial-planning addendum.

Agents who achieve one or both of these designations—and a CLU generally takes between three and five years to complete—agree to abide by the college's code of ethics and conduct.

A Chartered Property Casualty Underwriter (CPCU) is someone who has completed property and liability coverage education requirements. Awarded by the American Institute for Chartered Property Casualty Underwriters, a CPCU also agrees to conform to a code of professional ethics.

You may also prefer to work with an agent who is a member of the National Association of Life Underwriters (NALU), a sort of umbrella group for life-insurance agents. While membership does not require the kind of training of the other programs, there is a code of conduct and ethics that members must follow.

Beyond insurance credentials, insurance agents may pursue financial planning designations, such as the Certified Financial Planner (CFP) mark. This is helpful, but you need to make sure the agent understands the role you expect him to play and that you may already have a financial planner to oversee your general money-management needs.

Designations such as "Million Dollar Round Table" may be nothing more than sales awards or may combine a sales objective with educational and ethical baselines. Someone who can sell tons of insurance is a good salesman but not necessarily a successful one in terms of the relationships he develops with customers. Ask how a sales-oriented designation helps you as a customer.

If your prospective agent offers you credentials beyond these, find out what it took to earn them. The industry is churning out new designations quickly, and you will want to make sure the letters after an agent's name have meaning before you factor them into your hiring decision.

What kind of insurance do I want?

This applies, again, mostly to life insurance. It is not hard to figure out whether you need auto insurance—although you will want the coverage that is most efficient—but the choices in life coverage can be confusing.

Because insurance is sold more often than it is purchased—if you call agents out of the blue to buy insurance, some will wonder if you just flunked an annual physical—it helps to go in armed with information. Otherwise, you will be pitched products and will lack the knowledge to separate the cow from the manure.

"Universal life," "variable life" and any number of similarly named types of coverage are designed to provide both life insurance and investment growth. Policy restrictions and available investments will determine how the money grows; there will be strict rules for how you can touch or borrow against the cash value of the policy.

"Term insurance" is designed to provide coverage over a certain period of time. It does not build any investment value, but rather provides coverage for as long as you have a need; when the term ends—provided the policy is not converted into some other form of insurance—there are no premiums and nothing to cash in. Term is ideal for people who have a need for insurance, perhaps to pay off a mortgage or college education, but who have no need for insurance once their family is grown and home is paid for.

Term policies carry lower premiums than cash-value policies, the idea being that holders will invest the difference on their own, hopefully providing greater returns than might be available through an insurance policy.

There are a great many arguments for which type of policy is best, and for whom.

In my years covering personal finance, I have come to believe that insurance is best used to do what it is intended for, namely offer protection and not savings. That said, plenty of people would not save were it not for insurance policies, or they need the peace-of-mind of saving one big chunk of money they absolutely will never touch. And I have heard a great many insurance sales pitches that make very convincing arguments.

The idea, therefore, is to find what is most comfortable for you, realizing that cash-value policies will cost you more money and bring your agent a bigger commission. In addition, remember there may be flexibility in policies, such as term coverage that can be converted to cash-value if your needs (or opinions) change within a few years of signing the policy.

How do insurance agents charge for their services?

Most agents are paid on commission, which is not surprising given the fact that most policies are sold, not bought. Commissions can be hefty; depending on the type of insurance, fees can be up to 50 percent of first-year premiums, falling to 3 percent to 5 percent thereafter.

Commissions also depend on the quality of the insurer. A high-quality company does not pay as much in commissions as one that is in tougher financial straits, because the good company's high ratings make its products easier to sell. (Commission structure is why the low-load and fee-only adviser options are becoming increasingly popular.)

The differences between one company and the next are so minimal that good agents will simply bring you the best available policies; they aren't likely to gouge on commissions if it puts their reputation at risk for just a few dollars in extra take-home pay.

And while it is important to know how every financial adviser gets paid, it is less of a concern with insurance agents than with the other types of financial advisers. The reason: you are looking at a product and can make apples-to-apples comparisons.

Say an agent shows you two life policies charging, say, $200 per month in premiums; both policies offer virtually identical coverage and are sufficient for your needs. If the price is identical, the commission is irrelevant; you are getting what you paid for at a price that is reasonable and non-negotiable. Provided your agent has done his job in finding the best policies for you, the cost of the coverage and the quality of the insurer—rather than commissions—will be your determining factor.

Where do I start my search?

Nothing beats word of mouth, particularly if it comes from someone who has had claims experience with an agent. The best minds in the insurance business say the place to start is with friends, relatives and co-workers to determine who they use as an insurer.

Beyond that, call the national accreditation organizations for lists of members in your area. You can find a CLU in your area by calling the Society of Financial Service Professionals at 610-526-2500; you can find a CPCU by calling 800-644-2101.

Lastly, you might check with the independent insurance agents association in your state. (You will find addresses and phone numbers in Appendix 2.)

How do I check them out?

Always check with your state insurance commissioner's office to see if there have been complaints, disciplinary problems or licensing actions taken against an agent. (You will find the insurance commissioner's office for your state listed in Appendix 2 too.) In addition, if an agent shows you credentials such as the CLU or CPCU, call the issuing agency to make sure the adviser is up-to-date, in good standing and has no disciplinary history.

Finally, check with the local Better Business Bureau for a report on the agent, firm and insurer.

What should an agent ask me during an interview?

Regardless of the financial specialty, the adviser will have plenty of questions for you during an initial interview. But unlike the other specialties, the life insurance agent isn't doing his or her job if you don't hear certain queries.

An agent is not doing his job if he does not ask about your income, assets/net worth, the make-up of your investment portfolio, marital status and children to support, employment status, salary, insurance benefits offered by your company and how much money your family needs to maintain its standard of living if you die.

An agent who has not gotten this basic information can not adequately determine your needs.

With that in mind, save yourself time and energy if an agent starts talking about a policy's price or earning potential before asking you for this information.

Once the agent has gone over your needs, he can show you the variety of ways to meet your needs and help you integrate insurance coverage into your financial plan. Until he has gone over your needs, he is strictly a salesman.

What should I ask during an interview?

Once the agent is done interviewing you, it is back to your due diligence in selecting an adviser. That will mean asking most or all of the following:

Do you specialize in any particular area of insurance?

You want to find out if an agency is full-service or limited to specific lines and types of coverage. Some agencies specialize in high-risk drivers and securing coverage for the uninsured, others can sell boat, homeowners, automobile, life, health and business insurance.

You may pick individual agents for each specialty, but that gets complicated and cumbersome. Generally, you will want to pick one agent and go to a specialist only when the need arises, such as if you have one child who is a high-risk driver and who might not be insurable under the family policy (or whose coverage would cost a fortune).

If an agent is not full-service, you should not automatically disqualify him. Some agencies focus on property and casualty coverage for your home and cars and property, while others concentrate on life coverage. Picking one of each can be a perfect marriage. (In fact, a property insurance specialist often makes for a good referral to a life insurance agent; ask who his life insurance agent is.)

How long have you been involved in the insurance business?

How long with this particular agency?

Experience counts, but it's not everything. If an agent has bounced around from one firm to the next, there may be a reason. While there are many reasons why an agent would switch firms, anyone who has done it repeatedly—every two years or so—may have a problem.

At the very least, you will have to question whether the agent will be there to service your long-term needs or if he will be gone when you need an insurance check-up, leaving you with a policy that is in force but a surrogate agent to advise you on what to do next.

Like many financial services disputes, problem insurance agents can sometimes get off without a scratch to their records by settling cases and resolving complaints before problems reach the state insurance commissioner. The firm that employs the agent may not be so lenient, however.

If the agent has a checkerboard employment history, you may want the office manager at his previous firm to be a reference, answering whether he would hire your prospective agent back.

How many insurance companies do you represent and can you place my business with?

How long have you worked with each company?
The more insurers an agent represents, the more options he can present you with.

At the same time, he may have a few favorites that he knows well and prefers to work with. There are a lot of reasons why an insurer might drop an agent, not the least of which is state regulations that make a company decide to no longer participate in the market.

Still, if an agent has a long history in the business but a short time with each of his insurers, it should raise a concern that he has not been the kind of agent these insurers want to keep. If there have been a lot of changes in his product line, find out why.

Which companies get most of your business and why?
Independent agencies are a great idea, but that doesn't mean they won't play favorites.

That's okay, so long as the insurer is a good one—and not just paying the highest commission.

The reason to ask this question in advance, however, has more to do with how you will size up an agent's advice. If he comes back with several options but is recommending against his favorite company, you will want to know why. And if he comes back picking his fave, you will want him to convince you why it's a better policy than the others.

How are the companies you deal with rated?
Before buying an insurance policy, you are going to want to know about the financial strength of the company that is writing your policy. There are five major independent firms that rate the financial strength of insurers: A.M. Best, Duff & Phelps, Moody's Investors Service, Standard & Poor's Corp. and Weiss Research.

The ratings firms measure a company based on the depth of its reserves, the spread of its risks, profitability and investment income, the quality of management and more. After this analysis, each firm assigns a letter grade, although the scale varies from one company to the next. (Duff & Phelps and Standard & Poor's both make AAA their highest rating, while Weiss Research offers a simple A as its top grade.)

Your agent should be willing to give you at least two ratings reports on any insurer you consider. If he can't deliver those reports, question whether he is hiding something.

Unless you have a special need—such as a hard-to-insure driver who has limited choices for auto insurance—you will want to deal with insurers whose ratings are excellent or superior. Your adviser should not only show you the ratings, but also explain how the grade system works.

What continuing education classes have you taken? What credentials, if any, do you have?

Insurance, like the other financial services specialties, is evolving; you want someone who is current on the law and on the best procedures to follow to maximize your insurance dollar. With pricing being less of an issue in insurance than other specialties, expertise is at a premium (so to speak) and you will want to make sure your agent is an expert rather than merely a salesman.

Can I have your insurance license number?

Ask this one early in the process and you could save some time. It's a deal-breaker.

You must be licensed by the state in order to sell insurance. Getting the license number speeds up your background check with the state insurance commissioner (although not having it won't stop you), and it sends a clear message to the agent that you intend to do a background check.

You can laugh it off as being precautionary and being a waste of a phone call if that gets the agent to show you a license, but you should make it clear that you won't hire an agent who has not proven to you that he is currently licensed.

Some states give agents a card to show, others a certificate for the wall. It doesn't matter; ask for proof, look at the document, check the names and dates.

Refusal to give you the number—when he knows you are going to check—is as good as an admission of trouble. Without trouble, there is nothing to hide.

If an agent balks at showing his license or letting you take the number, call the interview off.

How do you charge for your services?
Every financial adviser must be asked to spell out his cost structure. In spite of the fact that, as described previously, insurance is a product or commodity in which the salesperson's commission is less important than the overall cost of the good, you still want to make sure there will be no surprises, particularly if you intend to develop a relationship and get on the phone periodically seeking advice.

Insurance agents get paid more for selling new policies than for maintaining older ones, and some recoup this decline by adding hourly costs for offering ancillary financial planning services. If an adviser will put you on the clock when you call for advice, you should know it upfront, especially if the charges are in addition to ongoing commissions from your insurance policies.

How much of my initial premium payment will go to commissions and fees, and how much of that commission do you get?
This is a big issue with life insurance products, for which the agent is going to get a big cut of what you spend upfront to buy coverage. A big chunk of your first premium payment is going to the adviser, no matter what, so be sure the agent has shown you several options and given you the information necessary to pick the best one for you. That won't necessarily be the policy that provides the agent with the biggest pay day.

How can I reduce my costs?
In all types of insurance, there are plenty of ways to cut costs, jettisoning unnecessary coverages, consolidating policies under one insurer, qualifying for discounts and more.

Ask for a list of all potential discounts. Insurers offer discounts for everything from people who stop smoking to those who enter a weight-loss program or get good grades.

In addition, discuss any situation that is "abnormal."

Say you have a child who is covered by your auto insurance. The child goes to college for several months at a time and has no access to a car. During the time when the student is at school, you can remove him from your policy and save on the premiums.

Likewise, if you stop driving to work for a long stretch of time—such as a maternity or sick leave, or if you leave a car in the garage while you travel—you may be able to stop coverages temporarily, saving on the cost of protection you don't need.

You should not be paying for any coverage you are not likely to use or need, and a good agent can unbundle standard policies to at least see if you are better off financially with a menu of services customized to your needs.

How does your firm operate?

When is it open? What about after-hours contacts?

How will claims reporting be handled?

These questions are the nuts-and-bolts of your relationship with an insurance adviser. There are plenty of reasons to get these answers long before you have to put the agent to the test.

Say you decide to buy a car on a Saturday afternoon, but don't know whether your current policy offers sufficient protection for the new car. If you drive off the lot and get in an accident, you could be in for a heap of financial troubles; if your agent isn't available until Monday, you may not have any way of knowing whether you are sufficiently covered on the new car.

Likewise, you have a car accident on the weekend and need to know if you can rent a car and bill it to the insurer, or you have a fire in your home and want to know how quickly you can get people working to weatherproof the parts of your home that survived.

And because insurance affects your spouse and family, you want to make sure they know how to deal with the agent if something unexpected happens to you.

With all of those things in mind, you want to find out how an agent pursues claims—some walk customers through the process, others leave everything to adjusters—and make sure you are comfortable not only with their sales pitch, but also with the service you can expect after the sale.

What is your philosophy on working with insurance companies and consumers in settling disputed claims?

This is one of those areas in which an independent agent may have an edge.

If your agent believes the insurer was wrong in denying a claim, he should step in and lobby on your behalf. When an agent represents one company, he may not want to put up too big a fight or he could wind up out of business. An independent agent, meanwhile, has the threat of moving the business to another company he or she represents.

Under any circumstances, you want to find out not only how an agent will help in processing claims, but also whether he will go to bat for you when a claim goes against you.

Who will have the primary responsibility for handling my account?

If an agency is big enough, the salesman may only close the deal. Subordinates or clerical staff do the actual paperwork and much of the research.

If that's the case, you will want to know who will have responsibility over your account.

After the initial sale, when will I hear from you, and why?

If the agent is transaction-oriented, you will get calls only when there are other products to pitch, most likely at policy renewal time when he might convince you to upgrade.

If the adviser wants to pursue a relationship, he should call periodically, notably when he notices a major life change in the offing (kids getting ready to leave for college, mortgage debt almost retired, etc.)

Good agents can be good salesmen, but they earn that distinction by taking care of their clients first and filling their sales ledgers second. If you plan to have a long-term relationship with an adviser, make sure he is willing to work with your other financial advisers and will meet with you at times when there is no pressing need for service, just to do an insurance check-up and make sure you have not outgrown your financial safety net.

How involved are you in the local community?

If you have decided to hire a local agent, a big part of your reasoning will be that he offers better service than someone from outside the area or a person working on a quote line.

Todd Muller, a vice president with the Independent Insurance Agents of America, notes that "the more ingrained in the community an agency is, the more they have a selfish reason to serve customers to their utmost ability. Preservation of their reputation is exceedingly important because they can not just get up and move one day, because they are tied into the community.

"In the end, every agent has that conflict of working for you and for the company. If there is a conflict, you want someone who is working for you, and if the company is located somewhere across the country, a guy who is tied into your town is going to be thinking `My customer lives here and I go to church with him or coach his son in Little League and, by golly, I am going to make sure the people in my town are taken care of."

Muller has a point. An agent tied to your town faces a lot of bad word-of-mouth if your house burns to the ground and he or his company is seen as the proverbial fiddlers orchestrating an unhappy settlement.

Could I get the names of a few recent clients who you have worked with?

At this point in the process, you are ready to get the names of some customers, preferably folks whose cases are similar to yours and who use the adviser for the same types of situations.

Have you ever been the subject of any complaints to the insurance commissioner or any lawsuits? If so, for what and how do we make sure that situation does not happen again?

By this time, the adviser knows you are going to check him out. That makes it pretty senseless to lie, because that would get him tossed from your list of candidates.

Still, if anything comes up, make sure the explanation jives with what you learn of his disciplinary history, and that it sits well with you and does not give you the shakes. If you believe the action that landed him in trouble is unforgivable, move on.

How will we resolve complaints if I am dissatisfied?

Most times, real problems will wind up in mediation, but find out how the process works and which chain of command your complaint will follow. That way, if problems do arise in the relationship, you can pursue redress immediately.

How can I terminate this relationship? How do I get out from under these insurance contracts?

You may be able to walk away from the agent, but not the insurer. Your contract may specify a period of time during which your policy is in force, with financial penalties for early cancellation.

If you are satisfied with the coverage but not the insurer, you might call the company and ask for names of other agents in your area; the insurer will be happy to oblige because it is less likely to lose your business.

As with any financial arrangement, however, it is important you know ahead of time how you can get out if you are not satisfied with products, service or performance.

What do I ask references?

The main thing you want from an insurance adviser is service. If all you cared about was price, it would not matter much who you picked.

With that in mind, ask not only the questions appropriate to all reference checks (as laid out in Chapter 11), but also ask what kind of claim experience a client has had and how involved the agent was in helping him get a satisfactory resolution.

What are the danger signs to a relationship gone sour?

Several years ago, a few prominent insurance groups got together and drafted what they called the insurance consumer's bill of rights. Essentially, as a customer, you have rights to protection, to be informed, to choose, to be heard, to redress and to services.

If your rights are being violated, then you've got problems with your agent.

Let's examine each situation individually.

The right to protection
Obviously, you are paying to receive adequate protection. If your policies do not meet your needs, or you find out through dealing with other financial advisers that your needs were not properly met, you have not received the guidance you were paying for.

The right to be informed
Insurance is a mysterious business, cloaked in jargon and with so many subjective, hard-to-assess judgments. If you are not kept abreast of changes in your policy, in state or federal laws that affect you, of the basic assumptions made in calculating your needs and in adjustments made to those assumptions over the years, you are operating in the

dark. If you are uninformed, then you truly become one of those customers to whom insurance is sold.

The right to choose

The choice may come down to finding another agent, but you always have options. If an agent says that you have no choice and no options—remember, giving up a policy and paying surrender charges is an option, no matter how unattractive—something is wrong.

The right to be heard

You should be the leading voice in any decisions that affect you, and you should be treated with the respect accorded the key decision maker. That means prompt response from your agent and insurance company. If your agent is not listening to your concerns or keeps pushing something at you that is not in accordance with your wishes—or if your agent is not quick to resolve problems—the agent has stopped listening to you.

The right to redress

If you have legitimate claims, they should be settled quickly. If not, and the agent isn't taking up your cause, get ready to pursue a case with your state insurance commissioner's office.

The right to service

Chances are the insurance salesman knows a lot more about policies and coverage than you do. That doesn't change the fact that you are entitled to prompt, fair attention. An insurance agent should want to be a part of your financial team and should never be afraid he can't justify your coverages to the other members of your advisory squad; if he can't show your other experts how he has served you well and acted in your best interests, something is amiss.

Beyond those basic rights, the other big sign that may underscore a problem in your relationship with an insurance agent is surprise.

The whole idea of insurance is protection. The catastrophe that forces you to make an insurance claim—whether it is an auto accident, a house fire or a death in the family is traumatic enough. If the coverage or service in those times of need does not live up to expectations, or if the protection you thought was sufficient turns out to be faulty, the relationship probably was based more on making a sale than protecting you as a client.

At that point, the relationship probably is past sour, because the agent will have a tough time regaining your trust.

If I have a complaint, where do I go?

If the agent is a sole practitioner, your first place to turn may be the insurance company to see if it is willing to intervene on your behalf, or step in and correct a perceived wrong.

With an agent at a large firm, your complaints will start with a supervisor.

In both cases, you may have signed an agreement to mediate any disputes between you and the adviser. Do not wait to start the ball rolling; if the agent's actions were so heinous that they can not be adequately settled in mediation, you will want to pursue other remedies (lawsuits) before any statutes of limitation expire.

If your problem is severe enough to require a mediator, it also warrants a call to the state insurance commissioner's office, which has the power to frighten most agents into at least reviewing tough cases.

Don't stop there. The insurance agent's responsibility is to sell you products in your best interest and suitable for your needs; if he has failed to do this, your remedy is likely to come in court.

How can I develop and build the relationship?

Like a will or an estate plan, insurance coverage must be reviewed periodically, particularly when there are major life changes.

Take the time to do this in person, to have an insurance check-up that brings the adviser up to date on your needs, desires and how your financial picture has changed over the last few years.

Make sure the adviser knows you welcome his input to your financial team; most will want to work with you in that fashion—and to interact with your other advisers—because it provides a refreshing change from the routine and it gives him the best chance to represent you well.

17   *Hiring an accountant or tax preparer/tax planner*

Former U.S. Senator Edward Gurney once noted that the United States is the only country in which "it takes more brains to figure your tax than to earn the money to pay it."

To be honest, that's not entirely true. It's only more complicated to pay your taxes if you earn a lot of money.

If you don't earn much or if you have a very simple situation—you are single and have no deductions, for example—then navigating through the tax code is pretty easy (or EZ, in the words of the tax forms you will have to prepare).

Once things get complicated, however, you must decide whether you are the best qualified person to represent yourself to the Internal Revenue Service. In addition, there is a real value-of-your-time issue when it comes to preparing a tax return; if you spend five or 10 hours gathering your materials, crunching the numbers and reading the forms so that you file by the book, you might actually be better off turning the paperwork over to a preparer. The loss of more than five hours of your time—depending on how you value it—and the aggravation of trying to sort out what the IRS passes off as English may be more costly than the price of paying someone to help you.

To a lot of people, a tax preparer is merely someone who processes paperwork. That's a bit shortsighted, considering that whoever prepares your tax return will learn your deepest secrets, things even your family may not know about you—household income, investment returns and more. It has to be someone who can draw out that information, be trusted to keep it confidential and use it to your advantage while staying securely within the boundaries of the law.

And while most people engage a tax preparer for the current year, there is good reason to want someone who will be around to defend both his math and tax logic in the event that the IRS comes calling.

The challenge for an individual looking to hire a tax preparer is finding the right match of competence, expertise, price and attitude toward dealing with the IRS.

That's not easy because, literally, anyone can be a tax preparer. By law, even you—feeling the need to hire help to do your own taxes—would be allowed to hang out a shingle and sell your services as a tax preparer.

Here are the questions you will want to answer as you search for a tax preparer or accountant who is right for you.

Can I do this myself?

Everyone is entitled to prepare his own tax return, so no one actually needs to hire a preparer or accountant to do the work.

The question you must answer is whether taxation without representation is stupidity.

In every tax situation, there are three solutions: the "right" way, the wrong way and your way.

The right way gets every allowable deduction without stretching the truth or making you vulnerable to penalties or a problem if you get audited. It generally involves not only doing the paperwork necessary to complete a tax return, but making occasional phone calls throughout the year to allow for tax planning.

The right way is not necessarily letter-of-the-IRS tax advice, because officials in that agency acknowledge that there are many ways to do a tax return. It depends on how aggressive you want to be in taking deductions and pursuing opportunities; go for too much, and you get into trouble, pursue too few opportunities and the IRS gladly will accept the extra money you are paying.

Every year, for example, Money magazine has a number of tax preparers do the same sample returns, almost all of them coming up with different amounts of taxes due. The trick is to get as close as possible to the one ideal solution; few tax advisers ever hit that target.

The wrong way is slap-dash and sloppy, thrown together to beat the deadline or simply to get out from under the pressure of filing. It may involve stretching the truth or trying to take deductions you have reason to expect the IRS will disallow. It will cost you interest charges and penalty payments or simply in paying more tax than you needed to pay (and would have paid had you done things the right way).

Then there is your way, which is probably somewhere in between. Like the Money magazine survey of tax preparers, you too will likely find that in aiming for the perfect tax return you are shooting at a moving target.

The result is that you will want to prepare a return—either yourself or with an adviser who can do it for you—that comes as close as possible to being ideal for your particular circumstances.

It's not easy. As Albert Einstein once put it: "The hardest thing in the world to understand is the income tax."

If you don't feel comfortable that you understand it on your own, it's time to at least consider hiring help. The following questions will guide you toward hiring the appropriate tax specialist.

What kind of tax preparer do I want?

Tax preparation advice runs from free-and-simple to costly-and-complex.

Your selection will depend on your needs.

You can start by considering the IRS itself as a counselor, since the agency offers free advice on figuring out the right way to fill out your forms. Sadly, free does not necessarily mean good, even when the IRS is the source of the data.

The IRS does not stand behind its preparers; if they give you the wrong information—and they sometimes do—you are responsible for the problems with your return. In addition, the IRS offices and phone lines are swamped during tax season, so free help is better left to those people who want only a quick clarification or rules interpretation before finishing the work on their own.

The next level of guidance is the local tax preparation specialist. This can range from someone looking to earn extra money during tax season to a real expert. The problem is that unless this prospective adviser has credentials, you will have very little to go on in making your decision. Worse yet, the most attractive thing many plain-vanilla preparers have to offer is the promise of a refund, a promise that is often kept by playing fast and loose with IRS rules.

Just because anyone is allowed to act as a tax preparer doesn't mean they are all good at it. If you are dealing with an individual who has no firm and no verifiable credentials—but who talks a good game—make sure everything about the person and his operation (is it an office or a kitchen table?) strikes you as competent. If not, don't risk it.

The next step up the ladder is a national tax preparation chain, the H&R Blocks of the tax world. These firms have locations across the country and may have multiple offices in your area.

They process so many tax returns that they can do instant estimates on what yours is likely to cost, and they offer refund-anticipation loans, essentially an advance on your refund (for which you will pay an outrageously high rate of interest).

National chains require their preparers to pass an annual course covering the bulk of what they will see during the tax season. They may also hire advisers with more advanced credentials.

Each year, my tax preparer—who is an enrolled agent, a credential we will get to in a moment—fills her calendar and makes a little extra money by working at a storefront return service, a regional equivalent of an H&R Block office. If you happen to walk into that shop in the middle of tax season and she is the next available preparer, you luck out and get a highly qualified, expert tax professional doing your work on the cheap.

Of course, if she is tied up, you might get the person at the next desk who, on any given winter's day, might be a high school dropout who slept through the company's annual tax-preparation class. Even if this person can do a decent tax return for you—and it's not that hard if your return is basic—he may not be able to do the best job for you, given his limited knowledge. And chances are he won't be around the next summer when you have a question on the tax treatment of one of your investments. (And he will be long gone by the time you get an audit notice from the IRS; if the firm promises you representation in an audit, it will offer someone else, not your actual tax preparer.)

And therein lies the problem with the walk-in tax preparation centers. To deal with the crush of people during the tax season, they may hire people who are inexperienced, who view tax preparation as a part-time job rather than a career opportunity.

Worse yet, many firms pay their preparers based on how many returns they complete, which is an incentive to get you finished and out the door fast. That is not conducive to sweating the details; since you pay the penalties and are responsible for all taxes due, YOU need to sweat those details and shouldn't settle for someone who wants to give you a rush job.

If you are looking for more than the basics from a national firm, inquire about its "executive tax services," which typically function more like a traditional accountant's office than a walk-in center. You will need to make appointments, you should be able to develop an ongoing relationship with a full-time, year-round adviser, and you pay about three times the going rate charged to walk-in clients. In other words, if you went to the national firm looking for a bargain but need to hire the executive-level preparers, you can probably kiss the bargain goodbye.

If you decide to kiss off the national firm at the same time, your next stop would be either an Accredited Tax Preparer (ATP) or Accredited Tax Advisor (ATA), credentials that signify that the adviser has completed a tax preparation course offered by the College of Financial Planning and passed an exam offered by the Accreditation Council for Accountancy and Taxation.

You should also consider "enrolled agents," possibly the most under-recognized specialist in any of the advisory fields. Enrolled agents are former IRS workers, people with extensive dealings with the IRS or folks who have passed a comprehensive exam entitling them to represent clients before Uncle Sam. Most spent at least five years working for the IRS, then passed a two-day exam. In order to retain the designation, an enrolled agent must complete a required number of hours of college-level continuing education each year; many fulfill this requirement by pursuing a master's degree in taxation or accounting.

You can find enrolled agents, like mine, who work independently, but you will also find them working with accounting firms and law practices. Like a certified public accountant, an enrolled agent is trained to be expert in all areas of tax preparation; the difference is that he is not certified, which often translates into lower-cost services.

Enrolled agents don't sound as glamorous as certified public accountants, but they aren't any less qualified as tax advisers. While anyone can be a paid tax preparer, only an enrolled agent, certified public accountant or tax attorney can represent you in an audit.

Certified public accountants (CPAs) must earn at least a bachelor's degree and pass a strict national exam in addition to meeting several requirements for continuing education. CPAs may specialize in areas besides tax preparation, so the credential itself does not make someone right for you. (You should be aware that someone may be an "accountant" without being a CPA; in some states, a licensed public accountant is considered the equivalent of a CPA, in others, no one who has not qualified for the CPA can even say he provides "accounting services." If an adviser mentions accounting but is not saying he is a CPA licensee, ask enough questions to be sure you are getting the expertise you expect.)

CPAs should be members of their state society of certified public accountants as well as the American Institute of Certified Public Accountants. As such, they are governed by a strict code of ethics and their firms must undergo regular quality reviews conducted by peers. They also should be licensed to practice in your state.

Tax attorneys generally do not prepare returns themselves. In fact, some tax attorneys don't even have anyone on staff who can handle that chore. Instead, the role of a tax attorney is to provide counsel in tricky areas of tax law, notably divorce, estate planning and business issues. If you get into those arenas, or are embroiled in any sort of dispute that might put you at the mercy of the Tax Court, you may at least want to consult with a tax attorney (preferably with a master's degree in taxation or some other advanced credential) to be certain you are on sure footing.

Picking between the various levels of expertise depends mostly on your individual situation. The more complex your needs, the higher up the scale you most likely will go to ensure qualified counsel. Be realistic in assessing your needs; you don't want to pay for a Rolls Royce when a Yugo can get you comfortably from here to there.

What can I expect to pay? How do tax preparers charge for their services?

There are no good numbers for what the average tax return costs, which is good reason to shop around before settling on the adviser you intend to hire.

Typically, tax preparers charge either by the form or by the hour. Expect less-personalized service if you are being charged by the form, because the preparer has an incentive to crank out the paperwork and move on to the next return; while this could also be an incentive to file more forms on your behalf, the only way an adviser can get away with that is if you have a tax situation that requires extra forms, such as a business-at-home expense.

On the hourly side, most preparers can give you an estimate of how much time your return will take by looking at last year's return and listening to whatever changes in circumstances you have gone through in the last 12 months.

Some preparers charge a flat fee per completed return. The problem is that flat rates put a premium on doing returns quickly, not necessarily correctly or with the best tax outcome.

You might save a few bucks now but owe big-time costs later; make sure any adviser who charges a flat rate per return tells you how he handles complex cases—in case yours falls into that gray area—and how much time he spends on the average return. Compare the hours he expects to spend per return to the estimated hours given by other advisers, and determine whether the flat-rate preparer spends too little time on the case (or the hourly adviser too much).

Remember, too, that you will pay less if you deliver your papers in good order, rather than dumping a cigar box full of receipts on the preparer's desk.

Clearly, pay scale is tied to expertise, but all enrolled agents aren't cheaper than all accountants, so shop around. And the national preparation services aren't always such a bargain either; my enrolled agent charges less in her individual practice than if you met her at the storefront practice because she has less overhead.

In addition, find out how a tax adviser will bill you for time spent during the year that does not translate directly to what appears on your tax return. If, for example, you want tax advice before selling an investment or want to make sure another adviser's take on tax law is correct, you could call your adviser in, say, June.

Find out upfront how you will be billed for that time.

As you schedule interviews with a preparer, ask whether an initial get-to-know-you meeting is free. If you wait until tax time to find a preparer, you could be paying for his time but the amount might be rebated if you hire him to do the tax return; at other times of the year, most tax advisers should be willing to schedule a how-do-you-do at no charge.

Where do I start my search?

As with all financial advisers, word-of-mouth recommendations carry a lot of weight. Still, go beyond your circle of friends to make sure you have gotten a good fit of expertise to needs.

The Accreditation Council for Accountancy and Taxation can give you a list of accredited tax preparers in your area—advisers who have earned the ATP or ATA credentials. Call 1-703-549-ACAT for a directory of preparers located near you.

Likewise, the National Association of Enrolled Agents will send a list of qualified members in your area. The group's referral line is 1-800-424-4339.

For accountants, the best place to turn is your state CPA organization. Most state associations have referral services (they are listed in Appendix 3).

In all cases, the referral services should not be perceived as endorsements. Depending on the group, it may simply offer an alphabetized list of practitioners in your area, or it may be a fee-based service charged to members. In addition, many practitioners take themselves off referral services when they are not actively seeking a rush of new clients, preferring to build their practice through word-of-mouth.

As one enrolled agent put it, "The people who can serve you when you call on April 1—right before your return is due—may be good preparers who simply have the ability to handle more clients, or they may be the folks who can't get clients any other way."

How do I check them out?

The very same organizations that you would call for a referral are the ones to contact to check out a tax preparer. Obviously, if you got the name from the referral service, you can assume the person is a member in good standing. If you got the name from a friend or an advertisement, however, this is a call you will want to make.

If your adviser works for a firm—whether it is a major firm, a storefront service or a small partnership, be sure to check on the reputation of both the individual and the company.

Sadly, there is no clearinghouse to call for information on practitioner penalties, but ask for that data anyway. Some state CPA boards will check their databases for complaints and disciplinary or licensing action. If you come across a CPA who has a licensing problem in his file, call the interview off; disciplinary actions and complaints are rare, but can be overlooked as long as the circumstances are explained to you and clarified by the adviser.

Lastly, check with your local Better Business Bureau.

What should I ask during an interview?

Elvis Presley once noted that he "had no use for bodyguards. But I have a very special use for two highly trained certified public accountants."

How Presley determined the credentials of those advisers was never made clear. The best way for you to determine that your adviser— whether he is a CPA, enrolled agent, local preparer or the college kid at the corner franchise—is qualified to meet your needs is to ask the following questions during an initial interview.

How long have you been preparing tax returns?

While tax law is always changing, experience counts for something. Think back to the first time you faced any given tax form and you'll understand why you don't want to be any preparer's test drive into a new area of the tax code.

"The first thing you want to know is how familiar the person is with your type of tax situation and whether he has done returns like this before," said Mike Snowdon, academic associate at the National Endowment for Financial Education in Denver. "You don't want to be the guy's first shot at some form, or even the second. If he isn't used to doing a return like yours, find someone who is."

Looking at my return from last year, how do I compare to your average client? Am I more or less complex, or about the same?

You should bring previous tax returns to an initial interview so the planner gets an idea of what is involved and can accurately forecast a cost.

By asking how you compare to a typical client, you should find out what concerns the adviser might have in preparing your returns. ("Well, most of my clients don't have self-employment income [or fill-in-the-blank unique need]" should raise a red flag.)

Make sure the adviser describes the average client to you, using specifics of age, family situation, average income and so on. His idea of what is average may come from the paperwork—a 1040 with Schedules A, B, D and other standard forms—rather than the people. If you want him to be able to give you advice beyond merely filing returns, if he is going to become an asset to your financial team, you will need to resemble the average client in more than just the forms you fill out.

Another way of getting at this information is to ask for the range of forms the preparer filed the previous year. He may have done a lot of Schedule A and B forms, but not a single Schedule SE, which affects people who are self-employed. If his range of forms experience is narrow, make sure your previous returns do not eclipse the adviser's comfort zone.

Are there any areas on which your practice is focused or in which you specialize?

Like most financial counselors, tax advisers can be generalists or specialists. They may focus on a particular clientele—small business owners, for example—or type of situation, such as divorce.

Just because an adviser has a specialty doesn't mean he won't branch off into other arenas depending on a client's needs. If you are considering an adviser with a particular area of expertise, make sure your needs fall in the trunk area of the practice, and not out in the tree limbs.

What continuing education classes have you taken? What credentials, if any, do you have?

As discussed previously, tax-preparation credentials require ongoing classes or certification exams. Find out what makes the preparer qualified to be your personal expert; you will find that many people with similar professional designations have different backgrounds, with some opting to do the minimum and others going back to school for master's degrees in taxation.

Regardless of credentials, your preparer must be current on the law, which changes almost daily. The IRS does not care if you—or your preparer—are unaware; ignorance is no defense for overzealous deductions or underpayment of taxes due, so be wary of advisers who haven't been to continuing education programs in more than a year. Remember, it's almost always going to be you who foots the bill if your adviser makes a mistake, even if the blunder was caused by not keeping current on the tax laws.

How many clients do you work with?

Most of the year this will not be a particular issue; you can almost always reach a tax preparer for advice over the summer.

This question looks at the crucial time of the year, when your paperwork is due. There are about 600 working hours in a tax season, and a busy firm with an office staff may do 600 or more returns. A small practitioner with little or no office support may handle a few dozen.

Make sure the adviser is not too busy to give you his full attention. If he has a big clientele, ask how that affects your return and whether that changes when you must have paperwork ready.

Are you open for business all year?
It's not just the storefronts or the local preparers out to make an extra buck who may be gone when your audit notice arrives. There are some enrolled agents and accredited tax preparers who shut down when it's not tax time.

That said, this is not a dumb question. If you want more information on a return—say to challenge an IRS ruling on your deductions—or if you want tax planning and have ongoing questions, you will want someone who is in the business for the long haul.

What percentage of your clients file for an extension?
Some advisers file extensions for everyone;, others make a habit of having all clients polished off by April 15.

An extension does not put off paying the IRS any taxes due. It simply gives you more time in which to file the paperwork.

If you are expecting a refund, it slows the process tremendously.

If an adviser has a lot of clients and files extensions as a matter of course—rather than need—you have a reason to question whether he has adequate time available to serve you.

How do you charge for your services? What do I get for my money?
Every financial adviser must be asked to spell out his cost structure. In addition, you want to find out if paying for a tax return simply means getting the paperwork completed or whether you can call throughout the year when you have a tax question, and whether the meter will be running during those phone calls.

Get billing details upfront, too. For instance, find out when you will be expected to pay—when the return is ready? in advance?—and how detailed the bill will be.

What other costs might I incur?
Like any other sort of financial advice, the level of service included in the return varies. Some tax preparers may charge you for filing a tax re-

turn electronically, others may charge you copying costs for the copies you take home.

It's a miserable feeling to get the bill for services and feel like you have been squeezed for every extra penny, so ask ahead of time what you could pay for in addition to the time spent meeting with you or preparing a return.

In addition, ask about research time. If a tax adviser needs to do research to prepare your return, will he bill you for that time? If so, make sure the research is specific to you, and that he is not double-billing, putting the research time needed to check out a fairly common issue on the bills of several clients. If the research was not required specifically by your circumstance—and if it is applicable to others—you shouldn't pay for it any more than you would pick up the tab on some continuing education classes.

How can I reduce my costs?

If you plan to take the shoebox and drop it on your adviser's desk, you are going to pay dearly to have someone go through your receipts and try to piece together your life. In fact, many advisers won't do it, particularly if you are hiring them in the middle of tax season.

But even if you think you have done all of the math yourself, you may be coming to them with material that requires more preparation time than you might have expected. Find out from them what you can do to make the process more efficient without reducing the accuracy of the return.

Most advisers will be happy to give you this information, because even though it cuts into their take on your return, it makes the filing process a whole lot easier.

If an adviser has a certain way he likes material organized and wants particular details in place before he works on your return, chances are you will cut your bill significantly if you can become the preparer's ideal client.

If you do not have the expertise to handle my return—or to advise me about the tax implications of financial moves that I may someday consider—where do you turn for help? Do you ever allow those other experts to take over a client?

This doesn't apply if your case is straightforward, but it is not uncommon for a tax situation to get sticky in a hurry. Inheritances, investment losses and changes in career, family or your health, for example, can take a simple tax return and make it a complicated mess overnight.

Find out where an adviser turns when situations get murky.

Will anyone else be working on my return?

You're the one paying the bill, so you should know what you are getting for your money.

If an accountant uses junior partners or enrolled agents to do tax returns, you will want to know. Not only will you want to be able to check out the subordinate's credentials, but you also want to ask about the return-review process and find out whether the big shots double-check all work before asking you to sign it.

It's dumb to pay for a figurehead. Find out what, if anything, the involvement of others does to your projected costs; you should pay less if an accountant merely oversees your return than if he does the math and the work on his own.

What can I do to lower my taxes, both for this year and in the future?

Don't expect detailed advice in an initial interview, but try to get a feel for whether the adviser is content to have you stay the course or whether he believes that actively managing your tax situation could save you some dough.

If all he wants to do is crunch the numbers, he might not be the right kind of adviser if you want someone who can help you over a lifetime.

What is your approach to deductions?

You are trying to find out just how aggressive a tax preparer intends to be. I once interviewed an enrolled agent, for example, who told me he would not file an office-at-home deduction because "those things wind up as a red flag that makes you more likely to be audited."

That would be great logic if I were worried about facing an audit and losing.

My office is a legitimate, meets-the-IRS-standard deduction, and a big one at that. Not taking it to avoid a potential audit would cost me thousands of dollars over the years; taking the deduction would not cost me in an audit because it's legitimate.

Clearly, that tax adviser was too conservative for me.

I agree with the late American jurist, Learned Hand (yes, that was really his name), who said "There is nothing sinister in so arranging one's affairs as to keep taxes as low as possible."

What you are looking for in a tax adviser is someone who is as aggressive or conservative as you are. Is he unafraid of incurring questions from the IRS or does he take a conservative approach that is less risky but possibly more costly?

Ask how the preparer deals with the gray areas of the tax code. If the preparer wants to push the envelope of legality and you don't—or vice versa—you don't have a good match.

Remember, you will pay the extra tax if you are too conservative but also will be responsible for the tax and penalties if the IRS quashes exuberant deductions made by your preparer. That's a reminder that there is a right way, a wrong way and your way to do these things, and you will want to find a preparer who does things your way.

Will you guarantee me a tax refund?
The answer you are listening for is NO.

Any adviser who says that he can always get you money back from Uncle Sam is prepared to bend the rules—particularly if he hasn't had a chance to dig into your files and see whether you (or previous advisers) have done well.

What are the potential outcomes of my return?
From a basic description of your current circumstances and a perusal of last year's tax return, an adviser should be able to tell you whether you are looking at a refund or taxes due. What you want is a realistic assessment of where you stand now; you do not want the tax equivalent of a "yes man" telling you what you want to hear.

Even if you don't have the expertise to do your own taxes, you have enough knowledge to know the shape you are in. You know whether your earnings have shot up, if you have withheld more of your salary, if you sold investments and realized capital gains, if you gained or lost deductions based on your marital status and circumstances surrounding your children, and more.

Presumably, the adviser should give you an answer that you expect, even if that's not the answer you would like to hear.

If you get this adviser's answer in a meeting held before tax season—which is always the best time to hire a tax planner—follow it up by asking:

Are you familiar with the laws of the states in which I am subject to tax?
Presumably, every adviser knows the rules of the state in which he lives.

But if you have financial interests in more than one state, you will want someone familiar with the rules in both places. This is particularly important for people who live in one state and work in another, who receive income from a partnership based in another state or who have moved and owe taxes to two state governments.

What percentage of the returns you filed last year were audited? What percentage of returns over the course of your career have been audited?

An abnormally high number, above 1 percent or 2 percent, warrants some explanation.

Periodically, the IRS focuses on certain occupations and industries and niches; specializing in returns on this hit list—a clientele composed primarily of doctors when the IRS decides to take a better look at that profession, for example—can dramatically inflate a preparer's audit numbers.

If those special circumstances do not exist, ask why the clients have been audited and what the outcomes were of most audits. Too many audits can be a sign that the IRS and the preparer don't see eye-to-eye on how certain rules are interpreted; the IRS generally wins those arguments.

Who will represent me in an audit?

You already know that only enrolled agents, CPAs and tax attorneys can actually represent you if the IRS comes calling. That said, even some of those advisers do not handle audits themselves, leaving the work to partners or others with more audit experience. In the case of storefront preparation services, you want to find out who the firm will send with you and how you will contact the firm in the event of an audit (some storefront services are open only during tax season; these temporary offices will be gone when the audit notice arrives, so you will want to find out who to call).

If your adviser plans to be with you during an audit, ask how much experience he has in handling audits. On the one hand, you'd like some experience; on the other, too much is not a good sign.

Be sure to ask about the cost of being represented in an audit. Just because an adviser can do it doesn't mean he will not charge you for it. Find out the costs involved, just in case; it may help you decide exactly how aggressive you want to be with those deductions.

If I am audited or notified of a problem with my return, who pays penalties and interest on the amount I owe?

There is no getting around the taxes; you are going to pay what the government determines you owe, as well as for any blunders for which you are responsible. That means if you do not withhold enough money from your paycheck and owe Uncle Sam taxes and penalties on April 15, it's your responsibility. But say your adviser whiffed on a portion of the tax code and a deduction was disallowed; you will owe the taxes on the income that is no longer tax-deductible, but the adviser may agree to pay any penalties and interest due on the amount you owe.

Find out what the adviser will do for you if he miscalculates your return. Most will make good on punishments you incur because of their mistakes.

When will I hear from you, and why?

If all you want is someone who can ease your paperwork burden one time, this year, then this question is not important. The adviser could be out of business in six months—and many are—and it wouldn't matter to you.

If, however, you want to integrate a tax adviser into your financial team and work with someone you trust for many years, you will want an adviser who is interested in dealing with you all year long. Just as importantly, you will want to know what to expect from the relationship after the paperwork is filed.

There are four basic functions you should expect from a tax adviser: Suggesting tax strategies, preparing returns, minimizing tax exposure and, if necessary, preparing you to meet authorities.

Find out whether an adviser will cover those bases. To do that, he must contact you periodically. It is not enough simply to tell you when to gather your paperwork and to call you when it's over.

A relationship-oriented adviser will want to handle all of the four major functions, plus review your estate planning and help manage investment and insurance decisions.

That may mean regular visits, phone calls when you plan to sell investments, end-of-the-year tax-reduction brainstorming or more. In any event, you want to find out how involved the adviser gets in helping clients prepare for the future. Armed with that information, you can decide whether this is the kind of person with whom you want a long-term professional relationship.

Could I get the names of a few recent clients who you have worked with?

At this point in the process, you are ready to get the names of some customers, preferably folks whose cases are similar to yours and who use the adviser for the same sorts of situations, whether simply putting together a tax return or seeking long-term tax counsel.

Have you ever been subject to any practitioner penalties? If so, for what?

Tax advisers do not have to tell you if they have been subject to practitioner penalties, and there may not be a way for you to track down that information.

Ask anyway.

If a preparer reacts funny, use your intuition.

How will we resolve complaints if I am dissatisfied?

There is no standard procedure for solving problems in the preparation of a tax return. If you are dealing with a sole practitioner, for example, there is no boss to go to.

Still, you want to find out what will happen if you are not satisfied with the work done on your behalf (and that means you are displeased with the quality of the advice, not with the fact that you owe Uncle Sam some money).

A tax adviser may not have a great answer to this question; that is saying that your only recourse may be some type of malpractice action.

How can I terminate this relationship if I am not satisfied?

Until you get to the level at which you are hiring an accountant, there may be no formal agreement to sign. Termination may be as simple as walking away, although you may need to make sure you get all of your paperwork back.

Most accountants ask you to sign a "letter of engagement." Never enter any financial arrangement without knowing how to get out of it.

What do I ask references?

Aside from the questions you would ask any adviser (as described in Chapter 11), there are several things you should learn about a tax adviser from a client's perspective. They include:

- Did the adviser seek deductions that might otherwise have been missed?

- Did the adviser suggest ways to lower taxes due?

- What kind of tax planning do you receive in mid-year reviews?

- Does the preparer work to keep bills down by listing in advance the data he requires?

- Has the adviser, in general, avoided nasty surprises so that, even if the news was bad, you were prepared for all possible outcomes?

- If you have ever had to pay any tax penalties because of something the adviser forgot to do, did the adviser correct—and pay for—the mistake at no cost? (Remember, the adviser is likely to pay only for penalties and, possibly, interest due; the actual tax liability always is the responsibility of the customer, even if it was the adviser who suggested, say, a deduction that was disallowed.)

What are the danger signs to a relationship gone sour?

Aside from guarantees, the biggest danger sign is some sort of *surprise.*

You may owe a monster tax bill, for example, but it should not be a surprise. You may have had to liquidate a retirement account and be facing major penalties, but that should not come as a shock; your adviser should have forewarned you about these things and even helped with the math.

Obviously, if a tax planner suggests moves that generate these bills—without warning you of the consequences—you have another problem, namely *lack of communication.*

A tax adviser should help you develop a strategy and work with you on implementing it; he should help you consider all of your options and the likely tax outcomes. Anything less than that and the relationship is headed for trouble, so don't let your adviser lose you in the tax code; make him explain everything necessary to your level so you can avoid those surprises.

Failure to meet deadlines is another potential problem with tax advisers. You have asked in the interview about extensions; if you wind up filing one that you were not prepared for—or which should not be necessary because you have a simple return—you might question whether the adviser has taken on more clients than he or she can adequately handle on time.

Recurring annual problems can be another sign of trouble. A tax refund is not a bonus, it's a sign that you withheld too much money. It represents an interest-free loan to Uncle Sam; conversely, having significant tax bills due every April could be either a strategy or a sign that you are headed for cash-flow problems.

A tax adviser should be able to tell you the correct amount to withhold or pay in estimated taxes so that, in any given year, you are as tax-efficient as possible, neither owing nor expecting a significant amount of money from the government. If an adviser can't get you on that even keel, either he doesn't have enough information from you, one (or both) of you is pursuing a particular tax strategy or he isn't working hard enough.

If I have a complaint, where do I go?

The answer depends on what kind of adviser you are hiring. If you are working with a national tax service, you will start with the office or regional manager. With an accountant or enrolled agent in a large firm, chances are you will first pursue a complaint with the managing partner.

If you work with a CPA, your next step will be to approach the state society to see if it can offer you any relief. At the very least, file a complaint in the hope that the group will make it available to others who call to check out the accountant's record.

If you can not work out some form of settlement, contact an attorney. Accountants can be guilty of malpractice as much as lawyers, brokers or doctors.

How can I develop and build the relationship?

The only way to turn a tax preparer into a tax planner is to seek out his counsel at other times of the year and involve him in your other financial relationships.

It makes sense, for example, for a tax adviser to question whether you are taking advantage of individual retirement accounts. You may not be because of the availability of other savings vehicles. That does not make IRAs a poor option, however; if the adviser asks you a question you can't answer, you will want him to work with your broker or financial planner to help determine a money management strategy that is both rewarding and tax-efficient.

No one gets tax planning in March or April. You get it the rest of the year, when there is still time to move money around and take advantage of your own personal tax circumstances. If you want to build a relationship with a tax adviser, make a regular appointment to sit down after tax season ends, and make it a point to call him for advice whenever taxes play a role in your other money-management decisions.

The idea, in this case, is to be like Elvis, and find the special uses for your tax preparers.

18 *Hiring a lawyer*

In investment circles, there is an old saying that goes:

Insurance salesmen profit on fear.

Stock brokers profit on greed.

Lawyers profit on everyone.

All jokes aside, there will come a day when you need a lawyer. In fact, the likelihood is that over your lifetime you might need several lawyers, so no matter how loathsome you find the profession and how many vicious lawyer jokes you swap with friends, you will at least want to know how to contact and select an attorney who can answer your questions.

Most of financial planning comes down to creating a safety net— finding help for growing, tending and protecting what you earn. Lawyers are a part of that safety net; just as insurance can protect you from accidents and catastrophes, so can lawyers protect you from trouble and help you retain your rights when something goes wrong.

In today's litigious society, the first thing you must do in any situation with legal ramifications is assess whether you need an attorney's special training. If the problem is complex enough that it could wind up in court, or if novice mistakes could cost you tons of money—as happens all the time with poorly drawn estate plans—it's probably time to consult a lawyer.

There was a day when lawyers were almost a one-size-fits-all group. The same guy who wrote your will also went to court with your cousin to defend against reckless driving charges. It's the country-lawyer image portrayed in old movies and it's about as current as those black-

and-white films; today, law is highly specialized and most attorneys concentrate in just a few areas.

That doesn't mean a lawyer won't take up almost any request that comes his or her way, but it puts the onus on you to gauge whether the lawyer has the skill to handle your specific needs. Since switching attorneys in the middle of a case is both complicated and costly, take the time to get comfortable with a lawyer before going forward as a client.

Here are the questions you will want to answer before hiring an attorney:

Can I do this myself?

The oldest axiom in law is that any man who acts as his own lawyer has a fool for a client.

Of course, it was lawyers who created that axiom, and they make money only when they have clients to represent.

There are many situations when you may not need or want a lawyer. Almost every community has some form of small claims court, through which you can resolve disputes valued up to a few thousand dollars by representing yourself in informal proceedings (and with minimal court costs).

Likewise, some situations can be resolved through arbitration, by which an impartial observer—generally former judges, current and former lawyers and business people—settles your dispute in a binding situation. The ground rules, including maximum allowable monetary damages, are set when you agree to arbitration; the process is quick and results are private, unlike court hearings.

Mediation is similar, except that the neutral mediator only offers suggestions to resolve the dispute. There is no settlement unless you and your opponent come to terms.

Then there is the do-it-yourself segment of the legal business, which includes reference work and software programs available at most bookstores. You can use those items for help to write your own will, handle a divorce, file for the protection of the bankruptcy court, establish various types of trusts and write basic business contracts. The books and programs produce documents that meet basic standards, but they may not go far enough to cover your individual circumstances.

Ironically, the best way to make sure that these programs measure up to the current legal standard is to do the work yourself and then hire a lawyer to review it; it may drive your costs up—though it will be cheaper than having the documents drawn up by the attorney—but your efforts still will be rewarded with dramatically reduced legal bills.

Most lawyers I talk with agree the decision to hire an attorney comes down to three factors:

1. How complicated is the situation? Complications can be caused by technicalities of the law, the number of parties involved in the suit (and the fact that some of them live out of state), or the complexities of the case.

Think of it this way: If the situation is complicated enough for the other side to have an attorney, chances are you should, too.

2. How much is at stake? That's not just a monetary question, since anything more serious than a traffic ticket could put your civil liberty at risk. Likewise, you probably wouldn't want to go through a foreclosure proceeding without an attorney on your side.

Ask yourself "Is this really so important to me?" If it is, then you probably don't want to risk going to court without counsel.

3. Do I need someone to speak for me? This is a personal decision, but if you are in an emotional situation that could provoke anger or rage, you should consider getting a lawyer to act as your mouthpiece.

On the one hand, being your own lawyer allows you to vent your frustrations; on the other hand, such venting might cause more harm than good in the eyes of the court.

What is the lawyer's job?

Once you have decided not to represent yourself, only a lawyer can represent you in legal proceedings. All lawyers must pass a state bar exam and a character review in order to receive a license to practice law. Because practicing law without a license is a crime in most states, lawyers are the only ones who can be your advocates, although paralegals, bankers and others may help draw up papers. (In some states, paralegals who work directly under the supervision of lawyers may handle minor matters and even offer direct consultation in a few, very limited areas.)

What a lawyer is supposed to bring to the table is knowledge of legal procedures and informed judgment. A good lawyer listens to your problem and searches for the best course of action, whether it be a recommendation on which type of trust to establish or if a personal-injury case is worth pursuing.

What kind of lawyer do I need?

There are legal specialists for almost every situation imaginable. In alphabetical order, here are the major areas of legal practice and a short description of what each type of lawyer provides:

Business lawyers give advice on general corporate matters, from start-ups to mergers and acquisitions, business taxation, contract and partnership issues.

Consumer lawyers represent clients in disputes with stores and consumer products companies.

Criminal lawyers do the obvious, defending or prosecuting cases of criminal wrongdoing.

Estate planning lawyers write wills, set up trusts, establish powers of attorney, and counsel clients on property management, inheritance, tax and probate issues. Some also act as executors on clients' estates.

Family lawyers— more widely known as *divorce attorneys or domestic-relations lawyers*—handle cases of divorce, separation, annulment, child custody and support. Many family lawyers (along with some estate planning attorneys) also work as *elder lawyers*, specializing in "elder law issues," the rights and rules that concern senior citizens.

Governmental lawyers are generally considered an extension of business lawyers, helping clients comply with (or dispute) local, state and federal rulings, regulations and statutes.

Immigration lawyers represent people in immigration and naturalization proceedings, helping them become citizens or avoid deportation.

Intellectual property lawyers, also known as "patent attorneys," advise clients on issues involving copyrights, trademarks and patents.

Labor lawyers cover a wide range of issues. They can represent employers, unions or individuals in cases involving workplace safety, compliance with government regulations and questions of allowable union activity, and also can get involved in workplace discrimination cases.

Personal injury lawyers take on the cases of people hurt through the intentional or negligent actions of a person or company. Many also specialize in workers' compensation claims for employees injured on the job.

Real estate lawyers help clients analyze real estate contracts, mortgage paperwork, and disputes with brokers, agents or contractors and process the paperwork involved in a closing. They can also get involved in neighbor disputes and other real-estate issues.

Tax lawyers counsel individuals and businesses in federal, state and local tax matters, interpreting the tax code when sticky situations arise. Most will not fill out your tax return, although some will be affiliated with accountants and others who handle the actual paperwork.

How is my lawyer going to be compensated?

Lord Henry Peter Brougham, a 19th-century British statesman, once noted that a lawyer is "a learned gentleman who rescues your estate from your enemies and keeps it for himself."

Indeed, one reason many people fear hiring a lawyer is the cost.

There is a real fear that it's too expensive to hire a lawyer, or that the only way to get good legal representation is to pay a lot of money. Sometimes, those fears turn out to be true.

Lawyers are paid in several different ways, and sometimes more than one depending on what they do for you.

Flat fees or *fee-for-service payments* are common when the procedure is straightforward and generally requires a routine amount of time. Many lawyers quote a flat rate on simple wills, title searches, review of a real estate contract and other common practices.

(Routine procedures also are perfect opportunities to use pre-paid legal plans and legal clinics. Pre-paid plans—which are being offered with increasing frequency as a benefit to employees—function as a kind of legal health maintenance organization, by which you pay an annual fee and are entitled to a specified amount of service from lawyers who take part in the network. Legal clinics tend to offer low-cost representation, often with less-experienced attorneys than those in private practices; simple procedures such as those billed at a flat rate generally can be handled cheaply by this kind of law office.)

If your legal needs are not routine and the amount of work involved is not predictable, chances are you will pay *hourly rates* for services. This is the most common form of billing and when most individuals worry their legal bills will escalate. Rates go from $25 to $500 or more per hour, depending on the expertise of the lawyer, the complexity of the case, the size of the firm and the amount of work the firm must turn down to accept your case.

Most lawyers keep a detailed record of how many hours they work for you, often breaking the time down into as little as tenths of hours. They keep a log of the time they spend on your case—and may charge a higher rate for courtroom time than for office or telephone minutes.

This is when it is important to understand exactly when and why your lawyer is charging you. If the meter is running every time the lawyer picks up the phone—even if it is just to tell you there is no progress on your case—that might wear your pocketbook thin.

Remember, too, that the lawyer's out-of-pocket expenses—from court fees to messenger services, faxes, copying and more—will show up on your bill too, added to the hourly tab.

If you fear an out-of-control hourly bill, find out if the lawyer will limit the amount you can be charged. Essentially, this combines flat-rate and hourly plans, setting a maximum rate for the service you need while saving you on hourly costs if necessary work can be done quickly.

(To cut costs further, ask what you can do to help. Some lawyers will let you pick up and deliver documents or make phone calls to help gather information. This could not only save time and routine expenses, it might also make you better informed on the status of your case.)

Some lawyers charge *asset-based* or *percentage fees,* which are simply a sliver of the assets being managed or distributed. For example, a lawyer may earn a percentage of the assets in a will that goes through probate.

The problem with percentage fees is that they aren't always commensurate with the work involved to earn them. If there are major assets involved but only routine legal work—say you are selling a $1 million home in a straightforward transaction—you will be overpaying for the service you get. In those situations, press the lawyer to use an hourly or flat rate for the service, or ask for a cut of the percentage fee so your bill is fair, given the amount of work involved.

Lawyers accept *contingent fees* on cases they believe they can win, usually for a client who can not afford to pay the other types of fees. Contingency fees apply only in situations in which money is being claimed, notably personal injury and workers' compensation cases;

some states forbid criminal and domestic-relations attorneys from accepting cases on a contingency basis.

If you win the case, the lawyer takes home a big cut, usually between 25 and 50 percent. Generally, the lawyer gets one-third of your winnings (many states limit the maximum allowable fee), although "sliding scale arrangements" in your contract may increase the attorney's cut if the case drags on or is appealed, or lower the percentage as the dollar value of the settlement rises.

If you lose the case, there are no winnings to split up and the lawyer gets nothing.

Win or lose, however, you will owe court costs. I recently saw a television ad for a lawyer who promised clients would "never pay a single cent out-of-pocket" to try their case. Unless the lawyer agrees to pick up filing fees and assorted court costs in the event of a loss, that statement most likely was false.

Those court costs are an important consideration in hiring a lawyer on contingency. To get the most for your money, you will want expenses to be deducted from the monetary award before the lawyer gets his or her cut. Say you win a $15,000 judgment and court costs are $3,000.

If the lawyer gets the first cut, he takes one-third of $15,000, which is $5,000. Then you pay the $3,000 in court costs and are left with $7,000.

If you pay the court costs first, you reduce your $15,000 award by the $3,000 in expenses. That leaves $12,000, of which the lawyer gets one-third, or $4,000. You take home $8,000. Many contingency lawyers prefer to be paid before expenses are taken from the award, but the point often is negotiable. Be sure to negotiate it.

Retainers are monies paid to lawyers on a regular basis to make sure an attorney is available when needed. Retainers are paid mostly by individuals and companies with a regular need for service. (Many lawyers agree to take work from individuals in exchange for an upfront payment for part or all of their services; they may call this a retainer but it typically amounts to a non-refundable advance.)

But retainers are merely a method of payment, and not a charge for service; as a result, you still must find out how you are being charged for the work being done.

If your lawyer asks for a retainer, consider this a down payment; if you have a big need for legal services, you could outspend the retainer and wind up with a bill. Make sure you have an idea how much service—hours of the lawyer's time—you should expect a retainer to cover.

Referral fees are paid if you go to a lawyer who refers your case to someone more expert in dealing with your problem. In exchange for the referral, the first lawyer may ask for a cut of the fee, an arrangement that may be prohibited by law depending on the circumstances of the case.

Both attorneys are entitled to a fee, as long as they both work the case. If the first lawyer steps out of the case completely, he should get no further payment.

If one lawyer refers you to another, ask if there will be a referral fee and, if so, how the arrangement is going to work. In most states, the ethical rules governing lawyers say a referral fee can not be charged unless the client is aware of the situation and each attorney works on the case and splits the fee proportionately to the work he performed. Equally important, the referral fee can not make the total bill unreasonably high.

One last thing to remember about fees: In some cases, you can recoup attorney's fees and ancillary costs from the other side, but there is no guarantee. If you lose the case, you're stuck paying whatever fees and costs you agreed to, and may also have to pay your adversary's court costs.

What credentials will I have to deal with, and how important are they?

Law is not an area in which you must see specific credentials to feel comfortable with a practitioner. The law degree and license speak volumes about someone having achieved the minimum standards for competency.

That said, there are some legal specialties—and more than 20 states— in which lawyers can become certified specialists, such as a "certified civil trial lawyer" or "certified tax lawyer." Nationally, for example, the American Trial Lawyers Organization has a credential for "certified trial lawyers," but most national law specialty groups are membership organizations rather than educational/credentialing institutions.

These credentials are valuable when you are looking for an attorney with a particular expertise, since maintaining these designations requires continuing education and some level of experience in the field. Still, they are hardly a necessity because they are not uniformly administered. (Traditionally, most lawyers were prohibited from calling themselves "specialists," even if they limited their practices; some states continue to adhere to this outdated custom, which could put the burden on you to find someone whose practice meets your needs.)

You are looking for someone who is experienced in the kind of matters you have; if you are presented with a credential, learn the educational and experience requirements and ask to see a code of ethics, if there is one.

The one time you will want to be picky about credentials is if your lawyer is going to wear two hats on your financial team. Some attorneys, for example, also are certified public accountants or financial planners. If you intend to hire an attorney-CPA, for example, make sure he has the appropriate accounting designations; if a lawyer doubles as a financial planner, look for an advisory credential (because, unlike law, there is no minimum standard of acumen to becoming a financial planner, and a lawyer can expand into that arena without being truly qualified).

Where do I start my search?

When you need a lawyer, ask relatives and trusted friends who have been in a similar situation. Their references will go a long way, although you must remember that each case is different.

There are legal referral services in many communities, which will recommend a lawyer to evaluate your situation—often at a reduced cost. Bar associations also make referrals according to specific areas of law. Many of the referral organizations have minimum competency or experience requirements.

Even that is no guarantee you will find the right lawyer, however. Some referral services are more advertising than substance, with lawyers paying to get a spot on the referral list. In those situations, there is no attention paid to a lawyer's skill.

Lawyers also can advertise on television, in newspapers, on the radio and in the phone book. This may help you remember their names, but it does not make them the best lawyer for your case. Moreover, be careful of pricing issues; advertising may talk about specific types of services and fees, but your case may not fall into the simple-and-straightforward category and you may not be able to get the advertised special.

Appendix 4 lists every state bar association; call yours or look at its web site to get a few names. From there, call and arrange interviews. Many lawyers offer a free initial consultation, although some charge a nominal fee for their time; find this out before you set up the interview.

How do I check them out?

If you got a referral to a lawyer from a bar association or referral service, you should have asked if there was any record of the lawyer's disciplinary history. But since many of those listings are actually supplied and paid for by the lawyer, there may not be any negatives to speak of.

The Martindale-Hubbell Law Directory is a complete listing of domestic and international lawyers by state and specialty. It is available in most public libraries and provides background information on how long a lawyer has been in practice, where and when they earned their degrees, and more. You can access it online at the company's web site, www.martindale.com, where the lawyer locator feature will help you find and research potential advisers.

Unfortunately, it's still just a surface measure of an attorney's background; you will not find out whether an adviser has had complaints and malpractice suits filed against him.

In fact, that kind of crucial information is lacking almost everywhere you turn. Few states make all complaints available to the public from the time allegations are filed. Most states will reveal grievance filings, but only once the state bar association's grievance committee has decided to issue charges against the attorney. Those committees can take years to make a decision, and those charges can end in "admonitions" or "private reprimands," in which only the lawyer—and possibly the aggrieved client—know what happened.

Regardless of those shortcomings, call your state or local bar association's grievance committee for any records it can provide pertaining to your prospective attorney. In addition, check with your local Better Business Bureau for any complaints.

What should I ask during an interview?

Financier J. Pierpont Morgan once described what he wanted from an attorney, saying, "I don't want a lawyer to tell me what I can not do, I hire him to tell me how to do what I want to do."

While none of us has Morgan's enormous fortune, we do want to hire his kind of lawyer, one who will be able to help us achieve our goals.

Unfortunately, that may mean telling us what we can not do. A good lawyer knows better than to waste time. You do not want a lawyer who is a "yes man," but rather someone who will argue on your behalf and also be ready to fight with you in order to keep you out of trouble. You need someone who pays attention to details and who does not let the little things slide.

As with every other type of financial adviser, you are shopping for trust, integrity and ability, all of which will be hard for you to gauge during an initial interview. Obviously, the way you make that determination depends on your needs. Someone seeking a divorce attorney is going to need different information than someone looking for defense counsel in a reckless driving case. Nevertheless, here are the questions to ask when sizing up a lawyer:

How long have you been practicing and in what areas of the law do you specialize?

In all financial relationships, you don't want to be a guinea pig. That's particularly true of law, when one misstep could put you on the wrong side of a judgment.

Find out the scope of the practice and whether your current needs are a good fit for either the individual lawyer or the firm. It's not that a patent attorney can't write a good will, but you might have regrets when someday you discover what years of practicing intellectual property law have done to his skills as an estate planning attorney.

If a lawyer has several specialities, ask how his workload is divided between those areas of the law. A lawyer might do real estate contracts and estate planning, for example, but his business may be heavily weighted toward the former. If you come in with a complex estate situation, he may not have the depth of experience you want—even though estate planning is supposed to be one of his specialties.

Be sure to find out how long a lawyer has worked in each specialty. He may have 10 years of practice experience as a business lawyer, for example, but might have branched into intellectual property only a year ago. Make sure he passes muster in your area of need.

What continuing education classes have you taken? What certifications, if any, do you have?

Again, you are looking to establish a lawyer's competency. The law is constantly changing and evolving; the lawyer who fails to keep up with it eventually becomes a danger to his clients.

Who is your typical client?

You don't want actual names, so this question does not violate attorney-client privilege. What you want to find out is whether the average client is an individual or a business, and whether the average job resembles what you need done, both in terms of the legal matters being covered and, when applicable, the dollars involved. If a book publisher wants to buy your memoirs, for example, and is offering a big six-figure advance, you would not want to hire an attorney whose experience negotiating book contracts was limited to deals worth only a few thousand dollars.

This is particularly important for any type of lawyer with whom you expect to have an ongoing relationship, during which important papers—such as wills and estate-planning documents—are re-examined and updated every few years. If you are not a good fit for a lawyer's practice today, you may be even further out of sync in the future.

If you do not have the expertise to handle my case on your own, do you work with other lawyers? Under what circumstances would you allow them to take over the case?

Determine what makes a lawyer nervous enough to seek help or back away from a case.

Ideally, you hire a lawyer who is as aggressive or conservative in his approach to work as you are in your approach to life. If you are the conservative type who likes everything buttoned down before proceeding, you might be concerned about a lawyer who never consults with others before making new maneuvers for clients.

Under what circumstances would you simply refer me to another lawyer?

There are good and bad answers to this question.

Good answers involve a lawyer passing you on to a partner—or even an outsider—who is better suited for the job or when he is too busy to give your case the attention it deserves. Bad answers are that your case is not interesting enough or not likely to generate enough in fees.

If you go to a firm to interview a senior partner and find a fresh-out-of-school rookie handling your case, that could be a problem. Let the lawyer know you intend to interview any lawyer to whom you are referred before signing up for that person's services.

Under all circumstances, find out if the lawyer charges a referral fee.

Will anyone else be working on the case?

You're the one paying the bill, and you want to get what you pay for.

If the lawyer uses paralegals or junior partners to do the work, you should find out just how involved your attorney intends to be. It's dumb to pay for a figurehead. You also want to find out what, if anything, the involvement of others does to your projected costs; some firms have additional charges when paralegals and researchers get involved in a case.

How many active cases/clients do you work with at one time?

This is another good indicator of how likely the attorney is to work on your case. If he has a heavy workload, your run-of-the-mill situation may not get the attention it deserves. Your will may be an everyday document to an attorney, but it is protection for your family, not something you want the lawyer to squeeze in between 20 clients with needs he perceives as more pressing.

There is one more major concern when it comes to a lawyer's caseload, namely "double-billing." This occurs when a lawyer goes to court for you and several other clients at the same time. While traveling, the lawyer catches up on other cases or reading—and sends bills for that time to every client whose file is in the briefcase.

You're paying for the lawyer's attention to your case, but it's not full attention.

The American Bar Association has condemned this practice but can't punish members for it.

If your lawyer's caseload seems heavy, ask whether he or she ever practices double-billing. It's not that the practice makes him a bad lawyer, necessarily, it's that you should get some sort of reduction in the hourly rate if you don't have his full attention.

What are the potential outcomes of my case?

Any time there's an adversarial situation, one side loses. If every lawyer in every situation guaranteed a victory, half would be wrong.

Before you engage an attorney—particularly if you are paying an hourly rate instead of a contingency—you want an honest assessment of the strength of your case. This includes knowing whether the lawyer expects to settle the case or go to court—and the pluses and minuses of each of those resolutions—as well as whether a loss can be appealed and under what circumstances the lawyer would recommend it.

If the lawyer expects the case to go to trial, ask about trial experience, as there are plenty of attorneys who almost never set foot in a courtroom.

How do you work with clients?

Make sure a lawyer contacts you in all situations that affect your case, explaining the proceedings in plain English. Try to establish how often and under what circumstances you will hear from the lawyer, so you can decide whether that contact is sufficient for you to be satisfied.

In addition, find out what paperwork, if any, the lawyer will give you copies of. A file of these papers can be a good thing to have if you must change lawyers mid-stream.

Just how tough are you?

Many legal issues come down to a test of will and nerves—which side is going to break first or move the furthest from its demands.

You may want an aggressive lawyer, but you also must be able to live with the outcome.

For example, some lawyers are particularly tough negotiating insurance settlements. If they can't get the desired amount from the insurer, they may walk away from a settlement and risk getting the money in court. That could tie the case up for years—delaying how long it takes for you to get the money and, potentially, increasing your costs.

While you want someone who fights tooth-and-nail on your side, you may not want to pay the price such an aggressive lawyer exacts. Some particularly tough real estate lawyers, for example, will walk away from a house rather than give up on the concessions they demand from buyers or sellers. Their desire to do the best deal is wonderful, but not at the cost of your dream house.

Hire a lawyer who is as tough as you are, and who will demand nothing less than you would expect from yourself.

How are fees charged? How much are your fees and for what are they paid?

With all of the ways lawyers bill clients, you want to know specifically what is involved. You are always entitled to an itemized bill for your lawyer's services, but you would prefer to know in advance how fees are calculated.

Some lawyers are always on the clock, meaning your call to check on your case sets the clock in motion, as does your few minutes of small-talk with the attorney. You do not want to be racking up charges while talking to your attorney about his family.

Find out the ground rules for being charged; will a five-minute phone call show up on your bill, or is that a free part of the lawyer's service? If you are charged, what's the rate going to be? Will you pay to have copies of important papers mailed to you?

If you are involved in a case that could have court costs, be sure to get a ballpark figure from the lawyer as to your out-of-pocket costs.

What other costs might I incur?

Just because a lawyer gives you a great hourly rate doesn't mean you will get off cheaply.

You might pay $1 per photocopy, $5 to receive a fax or pay inflated tabs for secretarial work.

Lawyers really aren't supposed to profit on costs, but many do. They build depreciation, secretarial time and anything they can think of into charges for using the copier, for instance; you could pay a lot more than the two-cents-per-page charge from the corner office supply store.

Again, there is nothing illegal about this, although the American Bar Association says lawyers should charge only for "actual costs." That makes it hard to complain about after the fact, because you agreed to pay the lawyer's costs.

Most lawyers do not want to sound like they are squeezing clients dry. They may "waive" some charges if you press them for details in advance. If you don't ask about these charges upfront, however, don't be shocked if your bill comes back more padded than a salesman's expense account.

How can I reduce my costs?

Most lawyers will tell you the easiest way to keep costs down is to tell the truth at all times, since anything else can come back to haunt you and make a case even harder.

That's not a bad answer, but it doesn't really apply to the cost-conscious consumer. If you want to keep costs down, let your lawyer know and find out if you can pick up and deliver papers, photocopy documents and do some of the more menial chores that can inflate a legal bill.

You also may be able to cut costs by reducing the lawyer's workload. You may want, for example, to have a lawyer review your real estate contract. If you have bought several homes over the years, however, you may not want to pay to have the attorney handle your closing (particularly if you live in a state where the lender's attorney generally does the work).

Be sure you pay for necessary services and not window-dressing.

Who are the best lawyers in town—besides yourself—and why?

The legal community is tightly knit, particularly within specialties. You want someone who knows the competition and gets along with those adversaries, because your case may boil down to cutting a settlement rather than going to court.

Use the list of lawyers who your prospective counsel admires as part of the hiring process, too. They become references and should be asked the very same question; you want other lawyers to want to do business with your attorney.

Could I get the names of a few recent clients who you have worked with?

Attorney-client privilege sometimes makes this a sticky issue, but someone who can act as a reference and tell you how this lawyer deals with clients would help cement your decision.

If he won't give you the names of clients, ask for professional references, perhaps the names of lawyers to whom he makes referrals. When you call those colleagues, do not identify the person who gave you their names at first, saying "I was told you could be a reference for my attorney. I was wondering who you consider to be the best attorneys in town."

If your lawyer's name comes up, then ask why the reference feels that way. If he's not on the list, then ask why not.

How often will I hear from you?

You want to make sure the lawyer's idea of the appropriate amount of time to spend with you is similar to your own. If you need hand-holding and a call from your attorney every day, then a lawyer who calls only when there is action on the case may not be active enough.

This helps forge your expectations for the relationship. If the adviser subsequently fails to call frequently enough, you will have set a standard that he is measurably under, which helps you decide if the lawyer is living up to his end of the agreement.

How can I terminate this relationship if I am not satisfied?

Never enter any financial arrangement without knowing how to get out of it.

How will we resolve complaints if I am dissatisfied?

Just because you know how to get out of the arrangement doesn't mean there won't be complaints to settle. That being the case, find out how potential disputes will be settled.

Most state bar associations offer arbitration committees that, for a fee, settle disputes between clients and lawyers (usually over expenses). At the same time, you could resolve those matters in small claims court.

Fees represent the biggest area of dispute between lawyers and their clients; find out whether the lawyer has had this kind of problem in the past and how it has been resolved. Then determine how it will be resolved if it happens in your case, preferably settling on fee arbitration as the most fair solution to potential problems.

Have complaints against you been filed with the bar association? Have you been sued for malpractice?

These questions may make a lawyer wince, because they're uncomfortable. But suits happen.

I know many outstanding lawyers who have had to defend themselves against clients whose expectations were not met and who decided to sue the lawyer because they did not get the outcome they wanted.

If your lawyer has been sued, ask what happened and how the case was resolved.

More important, this will solidify your discussions of what to expect from both the current legal situation you are handling and the relationship, as well as how you will resolve any problems that arise before they reach this extreme.

Remember, the lawyer is not obligated to provide details of problem cases. You will have to use your intuition to determine whether past problems should send you off to visit someone else.

What happens next?

Once you have engaged a lawyer and taken care of your current needs, how often will you have contact with him? Will he call periodically to see if your will needs updating, for example, or if you need a new health-care proxy? When something else comes up in your life, will you be able to call him with a question—just to get a sense of the direction you want to go in—and not be billed for it? Under what circumstances would a future telephone consultation—perhaps a second opinion on an estate planning issue—become billable advice?

By defining what you want and describing the kind of ongoing relationship you desire with a lawyer, you lay the framework on which a successful relationship with a lawyer is built.

What are the danger signs of a relationship gone sour?

Even Perry Mason once lost a case; in real life, the best lawyers sometimes lose.

You have the right to competent representation. Your lawyer is not always to blame if a case ends against you. If you are dissatisfied with your lawyer—whether he is doing a simple will or defending you in court—it is important to look at the reasons why. If a realistic view leaves you with a complaint about the quality of your representation, then you may have an honest beef.

You should worry about the relationship with your lawyer if:

He appears to have lost interest or stopped working on a case. Unhappy clients often complain that a lawyer is not devoting sufficient time to the case. In fact, the client might not be completely aware of the progress being made or of delays beyond the lawyer's control. Generally, this boils down to a communications issue.

If the problem is more than miscommunication, write your lawyer a letter. This generally serves as a wake-up call because lawyers know it is a prelude to building a case against them for not doing their work.

In addition, every case has a time limit, called a statute of limitations, within which it must be filed. And some paperwork must be filed immediately given the health and welfare concerns of the people involved. If your lawyer is in jeopardy of missing these deadlines, you must either apply pressure to get the ball rolling or simply find someone else to tackle your case now.

Your instructions are not being followed.   With the exception of doing something illegal, such as lying in court, the lawyer's job is to advise a client of possible actions and outcomes and then take the path chosen by the client, even if it is not the direction in which the lawyer wants the case to go.

If your lawyer is doing things in accordance with his own feelings, or pushing you hard to do things his way without explaining the situation so you come to the same conclusions on your own, question whether he respects you.

The bill is much more than you expected or was not properly explained. You have a right to an itemized bill. You should have discussed what those items would be ahead of time, so there should not be unhappy surprises in the end. If there are, contact the lawyer and ask about the unexpected charges; if the situation can not be resolved that way, contact the local or state bar association to ask about the fee arbitration process.

There are any apparent conflicts of interest.   A lawyer can't sit on both sides of the fence, representing clients on opposite sides of the same or related lawsuits. If the lawyer wants to do this, both clients must give permission; if you find out that your lawyer has breached this ethical standard, you will probably want to seek new counsel immediately.

One other thing to know about conflicts: A lawyer should not represent you if your interests conflict with his own. In other words, a lawyer should not write your will if you plan to leave the lawyer property or money in that will.

Your have not received your complete share of a settlement.   If you believe a lawyer has improperly taken or kept money owed you, it's a big problem. Contact the state and local bar associations—specifically its disciplinary board—if your money is not returned on short order; when you contact the bar association, ask about its funds for "client assistance" or "client security." These are funds put together by lawyers that may reimburse you if a court decides your lawyer is guilty of fraud.

If I have a complaint, where do I go?

If something appears to be going wrong, talk to your lawyer first. If you are not satisfied after that, you have several options.

▪ If the lawyer is part of a firm, go to the managing partner. If you are in a pre-paid legal plan, you would contact the plan administrator.

In either case, he should try to resolve the complaint and get you the kind of representation you seek. That does not mean you will come away satisfied.

▪ Your state or local bar association can help in several ways. The disciplinary committee can answer questions about whether your complaint is legitimate. The fee arbitration committee can help you if fees really are out of line, and may be able to help settle any disputes.

If you believe the lawyer has stolen money from you, you may pursue restitution from the bar's client security fund. (You will also want to contact the police or your local district attorney.)

▪ You can sue your lawyer for malpractice. If the lawyer has been negligent and you have been damaged as a result, you can pursue reimbursement. (Of course, suing for malpractice involves hiring another attorney, one involved in handling professional liability cases.)

How can I develop and build the relationship?

If you want to have a lawyer as part of your financial team, you need to plan regular visits as often as you have major life changes—having children, buying a house, moving, etc.—and as infrequently as once every other year.

Ask the lawyer how often he wants to be consulted with regard to your financial planning and other issues, and try to include him in estate planning discussions with your financial adviser. (The latter is particularly important because estate plans go awry if assets are not properly titled.)

And, if you like your lawyer, consult with him on other legal matters, if only to get a referral to another specialist likely to help you. All of these conversations help to ensure that you will feel comfortable with your attorney, regardless of when you actually need his services.

19 *Hiring a real estate agent*

My parents have owned the same home for nearly 30 years. It will take a lot for them to sell it.

But a few years back, my father told me he had pretty well picked out the person he would use as a real estate agent when the time came to sell.

During the same conversation, he said he planned to have a different person come in and do a market evaluation of the house.

When I asked why he wouldn't use the agent who would someday represent the property, he explained that he didn't want to trouble the guy when no sale was imminent. Instead, he would take up some stranger's offer for a free evaluation; that agent had no expectations, so would not be disappointed when my parents opted not to sign a contract.

That reaction is not uncommon. Most people work with a real estate agent only when they are buying or selling a home.

That makes sense. Real estate agents get paid on commission for doing a deal, so the idea of continuing the relationship past the point of a sale—when there is no commission to be made—is foreign to many people.

But a home is the single-biggest investment most people ever make, and having a specialist can help you determine the appropriate steps to take to get the most from that holding. You might think the $20,000 in renovations you put into a home will come back to you in the selling price, but an agent familiar with the local market may know better; you might have a particular type of house—say a townhouse—for which there seems to be an upper limit as to what local buyers will pay. If you bought near that upper limit, you may not recoup the $20,000 in improvements because prospective buyers may not be willing to pay that much for a townhouse.

Real estate agents are valuable members of your financial team because they can help you determine the monetary impact of altering the biggest piece of your investment portfolio. Just as many people wouldn't invest $10,000 in their stock portfolio without consulting a broker, it is prudent not to make a big change in your real estate portfolio without consulting an expert.

Obviously, most people work with real estate brokers only when buying or selling. In hiring an agent, however, you should look at both how he gets deals done and what happens afterwards.

If you work with a real estate agent only during sale periods, you treat your home entirely as a "use asset," akin to a car, using and repairing it and getting whatever value possible from it when it's time to sell. Unlike a car, however, you probably expect your home to appreciate in value. The pre-baby boom generation and the front edge of the boomers lived through tremendous home-price appreciation. In the late 1980s, however, real estate price growth slowed dramatically and even turned negative in some parts of the country. Prices began appreciating sharply again in the late 1990s, but only in certain popular locations.

If location alone won't make your house appreciate, that puts a premium on managing your property. It's not that every quart of paint trickles down to the bottom line—or that you might not want to spend money for your own comfort, even if you will not be rewarded with a better sales price—but it does make it smart to consult with an expert every now and again.

"Real estate is a part of your investment portfolio and more and more people are treating their house as if it were a financial asset," says John A. Tuccillo, chief economist for the National Association of Realtors. "They want an expert on their house the same way they want an expert on mutual funds or estate planning, to help them decide if it's a good time to refinance or borrow against their equity, to expand or buy something new. You may only hire a Realtor when you are buying or selling, but it's a good idea to have one who you can talk to every now and again."

Presumably, that agent will be the one who served you when you bought or sold a home in your community, or the one you are likely to work with years from now when it comes time to move. In a case like my parents', advice over several years could be a precursor to doing business down the road—which is why the real estate agent is willing to take the time now to have informal meetings and create a comfortable working relationship before the time comes to sign an actual listing contract.

Whether you are a buyer or seller or are just looking for someone to help you make smart decisions as a homeowner, here are the questions you will want answered before hiring a real estate agent:

Can I do this myself? If not, whom should I deal with?

The short answer to this question is yes; the longer answer may be "Why would you want to?"

While the law does not require you to hire a real estate adviser when buying or selling a home, this is one area in which the biased professionals actually present a pretty clear picture of what will happen to you if you go it alone.

Real estate agents typically say they can get you a better price and sell your home more quickly and with less hassle. To some extent, all of those points are probably true.

The main reason to represent yourself is to save money, generally a commission of between 5 and 7 percent of the sale price that is paid to the agents involved in the deal. On a $150,000 house, that's a savings of between $7,500 and $10,500, which is hardly insignificant; depending on individual circumstances, that money can be the difference between making a profit on the home or having to bring a checkbook to the closing to settle up your losses.

But that assumes you can actually get to a closing on your own. Selling without representation is not a go-to-closing-free card. You have to do your own market analysis in order to price your house reasonably (but not too cheaply), pay all marketing costs, organize any and all open houses, and you have to find buyers without using the Multiple Listing Service, a computerized system in which member real estate brokers and agents advertise and swap information on available homes.

And unless you have the cash to do a seller-financed deal, you probably lack the kind of financing muscle a good agent can produce for a prospective homebuyer.

In other words, there's a reason why experts say about 90 percent of all homes—give or take 5 percent and excluding new construction—are sold through an agent. Unless you have a strong desire, a lot of time and a hot seller's market in which buyers are flocking to new offerings, you probably will want to hire an adviser to help with the sale of your home.

For homebuyers, the issue is a bit different. There is no drawback to scouring the newspaper, finding the right home and making appointments on your own. You miss out on access to the Multiple Listing Service, but you do get to see the for-sale-by-owner homes (which an agent might not show you, since he can't get even a small commission from many do-it-yourselfers.)

Dealing with the agent who handles the listing means you are dealing with the seller's broker, otherwise known as a conventional agent. Conventional agents always represent the seller.

But even if you go into a real estate office and sit down with an agent who helps you find a home to bid on, he remains a conventional agent, unless you have specifically contracted with him to represent you as a "buyer broker." In real estate terms, the conventional agent who brings the buyer to the bargaining table is a "sub-agent;" don't be fooled by the jargon.

Say, for example, you found an agent who showed you available listings in town. You find a home on which you bid, say, $135,000—but tell the agent you would go to $150,000. By law, the agent's responsibility is to look out for the seller's best interest—even if the agent has never met the seller—which means your willingness to go higher must be communicated.

Obviously, that's not a great bidding strategy.

But the fact that an agent works for the seller should not discourage you. For years, conventional agents have been the only game in town and it didn't stop people from buying homes at fair market prices.

Indeed, most conventional agents do everything in their power to represent you well. It is in their best interest, after all, for you to be happy, to find a home you love, to refer other people to them and, perhaps, to someday sell your home through them.

What you should remember if you choose to work with a conventional agent is that he can not tell you which home to buy (if you are looking at more than one home in the area, he represents both sellers and is not allowed to favor one), how much to offer (his job is to get the seller the listing price) and—with the exception of hidden defects which, because they are invisible, must be pointed out—can not tell you what is wrong with the property (he is not allowed to influence you not to buy).

In addition, a conventional agent is not required to provide you with a comparative market analysis—although many do—unless you ask for it.

The apparent conflict of interest of having a buyer's agent actually working for the seller is as old as the profession itself, but if the potential biases worry you, consider a buyer broker.

With a buyer broker, you sign a contract that says you will not look for a house with any other agent for a specific period of time. The buyer broker comes to you with appropriate listings and handles every part of the negotiation, including pricing strategy. Many also help clients search for the best available financing and insurance and set up all inspections.

Shrewd buyer-brokers also watch the for-sale-by-owner market, meaning they may find homes a conventional agent would ignore. (They do this because you pay for their service, rather than the seller, so they get paid even if the house is sold by its owner.)

The drawbacks to buyer brokers are that they are sometimes discriminated against by conventional agents, which can affect how much (and how) you pay for their services, the exclusivity of the contract and potential conflicts of interest.

The discrimination issue is very big in some parts of the country, where resistance to the buyer-broker movement has been so strong that virtually no one attempts to work on behalf of buyers.

For anyone who has worked with conventional agents and jumped from one to the next, the exclusivity of a buyer-broker arrangement will seem a bit limiting. In addition, one frequent complaint from people who have used buyer brokers and have not been satisfied is that the broker got pushy as the exclusivity period neared its end.

As for the conflict of interest, that stems from the fact that most buyer brokers also work as sellers' agents. It is possible to have an agent who is doing both sides of the deal, selling you one of his own listings; in that case—and he must disclose the potential conflict—he is supposed to represent both you and the seller, which is close to impossible, since he probably has too much information from each side to cut an honest deal.

Is my only choice to go with a full-service agent or go it alone?

There are discount real estate brokerages; the question is whether there are any where you live.

For sellers, a discount brokerage works like this: The agent puts you into the Multi-List, you do virtually everything else.

That may be a bit harsh, but you get limited services, most revolving around the marketing of the house, and then you do the open houses, the showings, the price negotiations and the rest. The agent then gives back up to half of his share of the commission when the sale is completed.

Let's go back to that $150,000 example. The listing agent normally would get half of the $9,000 or so commission on the property (assuming there is a sub-agent or buyer broker for the bidder). That would make your take about $2,250.

For buyers, the system works roughly the same way. The agent gives you a listing of the available homes in the area, but you set up appointments, negotiate the contracts and all the rest. If you do all of the work, you get to split the commission.

In both cases, however, you really are working on a pay-as-you-go system. You get the full split of the commission if you do all the work; if you want the agent to step in and arrange for inspections, for example, that's going to cost you. If you want the agent to call your banker, *cha-ching!* goes the cash register.

That's not necessarily bad. You might be able to save money doing a lot of legwork and leaving the tasks you dislike to someone else. Just find out upfront how much those "extras" will cost you and what, exactly, you are being charged for.

Is there a difference between "brokers" and "agents?"

In terms of handling the purchase or sale of a piece of property, there is no real difference between a broker and an agent. A real estate broker, however, had to first qualify as an agent, taking the requisite classes and passing a licensing exam; moving up to broker requires additional class work, a certain amount of experience in the business and another test.

By earning a broker's license, an individual earns the right to work independently and open or operate a real estate office. An agent, meanwhile, must work for a broker.

Just because the broker is the Big Kahuna at the office does not make him a better adviser than one of his agents; plenty of agents have no desire to run an office, and plenty of brokers become office-bound and lose some of their feel for the community. You should worry more about an adviser's knowledge of the community than about the hierarchy in the real estate office.

Am I better off working with someone from a brand-name office?

Since all member agents have access to the Multiple Listing Service, bigger does not necessarily mean better when it comes to your agent's firm. Supply and demand in your market, the property itself and the initiative and energy of the agent will determine how quickly your home sells more than whether an agent runs a one-person shop or is affiliated with the local office of a giant national chain.

At the same time, one key factor for any agent is his contacts. If you are a buyer and you hire someone from the firm who does the most listings in the area, you are likely to get a chance to see those houses before they appear in the Multi-List. In a tight market, that can be an advantage.

There is no guarantee that the bigger firm does more business in your area than the mom-and-pop shop, so the agents there don't necessarily have more pull with local bankers. They may have more pull with the local media, however, if they have a big advertising budget; that can lead to better display in the paper, access to television shows spotlighting area homes and more. And though no one at a big firm would ever admit this, it's no secret that some big firms encourage agents to show prospective buyers the firm's listings first, meaning that a pool of prospects may see your property only after all of the alternatives have been reviewed.

The crucial elements, however, will be the people involved and the access to the Multiple Listing Service. Finding an agent you have confidence in—assuming all of your choices are members of the Multiple Listing Service—is more important than who the agent works for.

What credentials will I deal with, and how important are they?

While there are designations that mean something in the world of commercial real estate—such as the Counsellors of Real Estate designation that a select few members of the National Association of Realtors have earned—the truth is there is no specific credential that makes one residential real estate agent superior to another. Your hiring decision will be based more on what you perceive he can do for you than on what plaques hang on the wall.

That said, make sure your agent or broker is properly licensed by the state. Most states require brokers and agents to post their licenses in plain sight, but don't be afraid to ask for it.

The one designation most consumers look for is that of Realtor, which means an agent or broker is a member of the National Association of Realtors.

Of the two million real estate agents in the country, about 750,000 are Realtors. The big plus for consumers is that Realtors adhere to the national group's code of ethics and conduct.

The Realtist designation essentially is parallel to the Realtor. It is awarded by the National Association of Real Estate Brokers, a group that tries to meet the needs of real estate advisers who are African American or from other minority groups.

How does an agent get paid, and is it negotiable?

By this point, you know a real estate agent gets paid in commission, but that does not mean there is no room to negotiate.

A small-but-growing segment of real estate agents will make flat-fee arrangements—essentially a different form of discount brokerage—in which they agree to provide certain services for a pre-arranged fee. There still may be commission to pay for the broker who brings in the buyer, and there may be some work to do on your own behalf, but some experts believe this type of agreement represents the future of discount pricing for real estate advisers.

And in some of these cases, half of the flat fee must be paid upfront and is kept by the agent regardless of whether the home sells during the time of the listing agreement.

When it comes to buyer brokers, the commission issue also can get sticky. Technically, you sign a contract that specifies what the broker is to be paid either as a percentage of the purchase price or on an hourly or flat rate. In practice, however, the seller's agent agrees to split the commission with the buyer broker, just as he would with a conventional sub-agent.

But you can't bet on the fact that you won't have to come up with money to pay a buyer broker. In areas where "the Establishment" tries to discourage buyer brokers, many seller's agents structure listings so there is no splitting the commission with a buyer's agent. It's not fair—and it can often be negotiated around—but you still have to be prepared to pay up just in case. (There also would be no commission for a buyer broker if you buy a home sold by its owner, although this, too, can be negotiated.) Many sellers—and seller's agents—come around and pay for the buyer broker's services if they see a deal walking out the door.

As for negotiating commissions, that's a sticky issue with many real estate advisers. The problem with reducing the commission is that you may not get the same level of service or traffic; I have had a scary number of real estate agents say they don't work as hard when the commission is reduced, and that they are reluctant to show buyers homes for which a less-than-normal commission is being paid.

Still, if you have a seller's market for homes—in which it is easy to make properties move and there are not many homes listed—there may be the leverage necessary for agents to compete for business.

There are a lot of ways to play with commissions without necessarily insulting an agent. Find out if commissions can be shaved if the firm handles both sides of the deal; if the firm lines up the buyer, it doesn't have to share the seller's commission, so it might be willing to take a bit off to entice you to sign up.

If you have an expensive home, ask for a commission that is staggered. For example, the commission could be structured to equal 6 percent of the first $100,000 in sale price, 5 percent on the second $100,000 and 4 percent thereafter. If the house is worth enough to generate a big commission—particularly in a seller's market when there are few available houses—this kind of structure may be appealing. In addition, many brokers and agents won't negotiate commission because they don't like the principle of taking less money for their services; this may be a fair compromise, since it is not necessarily harder to sell a $400,000 home than a $250,000 home.

Lastly, if you have a home that is hard to sell—you live next to a toxic waste dump or, hopefully, some lesser evil—you might actually consider raising the commission. It is not out of line to pay a 10 percent commission for a home that is particularly tough to unload. Raising commissions also helps generate traffic if you have a short time to move the house; just as brokers and agents don't like to work in situations in which their rates are cut, they love situations that bring home extra money.

What should I ask during an interview?

If you are picking an agent to sell your home, the interview should occur at home, or at least after the agent has seen the property. Invite several agents to do a comparative market analysis.

Even if there is no imminent sale and you just want some advice and the chance to start building a relationship with an agent, a market evaluation is the place to start. It's a service most agents gladly provide because they know it can lead to future business and referrals (which is precisely why the agent my father had never met before offered him the service in the first place).

Essentially, you want the agent to walk through your home and get an idea of its pluses and minuses and to look for what you can do to make it more saleable.

It will generally take the agent a few days to put together a market evaluation, which includes checking the prices of similar properties currently on the market, as well as prices of similar homes that have sold in recent months.

You can interview a real estate agent either when he does the walk-through or when he delivers the analysis; I prefer the latter because the evaluation always brings up more questions.

Here are some things you will want to go over with an agent. Some apply only to seller or buyer agents, others to both; some must be altered slightly to fit both types of agents.

How long have you been in the business? Is this your full-time job?

Full-time, experienced people generally are the way to go, although there may be nothing wrong with folks who have less experience but know the area very well.

Part-time agents are the best option only if you are looking to buy a home and don't want your search to be too active—if you could be satisfied seeing only one or two homes a month—but the problem is that they are not always going to be available when you need them. Remember, too, that a real estate agent's life heats up when a sale is pending; if he squeezes business in between a lot of other activities, he may not have sufficient time to handle the demands of the deal at its most delicate time.

Are you a broker or a sales agent?

As stated earlier, this is a minor concern. The reason you ask is to be sure a broker has sufficient time to represent you effectively. If he is too busy managing the office or keeping tabs on associates, he might be too much of an administrator to meet your day-to-day demands.

What continuing education classes have you taken?

Real estate sales practices keep changing. So do the laws governing many specific aspects of land ownership. You are always best off working with someone who keeps his education current and is trying to make himself a better representative for you.

As long as you are asking about education and background in the business, don't be shy about asking for a resume. There is no reason for a real estate agent to withhold that information.

How far afield do you go to get clients?

If you are a buyer and want to look in a region—such as Boston's South Shore where I live—you want someone who knows more than one community. If, however, you want to live in a specific town or neighborhood, you may want someone who really specializes in local estate and has superior knowledge of the community you want to call home.

As a seller, your concern when someone is spread out is time. Since an agent can't be two places at once, having listings spread over a 25-mile radius can be a problem, particularly if you want your adviser to attend every showing of your home.

How many sellers or buyers do you work with at one time?

I know agents who say they can handle eight listings at once; I know others who claim to comfortably handle twice that many. There is no right number, but the amount of business an agent has right now does affect your service, ranging from how much time an agent might have to communicate with you to how often he will be able to show your home.

As with all advisory relationships, a lot of your decision will be based on instinct and who you feel you can trust. If you think a workload sounds unreasonable, ask about it.

How many homes have you listed and sold in the last year? (Or, how many buyers have you represented in the last year?)

Ask for a list of the homes the agent has sold in the last year, including both the list and sale prices. Real estate is not unlike financial planning or insurance, in that you want to be a lot like an adviser's average client.

If you have a $150,000 home (or that amount to spend on a new home) and the agent's sales sheet includes mostly homes valued at three times that much, you're not a good match.

Similarly, you want to make sure the agent sells your kinds of properties. If his sales in the last year have been mostly single-family homes and you own a condo (or want to buy a condo), he may not be an expert at dealing in your kind of property.

Have any of your showings or sales included homes in my neighborhood?

Just because someone is the top agent at his firm does not make him the best one for you. If he is not familiar with your neighborhood, if he can't describe it knowledgeably to a seller, you may be better off with someone else.

What is your standard commission?

You MUST ask. Enough said.

Do you accompany all buyers through my home?

This is a personal preference issue, but one that you want settled in advance. Many real estate agents use a "lock box," essentially a special key holder with a combination that is given to a buyer's agent. The buyer's agent brings clients to your home, opens the box and uses the key to show people around your empty home.

It's convenient, particularly if you live a busy life and can't always be home to open the door for a showing.

Still, many selling agents prefer to be present—or send associates—for walk-throughs, hanging around to answer questions about the house.

You can consider it either a service or a privacy issue, but consider it in advance so that you can let the agent know your preference. Remember, you want him to hire you as a client; if trekking to your house for each showing is more work than he cares to do—but you think his presence is important—neither you nor the agent is going to be happy with the relationship.

What are you going to do to help the house sell?

The Multiple Listing Service is a no-brainer. You want to find out if the rest of the advertising will consist of newspaper ads, exposure on a local television show, glossy advertising giveaways or, maybe, a radio transmitter that lets passers-by get a description of the house 24 hours a day.

Agents are paid to market your house; if they don't have a marketing plan, you'd be better off doing this yourself.

Are you going to hold a broker's open house?

A broker's open house shows your home to every other agent in town. Your agent will send a notice to every firm in the area, inviting interested agents to come for lunch and a look-see.

Don't kid yourself; there are plenty of agents who just come to eat, especially if your broker is known for putting out a good spread. Still, for a few hours on a weekday afternoon, you will get some agents in your home who could decide it is perfect for one of their clients.

Many agents choose not to do a "broker's open," particularly if the customer doesn't request it.

How often will you have weekend open houses?

This is both a marketing and lifestyle decision. For most busy people, there are only so many weekends in a month when they can disappear from home for five hours without falling behind on housework, yardwork or homework.

Too many open houses smacks of desperation, too few means you aren't bringing potential buyers through your door. Find a happy medium.

What are the positives and negatives of this house?

Few of us have a perfect house, no matter how much we love it. Ask an agent to tell you the home's best selling points and biggest drawbacks; you want to make sure the two of you perceive the house the same way, otherwise you could be in for a big disagreement on pricing.

What can I do to improve the house and make it easier to sell?

No one likes dumping money into a home he is about to sell, but a coat of paint can do a lot to refresh an older home. And while prospective buyers generally don't purchase your furniture, they do notice the way you live; cluttered closets, for example, look small and make people wonder if they will run out of shelf space.

Ask what can be done to get your house in the best condition to be shown. Plan to do the work early, so you don't have to rush around at the last minute before a prospective buyer shows up.

What price range would you suggest for my home and why? If the house stays on the market, when and by how much will we lower the asking price?

This is when he details the comparative market analysis and tells you what he thinks you can get for your house. Obviously, some level of agreement between you and the adviser is necessary.

What you are listening for is a fair market price based on current market conditions and the urgency of your need to sell, as well as a strategy that makes sense if you need to cut your price.

Don't be impressed by big numbers; some agents price everything high to impress potential clients. After the contract is signed, the house goes on the market at an inflated price before dropping to the more reasonable price suggested by less-aggressive (or, perhaps, more scrupulous) agents.

If the projected price is below your expectations, find out whether the agent's calculations or your impressions of the home are askew.

Make sure you know his feelings about how long a home should sit on the market before dropping a price, because you do not want the relationship with the agent to deteriorate later if there are pricing surprises. Many homeowner-broker relationships sour when the parties disagree on the next pricing move; since you both make money on the sale of the home, you are teammates and you will function best if you agree on strategies before the game begins.

Who are the best agents in town—besides yourself—and why?

Unlike virtually every other form of financial adviser, real estate agents are in a cooperative situation. A lawyer can sit in a corner office and write and file paperwork for you, an accountant can crunch numbers and a financial planner can develop a strategy all without consulting anyone.

But real estate agents can't close the deal without working with their peers. Real estate is a small community in which most of the local players know of each other (at least by reputation). If your agent can't say a nice thing about anyone else in the field, chances are he doesn't work well with those people. That is not good.

Asking this question lets you see what an agent admires in his peers. It's also a pretty good list of professional references, because the names you get represent the competition. If you call, say, a lawyer who the agent works with, there is a potential bias because the agent may routinely refer clients and the lawyer doesn't want to lose that business. The competition has no reason to say something nice, especially if they might be interested in your business themselves.

Could I get the names of a few recent sellers (or buyers) with whom you have worked?

Unlike many other financial advisory relationships, in which confidentiality and privacy are major concerns, you should have little trouble getting the names of references from a real estate agent. Property transactions are public record, so the confidentiality issue is moot.

Don't accept just the names of friends or relatives who referred you in the first place, as in "Why don't you just talk to Uncle Morty about that. You know how he feels about me."

This is your biggest investment and a bad adviser can cost you a lot of money, so make sure you talk to more than one reference. In fact, try to find references who had to deal with this agent under different circumstances, possibly one whose home sold quickly and another whose house sat on the market for months. (See Chapter 11 for a reminder of what to ask in reference checks.)

What can I do to make myself a better buyer?

If you are buying a home, there are ways to make bids more attractive, such as being pre-approved for a mortgage so the deal can be written without a mortgage contingency.

This question will give you insight into the kinds of strategies a buyer broker thinks will work, both with lenders and sellers.

Can you assist with financing?

Real estate agents often track interest rates and have contacts with favorite lenders who can speed the application process. That comes in handy not only when you buy a home, but also years later when your agent may be able to recommend lenders for refinancing, home-equity lines of credit, reverse mortgages and other options. (A good real estate agent knows which bankers bend the rules, going against standard industry formulas to improve your chances of getting, say, a home-equity loan.)

Do I need a "reality check?"

A reality check is when an agent puts you in the car and drives you around to look at other properties. If you're a seller, he is showing you that your expectations are unreasonable compared prices of to similar homes in similar neighborhoods. For buyers, a reality check may prove that you have too little money to afford the neighborhood and perhaps you need to adjust your hopes and dreams down to the size of your wallet.

How often will I hear from you?

Obviously, the agent should contact you the moment he has an offer (or a home he thinks might be right for you). The question is what happens when nothing is happening.

You should hear from your agent enough to quell your fears and to strategize about the price and marketing strategy (or whether to widen your search area because no homes are available in neighborhoods you desire). Generally, those conversations take place weekly, but you should know what to expect because lack of communication is how real estate relationships falter.

Are you planning a vacation soon?

Yes, it's a personal question and one that only a seller will ask. Brokers and agents are entitled to vacations like everyone else, but the hot time for activity on a home is when the listing is new, generally in the first three to four weeks after it is listed.

That's when every buyer in your price range and interested in your community—and every broker working with a prospective client in your area—will want to see the house. If you are putting your house on the market and need it to sell quickly, you may not be comfortable having your agent on the road during the first few weeks.

Does a vacation automatically disqualify an agent? Absolutely not. There is an adage in the real estate business that when brokers go on vacation, all of their listings sell.

If I sign a contract, how long is the listing agreement good for? Can I change agents without paying a double commission (or would you get a piece of the deal no matter what)? How can I terminate the listing, and for how long after that are you entitled to payment?

The listing agreement is fraught with terms to the agent's advantage. Ask about them and read the agreement carefully. Picking the wrong agent is bad enough, but signing a restrictive contract can actually make the situation worse.

Some contracts force you to list with the agent for six months—try to cut that to no more than three—and have no termination clause. Before signing a contract, you want to know exactly how to get out of it if you change your mind or dislike the service.

Paying a double commission can occur when you switch brokers. Brokers know that lost listings mean lost commissions and they want to cash in on their work even if you didn't think it was so great. Say someone sees the house today and comes back to see it again in six months—when you have a new agent. If he buys the home, the first agent may try to get paid for having "brought you the buyer." This is the kind of language you do not want in your listing agreement.

Similarly, say you decide to test the waters—hoping, perhaps, to move to a better place in town—and put your home on the market. A few people come through , but no one makes a worthy offer and you decide to terminate the listing. Five months later, one of the prospective buyers knocks on your door, wondering if you are still interested in selling and makes a great offer. If your listing agreement specifies that the agent gets a commission for six months after termination, you are going to pay a commission on the deal.

There are even listing agreements that can force you to pay a commission without selling the house, rewarding the agent for landing a "ready, willing and able buyer." If that buyer backs out—say he gets a job offer or transfer or simply gets cold feet—you could be on the hook for the commission. Make sure the agreement language does not force you to pay if the deal collapses.

If you go over a standard agreement line by line, you can find at least the potential for unfavorable terms.

In general, listing agreements are designed to discourage you from taking advantage of an agent's time, then bolting to stiff the agent and do the deal on your own. That's fair and reasonable, up to a point;

there's a fine line between the planning to stiff a broker—which presumably you will not do—and protecting yourself and your options.

What happens when there is an offer? What's the drill when we find a house to bid on?

For sellers, you want to be walked through the process of what will happen once a bid comes in, how the agent feels about counter-offers and pricing strategy and what he does to get the deal from start—the first contract with an acceptable offer—to closing.

Buyers, too, want to go over how a bid works and what the broker's responsibility is when it comes to helping push the deal through.

Describe your nightmare client/house

This is a good opportunity to hear some funny stories about an agent's worst client, the house that had the ugly shag carpeting badly soiled by pets, and so on. In between cringing and laughing, however, listen carefully to hear if the agent is describing you and/or your house.

If you fit the description of his worst nightmare, find someone else to work with.

What happens after the sale?

This gets back to the concept of developing a relationship so your real estate adviser is with you after you have moved in.

When my wife Susan and I bought our first home, it had an attic that was perfect for a master bedroom suite. The previous owners had started the work, we just needed to finish the job.

Before hiring a contractor, however, we went back to the agent who helped us buy the house (the same agent we planned to use to sell it when the time came), and she advised against fixing up the room, warning that we would never recoup the money. She provided a very compelling comparative analysis that saved us thousands of dollars, because we took a loss on the house and are convinced the extra room would not have generated enough additional sale price to pay for itself.

Find out if an agent is willing to consult with you periodically to "come see what you've done to the house" and advise you about the value of adding a fill-in-the-blank (fireplace, new kitchen, addition, swimming pool, etc.). His knowledge of the market can be a major asset to you, provided he is interested in you for more than your current transaction.

You are not talking about decorating tips or asking him to pick the color of your new shutters, so you won't see him often. It may be a once-a-year cup of coffee or lunch.

Most agents like doing this because they are always curious to see what happens to a house after the sale. It's good for you as a homeowner because it helps you set your priorities, particularly as you near a selling period. If you expect to stay in a house for only a few years but have the choice of which repairs to make next—say, replacement windows versus a replacement kitchen—the agent would probably advise you to make the repairs that will add the most to the selling price (the kitchen). If you plan to live in the house for 20 more years, the windows might be the better investment now, because they will save money on the heating bill.

Lastly, one reason to keep in touch with an agent is that it never hurts to have representation. You may not be in the market to sell your home, but few people would turn away an offer without at least reviewing it. If an agent knows your house and meets someone tomorrow who wants to move to your town and describes your house as his dream home, the agent may pick up the phone and call with an unsolicited offer. If it's good enough, you might decide it's a good time to move. At the very least, it never hurts to listen—and you will never have a shot at an unsolicited offer if a broker or agent is not familiar with your home.

How do I check out a broker or agent?

Check with your state to make sure an agent still has a license, although that is generally unnecessary (since agents work for brokers, the brokers have a vested interest in keeping you away from scoundrels).

Contact the local Board of Realtors to see if there is a record of disciplinary action against either the agent or the firm. (Not all Boards of Realtors give out information on member firms.)

Last, check with the local Better Business Bureau; if there has been any pattern of problems, it will show up in the files.

If you find problems, ask about them during your interview. You want to know what happened, how it was resolved and what can be done to make sure these problems don't happen to you.

What do I ask references?

Ask client references all of the character questions you asked the agent during your interview. Find out how often they heard from the agent, how quickly the price was dropped, how they felt about pricing and marketing strategy, whether there were unpleasant surprises—or pleasant ones, for that matter—in the process, and whether the agent smoothed over any rough edges and trouble spots while the sale was pending or during the closing.

Then ask what is always the most important question: "If you were selling (or buying) again today, would you hire this agent again? If so, would you do anything differently that would make things even better the second time around?"

You want references to alert you to anything you must incorporate into pre-hiring discussions with an agent to be certain he understands—and is willing to meet—your expectations.

From professional references, including those competing agents whose names you got during the interview, you want their opinion. What are the strengths and weaknesses they see in this agent. The most important question here is "If you were selling (or buying) a home and could not act as your own agent, would you this agent be one of the three top candidates to get the job?"

You can't expect them to say this person is "the one," because they have a lot of professional ties to maintain. If they tell you this person would be one of "five or six" they would consider, ask why they would consider so many people; listen for whether they are trying not to break wide-ranging ties, or if they are hemming and hawing, trying not to say your prospective agent does not have their full faith and confidence.

Remember, too, that in all reference situations, you would expect the agent to have given you the names of people who are going to say the right thing. If that does not happen, if the agent has misjudged how he is viewed by clients, colleagues and/or competitors, then you need to consider where else his judgment might be off when it comes to business relationships.

What are the danger signs to a relationship gone sour?

Big problems in real estate relationships often involve personality, communication and interest.

Obviously, you should not sign on with an agent—no matter how great his credentials or sparkling his resume—if you don't click. Chemistry is important, because it is hard to build a trusting relationship when the person across the table gives you the willies.

Going through a detailed interview and following the tenets put forth in this book should help you uncover personality conflicts before signing an agreement. If personality problems arise later, arrange a meeting between you, your agent and the firm's managing broker. The managing broker may be willing to reassign you to another agent rather than risk you terminating the contract.

While personality clashes account for the major problems, they are not the only warning signs. Others include:

▪ Loss of interest. Almost every broker is excited about your business after he first signs you as a client. But he may not be so excited when there is no movement. If your house isn't selling (or you, as a buyer, are extremely picky and not willing to bid on any number of houses that meet your own definition of what you're looking for), keep an eye on whether your broker or agent is doing everything possible to make things work.

For sellers, that means the agent continues to place ads, hold open houses and search for ways to make your home show better.

For buyers, it means trying to do a better job pinpointing exactly what it is you are looking for, reviewing your financial situation to see if there are other ways to help do a deal and continuing to scour the area for new listings to show you.

One other point: Loss of interest may not have anything to do with you. While there are many long-time real estate agents, there also are many transients who come into the field for a while and then pursue other careers. Just as you probably want to work with a full-time agent, you might be wary of an agent whose other interests make him so busy that he doesn't have the time or energy to work on your behalf.

▪ Lack of communication. During your interview, you set a standard for how often you should hear from the agent. Even if nothing is happening, there should be a phone call every week, assuming that is what you have agreed to.

Even if infrequent calls are acceptable, there could be a communication problem—and a loss of interest, for that matter—if your agent does not return phone calls within six hours.

And, obviously, you do not want any surprises. If you call and find out your broker has gone on vacation without telling you, that's a problem.

If you are a buyer, lack of communication can result in missed opportunities. By asking you a lot of questions, the broker gets an idea of how flexible you are in your needs—you need that fifth bedroom for an office, for example, but could get by with four bedrooms and some other space to work in—as well as your willingness to do work, make renovations and more. If he doesn't ask a lot of questions, particularly after you start looking at houses and your reactions tip him to the elements you consider crucial, then he is stuck with a rudimentary picture of what you want. He will never find out how your thinking is changing as you go through the buying process, and that makes it more difficult to find a home that meets your needs.

▪ Failure to follow instructions. If you are buying a home and the first few houses the agent shows you are out of your price range or not even close to the description of what you want, the agent is trying to make you more like his average client and fit you into his comfort zone.

Don't go there. You control the relationship.

My wife Susan and I once worked with an agent—very briefly—when we were just starting to search for a home. We had very little free time and figured we were at least six to 12 months away from being financially ready to buy. We also had a very specific price range.

When the agent wanted to show us four homes a week, all of them just slightly above our price range, and kept trying to convince us we could find a way to finance these homes, we felt pressured. The agent had stopped listening to what we wanted and was trying to bring us around to what she wanted, which was to sell a house in her favored price range.

▪ Maximum commission at your expense. It's understandable that agents hate the idea of reducing commissions, but it's shameful the way some unscrupulous agents nickel-and-dime buyers and sellers.

Say you have agreed on a deal, but the home inspection brings up a few issues. The buyer wants the price reduced and the seller agrees to make up the difference, but the real estate agent pushes to keep the original selling price and have the seller "credit back" money at the closing.

That keeps the agent's commission the same but benefits neither the buyer nor the seller. The buyer is not only taking a bigger mortgage to meet the higher price, but also could face higher property taxes, since many communities use sales price as part of their home valuation. The seller faces a larger capital gain on the home, plus the higher commission.

Some agents will argue that they should keep the higher commission, even if the price is adjusted from the original deal. That's a compromise, but it still smacks of an adviser who is not putting your interests first. It is the agent's job to represent the house properly and if anything comes up that alters the deal, that's a circumstance an experienced agent should be prepared to deal with in the best interest of the customer. If you have problems like this one, contact the managing broker and complain.

▪ Incomplete disclosure or conflicts of interest. We have already covered the potential conflicts of interest in most real estate relationships. These days, however, there are plenty of agents who function as both a buyer broker and seller's agent, depending on the needs of their clients. When an agent is listing your house and brings you a bidder who is not working with another real estate agent—or if he is your buyer broker and shows you a house which he is listing for the seller— he is functioning as a "dual agent."

If that sounds like something you read in a spy novel, then you understand why you need to be careful around double agents.

As a seller, your concern will be if the agent is acting as a buyer broker. If not, then he is a conventional agent, which means he represents the seller. As a result, at least technically, there is no conflict of interest because all of his fiduciary responsibility is to you. (Be aware, however, that being a dual agent means not splitting the commission, which is why an agent may be particularly sweet on an offer that comes from someone he represents; if there are two offers on the table, or you believe a second offer is about to be made, you will have to gauge whether your agent's desire to seal the deal is in your best interest.)

If your agent has a contract to act as a buyer broker and as your selling agent, there is a big conflict of interest. Effectively, the agent has a fiduciary duty to each of you, and it's tough to wear two hats. The agent may want you to sign a disclosure statement acknowledging that you understand the conflict of interest; that's fine and good, provided you believe you are getting the advice you are paying for. If, for example, the agent can not talk pricing strategy with you—he can't say how much the buyer is prepared to bid because that would break the trust of his buyer-broker client—then you may want to ask the managing broker of the office for someone else to step in on your side during these negotiations.

If you are the buyer and your agent has the listing of the seller, that's also a big conflict. Remember, the agent wants you to buy the house because he gets to keep the entire commission.

Any time there is a dual agency situation, be critical of your adviser's actions and make sure he has your best interest at heart. If he does not—if he keeps trying to steer you into a deal that benefits his other client or himself—then you will have lost the trust that is a cornerstone of the relationship, and it's probably time to find a new agent.

Where do I start my search to find the right agent?

Unlike most other financial advisers, there is not necessarily anywhere to go for a professional referral. Instead, most people find their agents by word of mouth, asking friends and neighbors who they worked with.

One suggestion for finding an agent is to start with your local Board of Realtors and find out which firms do the most business, then schedule appointments with the top-selling agents in those firms. That is no guarantee that you and the agent will be a match, but it does ensure that your candidates will all be very active members of the local real estate community. The big plus to this method for a buyer is that the most active agencies are likely to have the most listings and give you the chance to see the most houses before they go out to the rest of the world.

My favorite way to find an agent is to attend a few open houses in your neighborhood. As a seller, this helps you see how the agent represents a home and helps the owners get ready for a showing. In addition, going to open houses and looking at homes through the eyes of a buyer is a kind of reality check.

Attending an open house is also the best way to develop a relationship with an agent if you are looking for advice on managing your property but are not interested in selling right now.

After you have done a walk-through of a house—preferably some-thing in a similar price range to your own—talk to the agent. Chat with him about the local market and some of the broad home ownership is-sues in the area. He will invariably ask what you are looking for—he thinks you are a buyer and wants your business, even if it is not to buy the house you are visiting—and then you can tell him you are shop-ping for an agent or you want advice on prioritizing your home im-provements so you get the most for your home-ownership dollar.

This informal time will tell you a lot about chemistry. Coupled with the interview and market evaluation, it should be the beginning of a good, long relationship.

20   *Hiring a banker*

There are banks in this country that charge customers a fee for talking to a real person.

As callous as that sounds—and it applies only to certain routine transactions—that is actually an almost perfect marriage between a typical bank and a typical customer.

Banks, like any business, generally want to keep transaction costs low and stick to the formulas that generate profits.

At the same time, consumers choose their banker on the basis of convenient branches, locations of automated teller machines or the cost of a checking account. The customers then do their banking without ever leaving their car or talking to a person.

In other words, most people would never run up against that real-person fee.

Frequently, I ask consumers if they "know" their banker. To my way of thinking, that's being on a "name basis" with someone who can greet me by name without looking at my deposit ticket.

Most people do not know anyone in their bank by name.

If all you ever intend to do is run a checking account, that is perfectly appropriate. But it also means you are probably missing out on a higher level of service, and the lack of a relationship with your banker can cost you.

"I don't think people think of what they use a bank for before they choose a bank," says Tom Curry, commissioner of banking in Massachusetts. "Do you want a large multi-state operation or do you want more personalized service from a community bank? Do you value a large regional ATM network over being able to walk into a local branch and have someone know your name?

"What's more, with the bank failures and mergers of the 1980s and 90s, people have ended up in banks that they never chose in the first place, and they never looked to see if the bank that took over their account meets their needs."

For most people, the bank is their depository institution and maybe their lender when they need a mortgage or car loan. While they might be aware of a bank's trust department or available insurance coverage or mutual funds, those extras are not why they chose the bank.

Most people never interview a banker, and say the first time they met with anyone from the institution was to open an account. On that day, the banker they met with took the data to open an account and gave them starter checks. There may have been a cursory mention of other services—"Would you like a safe-deposit box?" or "Would you be interested in our trust department?"—but the entire experience didn't qualify as a mental handshake between consumer and adviser.

Of course, the big question is whether the average person needs to "have" a banker. After all, unlike a business that must find new and different ways to leverage assets to cut deals, or which needs to finesse financing so that it meshes with cash flow, an individual generally does not have those kinds of needs. Beyond a checking and savings account, perhaps some certificates of deposit or a money market and a safe-deposit box, typical consumer needs start to dwindle.

And while having a personal banker can be a big plus, it is hardly a necessity.

That said, you ought to know how to shop for a banking adviser so you can decide if you want a personal banking relationship.

More than virtually any other type of financial adviser, bankers clearly break into the two categories, concerned either about doing transactions or developing relationships.

Transaction-oriented bankers want to get the job done, from the easiest services to more complex offerings, by keeping the vast majority of customer business "within the box." The box is the safe zone in which the financial ratios work out to the bank's liking. If your numbers fit into the box, you get the loan; if not, hit the road.

Relationship bankers, as the name implies, want relationships.

They don't want just your checking account business, but as much of your money as possible, from mortgages and car loans to establishing trusts and selling insurance or mutual funds.

Obviously, you may not be comfortable with all of that—especially if you have an insurance agent and financial planner on your advisory team.

But if you ever want any treatment that is beyond the box—you want to buy an older used car, find out about lesser-known mortgages or simply try to get the most for your banking dollar, you will want to find a banker with whom you can have a relationship.

Very often—but not always—that means turning to a community banker. Unlike the giants, who thrive on cookie-cutter offices churning out the standard deals, smaller banks tend to thrive on relationships. But whether it is a large or small institution, relationship banking is unique enough that you will have to ask for a meeting and the chance to sit down with the branch manager or vice president running the office.

My own case proves the benefit of this kind of approach to banking. My wife and I lived in Pennsylvania before moving to Boston; at the time of our move, interest rates had fallen to the point at which a refinancing was attractive. In addition, we had been unable to sell our house and wanted to lower the payments so it could be rented more easily.

I had been working with a local bank, where I had moved our accounts, established our children's accounts and taken a car loan. Moreover, since it was a small local bank, I knew the executives and was comfortable calling.

When I started mortgage shopping, I had been looking simply for the best rate and had called the institutions that offered the best rates in the area. My bank was not among them.

In each case, the banks were going to charge me three points—a point is an upfront payment of a percentage of the loan—because the house was going to be a rental instead of a primary residence. While I was in the box as a customer—each bank wanted my business because I represented a good credit risk—I was out of the box on no points/no closing costs deals.

This was a distinct problem, as we hoped the house would sell within a year, meaning we would never pay off the points. Our choices appeared to be losing money on the rental or losing money on the points.

So I called "my banker" and told him of the situation and asked if there was anything he could do. Essentially, I needed a short-term mortgage with no points or closing costs.

A day later, my banker returned my call. His institution had been considering offering "interest-only mortgages," in which the borrower simply pays the interest due and does not reduce principal. This would dramatically cut my payments—to the point that the home could be rented easily without being a drag on the family finances—and stop me from pouring more equity into a house on which I expected to lose money. The loan, in essence, was a one-year loan that could be rolled-over if the home didn't sell.

The benefit to the bank was that it was getting a good credit risk and lending money at a rate higher than it could get by keeping the cash in its vault.

That banker's diligence in looking outside the box to solve my problems was a lifesaver. And the banker admitted afterwards that had I not been the type of customer who came in and asked questions and sought out solutions, I never would have gotten the loan.

Therein lies one of the primary benefits of working with a banker. But bankers function in many different arenas. Because they sell so many products, they can offer a good counterbalance to other advisers; in some instances, banks offer low-priced products too, particularly when it comes to basic term life insurance policies.

Here, again, there will be a difference between a relationship banker and a transaction banker. A relationship banker might notice an unusually large balance in your checking or savings account and call to suggest that perhaps you might be better served by putting the money elsewhere; if you approve, he may even call your accountant or financial planner with questions to integrate that cash into your money management agenda.

The result of this for the banker might be losing some of that money, as you could take tens of thousands of dollars and move it to the management of another adviser or into other products.

The transaction-oriented banker would not give you the call because he would rather have the money sit in your account, where it makes the most money for the bank.

If you are considering whether you need a relationship with a banker, here are the questions you will want to have answered:

Can I do this myself?

The answer to this question is "Probably not when it comes to having the money necessary to meet my own financing needs, but that may not matter much."

No consumer—as opposed to business accounts—absolutely must have a banker on his financial team. Indeed, of all of the advisory positions you need to fill, banker is in many ways the least essential.

You can find someone to make loans or extend you credit and offer some counseling in a time of need, so you don't necessarily need to be working with a banker at all times.

Indeed, if you are a transaction-oriented customer, you can simply seek out the services of a lender if and when you need one. You might decide to work with a mortgage broker—someone who originates loans for other institutions—or get a car loan through the dealership and keep your accounts on a drive-thru/by-machine/no-real-people basis.

Even if you have a relationship with a banker, you may still shop around with others when making transactions, if only because it is easy to shop rates online or by phone and you want to make sure you have a good deal.

But if your goals and objectives are the least bit out of the ordinary, or if you simply want a financial adviser whose help is generally a no-cost add-on to a service you need anyway, then you will not want to do your banking in a vacuum.

Where do I start my search for a relationship banker?

Word-of-mouth is the best advertising for good bankers. Ask around, then try to mesh your needs with your desires.

You may need to find the lowest available mortgage rate but want a banker who will do a lot of hand-holding throughout the buying process. That service may not come cheaply; you could be facing an interest rate that is a fraction higher.

Look at the advertisements and newspaper or online lists of the best available loan rates and the best account yields, then compare that to suggestions from friends, relatives and other financial intermediaries to see what banks score well on both counts.

Am I better off working with someone from a big or small bank?

Generally, community bankers have the most interest in developing special relationships with ordinary customers. Their charters proscribe that they do the majority of work in the community in which they are located, as opposed to a large regional bank that has a greater area in which to meet service requirements.

The other benefit to working with a small bank is that you generally will have a chance to meet the decision-makers, as opposed to working with a giant operation in which cut-and-dried decisions on loans are made in some centralized location miles away from your branch.

That said, however, the truth is that it will be the people you work with, rather than the size of the bank, that counts.

Many large banks have private banking services and will assign you an individual banker if you have sufficient money with the institution. Others simply have individuals who are willing to work with people because it presents an unusual opportunity in a transaction-oriented institution.

The bottom line is that all banks provide roughly the same types of services, so remember that you are selecting a banker, not just a bank.

What credentials will I deal with, and how important are they?

For the most part, the credentials of your banker will not be particularly important unless he is offering specific services that cross over into the realm of your other experts. If he offers to do financial planning or accounting—which might be included in some private banking services—you will want to qualify him the same way you would a financial planner.

How does a banker get paid?

Generally, bankers offer basic services for free, as a value-added part of having an account. Of course, the idea is to have you keep your money at the bank and take your loans there because that is how the bank makes its money.

That said, there may be charges for ancillary services, such as selling insurance or investments. If you cross the line from plain-vanilla banking services with clearly defined account charges into advice and sales-manship, be sure to find out if the banker will receive any special compensation.

What should I ask during an interview?

You will be able to distinguish transaction from relationship bankers almost immediately. If you walk in to open a new account and say you want to take a few minutes interviewing the manager and talking about your banking needs and the bankers are not particularly eager or responsive, chances are you are not in the office of a relationship-oriented banker.

After all, if they can't be responsive when you are opening a new account—or just considering opening an account or taking a loan—then when ARE they going to be responsive to you?

Because the interview is unusual for the banker, help your cause by bringing along some form of financial statement so you can talk about your assets, investments, cash flow and more.

On the assumption that a banker will be interested in your business, however, you will want to ask these questions:

How long have you been at the bank?

In every advisory circumstance, you want to know the breadth of experience of the person helping you. The longer your banker has been with the institution, the more he knows the ins and outs of the bank's philosophy and the better he can finesse your uique circumstances into "the box" in which the institution is comfortable doing business with you.

What are the basic accounts and services available?

You may already have this information by the time you sit down with a banker to find out what ELSE he or she can do for you. Take a look at the menu anyway.

From that, you must cover ground germane to the opening of any account: minimum balance requirements and penalties, types of accounts offered, the ways those accounts work and ancillary fees (such as the charge for talking to a live person).

Next, ask what else the bank can do for you, in terms of insurance, investments, credit cards and more—and ask after what kinds of discounts you can get if you do business with the bank in more than one area (does it give account holders a discount on insurance?).

You may not be interested in services such as private banking and estate planning now, but you will be if you remain a customer long enough.

Will I be dealing with you or someone else?

When you first walk into a bank and ask for a sit-down meeting, you likely will meet the manager on duty. When you explain that you'd like to have a personal relationship with a banker, someone you can bounce ideas off and who may get involved in helping to manage your money, make sure you find out who would become your personal banking adviser.

You may want to meet that person or have him sit in on your initial interview.

In addition, many banks refer customers to other financial advisers. If a bank offers other advisory services but sub-contracts the work out to others, you will want to know who those people are and complete a background check before accepting them on to your financial team.

Having reviewed briefly my financial statement, what suggestions would you have for me?

A big part of the reason to talk with a banker is to see what kind of creativity he brings to the table. You want someone who can offer a variety of solutions, preferably including some you and your other financial helpers haven't thought of.

If you keep a high balance in your checking account, you would hope he might notice and ask whether you need that money to live month-to-month or if you could put it into something that would provide a bit more yield.

If your financial planning is airtight, the bank's adviser won't have much to offer you. If it isn't, he should be able to come up with suggestions; after all, he wants your business.

Are there any special costs or charges I need to be aware of?

Always get a confirmation of costs, regardless of the financial adviser you are dealing with.

This is particularly true when you are doing some sort of transaction with your banker, such as a mortgage or refinancing. You may not pay a specific hourly charge as you do with many other forms of advisers, but high account fees, closing costs or points could make a financing deal less attractive than it sounds.

Does the bank stick to set formulas for determining who is eligible for a mortgage, home-equity loan, car loan, etc.?

Bankers have plenty of reasons to turn a loan down, and very few reasons to approve one. If a banker is bound and determined to stick to formulas, you are out of luck if your situation falls outside those parameters. If you are interested in a particular type of financing, ask about the formulas that apply and whether there is anything you can do to make yourself (or the property involved in the deal) fall within the bank's guidelines.

In general, you always should ask the banker for suggestions on how to make yourself a better candidate for a loan and a better credit risk.

Can I get a copy of the bank's financial statements? How about bank-ratings reports?

This is public information you can get on your own if you call the state banking commissioner for a "call report." The bank shouldn't put you through the trouble; if you are sharing your finances with a banker, he should give you a peek at its numbers.

As for bank ratings, there are several services that rate the financial strength of banking institutions, notably Sheshunoff Ratings Services, Veri-banc and Bauer Financial Reports. Ask about the highest possible rating for the service the bank shows you. If the bank does not get the best rating, ask why not; it's probably nothing to worry about—unless it gets very low ratings—but you'd like to be aware of potential problems in advance.

(When you ask this question, you should hear, pro forma, an explanation of bank insurance and how the protection applies to your accounts. If not, you will want to make sure you are protected—and you should remember that mutual funds sold through a bank do not have the deposit insurance of a savings account.)

You are looking for signs of a healthy institution, particularly because troubled institutions often tighten up lending practices down the road and can make life miserable for borrowers who got in under the old rules.

How are decisions made here?

Find out who pushes the buttons, whether the person you are talking to is actually involved in, say, the loan-review process or if decisions are made in some remote office.

Obviously, you tend to get the most options when you can work with the decision-makers and be involved in the process of deciding what choices appeal to you most, instead of just being thrown into the box for one-size-fits-all options that may not fit you.

This is one edge small banks and thrifts tend to have over regional giants; decisions are made locally by people who know the value of your business to both the bank and the community.

How will you work with my other advisers?

One key role a banker can play is to offer some options that might otherwise be overlooked.

A banker friend of mine recounted the story of a professional client whose accountant called. The client had a house, some investment properties and some good assets, but also some unsecured debt, such as credit-card expenses. The accountant knew that the $15,000 in unsecured debt was accruing interest at a rate of about 18 percent, or $2,700 per year.

The credit-card debt is not tax deductible.

The accountant wanted to know what the banker could do, and the answer was to refinance the mortgage on the home, with the unsecured debt added to the small amount the executive owed. The result was that the unsecured debt became tax deductible and the client saved money.

That kind of work is not unusual.

If you talk to a banker about your options, he may have some ideas on ways to save money or trim costs. If that happens, you may want the banker to talk directly to your other advisers, particularly if you must establish any accounts with specific tax or titling considerations.

What bankers in town—besides yourself—do the best job for their customers and why?

I like to ask this question to all advisers. Banking is a small community, and you will find out which qualities your banker admires in other bankers. If he does not place importance on the same things you do, it may be a sign of what you can (or can't) expect in the future.

What am I going to get from you that I can't get from every other bank in town clamoring for my business?

You may be a small fry today, but a smart banker will see you as a lifetime customer, someone he can make money from in many ways. Most banks are interchangeable, and a few are exceptional; make sure the banker convinces you that his institution falls into the latter camp.

How do I check out a banker?

You've already done this, in the interview when you asked about financial ratings and discussed bank insurance. Learn how federal deposit insurance works—all of your accounts with one institution qualify for a total of $100,000 in coverage—and exercise caution in crossing those limits, particularly if the bank-rating agencies do not give the institution its top grade.

What do I ask references?

When it comes to a bank, in which so much of the business is cookie-cutter transactions, you would want a reference only in situations in which you are either doing an important transaction or you have some unusual circumstance that requires special attention.

In that case, chances are good the person who gave you a referral to a banker may suffice.

Specifically, you might want to know how accommodating and easy-to-work-with the bank is as you get ready to close on a home. Likewise, if you know you have a debt problem and are looking for a consolidation loan, a friend with similar circumstances can probably give you all the information you need to be able to work with the banker comfortably.

How can I build a relationship with a banker? Where does it go after I open an account?

Even relationship-oriented bankers may not rush to call you all the time, but they will be happy to see your face when you stick it in their office door.

The more you stay in touch with the banker, the more you will get from the relationship.

This might mean bringing in updated financial statements every year or two or bringing a copy of your tax return and asking for your banker's opinion of any moves you might make.

Banking is a mix of objective and subjective decisions. The more someone knows you and knows of you, the easier it is to take those subjective factors and make them work in your favor.

What are the danger signs to a relationship gone sour?

Bankers are no different than most other advisers. There are three key trouble spots:

- Loss of interest. If you complete your immediate transactions and the banker is no longer interested in you, assume he was most interested in filling your pressing need.

  If you are trying to develop a relationship, you will want more than that.

- Lack of communication or incomplete disclosure. There should never be any surprises in a banking relationship. By law, most fees and costs must be explained in advance. If any banking service winds up with more out-of-pocket costs than anticipated, something is wrong.

  The same applies to the returns on bank products such as certificates of deposit. In most cases, rates and yields can be clearly explained; you should be able to say "Here is my money, what will it be worth at the end of X period of time?" and get a direct and concrete answer.

  Another key element of communication involves explanation of how various products sold by the bank actually work. A money market account, for example, is covered by federal deposit insurance. A money market mutual fund is not. You should know the status of each investment, particularly if you have multiple products from the bank.

- Lastly, if your banker won't give you a heads-up, he is not serving you appropriately.

  Say, for example, you have a CD coming due with a finite window in which to withdraw the money or roll it over. If you could do better by changing the term of the CD or moving the money elsewhere, or if you will not get interest during the make-up-your-mind period when the certificate comes due and before you reinvest, you should be aware of that.

Likewise, if a loan has restrictions penalizing early repayments, it should not be a surprise.

A banker is a valuable member of your advisory team only if he takes part; when a banker proves to you that he cares only about the next money-making transaction, you'll probably be better off limiting your contact to machines and drive-thru windows until you find a new banker.

21 *How to get a bunch of individuals to function as one unit*

Donald Trump practices the art of the deal with a cadre of support people in tow.

Warren Buffett, considered by many to be the greatest investor of all time, has a financial team that includes Charles Munger, one of the nation's most astute business observers in his own right. Buffett's former stockbroker, Bill Ruane, runs the Sequoia Fund, one of the most successful mutual funds in history.

In fact, virtually every famous financier and member of the money elite has a financial team.

Their dealings, of course, are far from those of the average person trying to figure out which mortgage is best or what stock or fund to buy with the annual Christmas bonus.

Still, they are cut from the same cloth—people seeking counsel on their decisions.

Why not the rest of us? We need a financial team as much as or more than the people on the Forbes magazine list of the richest people in the world, if only because we can't afford to make as many money mistakes.

If you expect to hire a multitude of experts to meet your needs at various times in your life, then it makes sense to build and manage a team of experts, coordinating your efforts and getting a cohesive strategy instead of piecing together a patchwork of different ideas and philosophies.

Let's face it, the vast majority of people—no matter how determined they are to manage their own affairs—will need to work with bankers, lawyers, investment consultants (brokers, financial planners and assorted others), accountants or tax preparers, insurance providers and real estate agents. The advisers will help manage your money, secure or work out loan agreements, buy real estate, insure the whole kit and caboodle and pay taxes on whatever can't be sheltered.

With the team approach, you cover all of the angles in each of those transactions, making sure you not only think of the investment possibilities of what to do with, say, an inheritance, but also the tax liabilities. You look not only at the legal ramifications of setting up a trust, but also at the financial options for managing the money within it.

As your lifestyle, finances and goals change, you have a team that knows you and can make sure that your moves fit in with an overall strategy, rather than merely buying products that may solve your current needs but not maximize your long-term earnings or savings potential.

And by developing a network, you should get superior counsel and expertise from advisers who will come to know you as more than just another file number.

The team-building process does not change the way you hire your specialists, but rather how you work with them. Even there, the modification is minor; you interact with these people individually, but also schedule the occasional brainstorming session at which they meet and work with your other helpers.

The only additional burden the team approach puts on your advisers is that each must be able to work well with the others. Anyone who, for the benefit of a client, is not willing to check his ego at the door probably does not deserve a spot on your financial team.

After all, even if your players are top experts in their fields, your lifetime needs are likely to encompass their knowledge and beyond.

Take a case I once heard from a leading financial planner, who was brought in to consult with an insurance agent and estate planning attorney.

The client had been lucky enough to amass a lot of money and wanted to donate a substantial amount of it to charity.

The attorney suggested a "charitable-remainder trust," an instrument designed to let the client (and his spouse, upon his death) make a donation yet retain a flow of income from the money. Once both spouses died, the money set aside for the trust would then go to charity.

To fund the trust, the client was told to transfer some of his stock portfolio. While most of the stocks had capital gains—he had been lucky enough to pick long-term winners—a few issues had losses, amounting to about $20,000.

The client was just about to complete the move when he brought in the planner for a second opinion. The planner recognized that putting the stocks with losses directly into the trust would mean missing out on a tax deduction. Instead of simply moving the assets, the client sold them, realizing the losses—which he could then use to offset other winnings for tax purposes—and then put the proceeds of the stock sale into the trust. (He correctly chose not to sell the stocks with the gains, however, because that would have triggered a tax bill.)

Complicated? Yes.

Ordinary? Absolutely.

Many situations cross disciplines, flowing from insurance to investing to law to taxation.

Let's look at a more common situation, one that doesn't require a huge estate.

Say, for example, you have a bank certificate of deposit coming due. Your banker, doing his job as your adviser, contacts you before the rollover date. In reviewing your options, the banker suggests you do something more aggressive with the money and shows you several attractive options, running from safe tax-free mutual funds to more aggressive stock funds.

By itself, the advice sounds good, because you are goosing the returns of a slow-moving asset.

There are countless people who take advice like this without consulting any other experts, including those they already have hired. Hundreds of financial advisers have had cases of well-meaning friends, relatives and advisers messing up the best-laid of financial foundations.

Armed with the banker's advice, the right thing to do might be to consult with your broker, accountant or financial planner. A quick phone call might reveal that moving the certificate-of-deposit money into mutual funds would lower a cash cushion built into your planning for liquidity purposes, or that a move into a tax-free fund is not needed given your tax circumstances.

The banker in this case isn't overstepping his role by making the suggestion. Ideally, however, the banker would know that you pursue a team approach, see the CD coming due and call you, possibly with the intent of talking with your other team members.

If that sounds like a Pollyanna situation—that such consultations and basic advice simply never happen in the real world—it should. It almost never does happen, not because advisers are unwilling to work as a team, but because investors don't ask them to.

"Some people get partial planning from a lot of people," explains Ross Levin of Accredited Investors in Minneapolis. "They do a little bit of everything that sounds good, and wind up with a hodge-podge, a collection of investment advice instead of a plan.

"They may just take sales advice from a few different people, without ever getting a second opinion. Or it might be that they have jumped around from adviser to adviser, keeping from each whatever sounded good or performed well, but never keeping their plans—financial, tax and estate—up to date. Or maybe they aren't happy with the way their investments are going, so when an insurance agent or banker offers investment advice, they take it and it goes against what they had set up with their financial planner. Then, to fix it, they wind up paying taxes or penalties or they give up interest (income)."

Over your financial lifetime, you will undoubtedly find advisers who claim to be able to do more than one job (the next chapter explains how to decide whether to take that bait) or who say they (or their firm) can offer one-stop shopping.

They may indeed be able to deliver, but having multiple team members allows you to view each situation from a different perspective, get second opinions, bring in additional specialists when unique needs arise and get the most from your advisory relationships.

Best of all, good advisers like working in a team approach, because they know the process stimulates discussions that will help not only you but also their other clients.

"Every adviser you hire has their own level of expertise," explains financial author and adviser Ginger Applegarth of First Financial Trust in Winchester, Mass. "When they work together, they raise that collective level. Everyone becomes more aware of what you want, and the different advisers all want to make sure that you get the best help and protection, so they will raise questions and try to make sure that everything gets taken care of to your best advantage.

"Good advisers want to learn from each other; they don't just want you to do better, they want to take the practical knowledge they gain from your case and apply it, if it is applicable, to their other clients."

At a bare minimum, your financial team should consist of an investment adviser, an accountant or tax preparer, an insurance adviser and an estate-planning lawyer.

A banker may also have a role on the team, depending on whether he provides real personal services, as opposed to being merely a conduit to the institution. A real estate agent probably will not work with your financial team on a regular basis, unless you are managing multiple properties or making estate plans that involve your home.

Stockbrokers are a question mark for your financial team. If they are securities salesmen working strictly on commission, their interests may not be in sync with the rest of the team (they will obviously want to see as much money as possible diverted toward your stock portfolio and will have little concern for the rest). But if they function as investment advisers or money managers, or if they need to be aware of specific long-term strategies that could affect the suitability of their investment selections, you might want to include them in the process.

(It is worth noting that insurance agents also get paid on commission and could have the same conflicts as brokers. Still, they have a role on the team, particularly as you move toward estate planning and asset-protection strategies.)

And if you are among those people who still believe a financial team is only for the Donald Trumps of this world, consider the cost of maintaining those advisers each year. A financial planner, for example, might charge 1 percent of the assets he manages, while an accountant could charge up to $200 per hour (it could be significantly less than that, depending largely on where you live and the supply-and-demand factors at work), an insurance adviser could charge either straight commission or $100 to $200 an hour if you are dealing with a fee-only adviser, and lawyer fees vary widely.

In general, you will spend more on an adviser when you first hire him than in subsequent years. But as you get your team up to speed— and depending on your assets—an annual outlay of $1,500 to $3,000 per year should be all it takes to have a complete team of advisers.

That may be more than you would like, but it's not bad considering that the team approach provides comprehensive services and maximizes the money expertise in each specialty.

As you hire advisers, here are some things to consider that will allow you to manage them as a team and maximize their potential not only in an individual specialty, but as a safety net to make sure you are always moving in the most efficient path toward your goals.

Make sure each adviser is aware of the others

Throughout the hiring process and as you develop a relationships, you want each of your advisers to know about the others. For the most part, that will be easy because you may involve your advisers in the selection process.

Say the first adviser you hire is a lawyer. That relationship is developing when you decide it is time to hire someone to do your taxes. One logical person to contact for a referral is the lawyer, who automatically knows you are planning a change in your financial situation.

Once you have the referral, make sure the lawyer knows you may, at some point, want a group consultation.

If an adviser is uncomfortable with the idea of working with a particular person you have hired, find out why. If an adviser has had past problems dealing with a prospective new team member or if something he has heard makes them reticent to deal with that person, that should raise a red flag over your selection.

Each adviser will know a few players in another specialty; you may be introducing him to someone new or simply providing him with a chance to catch up with old friends, but the one thing you can be sure of is that any adviser who knows he will be part of a team is going to want to make sure all of your other financial helpers know what they are doing.

Define each adviser's role. Make sure all advisers are fully aware of your wishes

Some advisers are true specialists. You may hire a lawyer, for example, who writes wills but doesn't handle insurance and charitable trusts (often key areas for a team).

Other advisers are generalists, crossing divergent lines because that is where their own interests—or those of their clients—have led them.

No matter which type of adviser you hire, you want each one to know exactly what he was hired for. You do not want the insurance adviser second-guessing the financial planner, or vice versa. You want them working in concert.

That means each should not cross the lines and recommend or sell you another financial product or service without consulting the others. Let's go back to the earlier example of the banker, the one who advised you how to handle a maturing CD, and assume the banker knows you have a financial team in place.

If the banker starts pushing other products without consulting the rest of the team—or if he encourages you to make your decision without contacting your other advisers—he obviously has his own interests at heart. It's not just that he is not a good team player, it's that he probably isn't a good adviser.

If, however, the banker encourages you to contact the others and in-forms you of the products he would recommend at the bank, you can consider those products if and when the other advisers agree moving the money is in keeping with the rest of your plan.

Throughout the hiring process, you worked to determine what an adviser can and should do for you. Make sure each one understands that role, particularly as you plan to have the whole team confer occa-sionally and would not want one of your helpers to discover then that he plays a more limited role in your financial life than you had led him to believe.

Hire a quarterback

One adviser is going to have to become the captain of your team, the person who coordinates the overall efforts of everyone to make sure you are going in the right direction.

While the next chapter warns about picking double agents, many people agree the best kind of leader for an advisory team is either a financial planner who also is a tax expert or an accountant who has a financial planning credential. (Of all the specialties, financial planning and accounting are the two that have their hands in virtually every as-pect of your life.)

The job of your quarterback or captain is to make sure all planning is properly constructed and implemented. If you are saving to pay for a college education, for example, he would make sure your plans not only maximize your savings but also potentially keep you eligible for grant or assistance programs; if you are doing estate planing, he would make sure your assets are re-titled so the plan can be carried out or, as mentioned earlier in this chapter, so the execution of your plan maxi-mizes your potential tax savings.

The quarterback is the person who will make sure everything is in order, that the efforts of your advisers are coordinated and nothing has been overlooked. Of all members of your financial team, this is the one you will meet with most often, perhaps once every quarter or six months compared to an annual or biannual checkup with the rest of your counselors.

Ideally, your quarterback will be well-connected in the local com-munity, so he knows many people in other advisory roles; not only will this make him more likely to know the helpers you have chosen, but it will allow him to get qualified second opinions if he feels the need to consult with someone outside your team. In spite of all your efforts to hire the best advisers, this kind of outside consultation may still be necessary; you can't expect anyone—even your team captain—to be an expert in every aspect of managing your affairs.

Have occasional group meetings

About once a year, you should get together with your team to review your progress toward your financial goals, discuss any changes in lifestyle or major events that have occurred since the last meeting and make sure everything is up to date.

The team approach may actually save you time in this manner; if not for this one meeting, you would be calling or meeting with the other advisers whenever there is a significant change in your life.

If a group meeting is not practical, consider meeting with each expert individually, with your team captain in tow.

A group meeting allows you to go over your finances specialty by specialty, and lets each adviser hear why moves were made, and your goals for each specialist and allows them to ask questions and review one anothers work. Effectively, you will get second opinions and questions and double-checks by having the advisers interact, because your players will want to know what the others are doing. They also will want to make sure they are giving you the best advice going forward so that, for example, the banker will want to know what is going on so that he doesn't tell you the wrong thing to do the next time a CD comes due.

Never let advisers argue in front of you

Whether you bring the advisers together for a face-to-face meeting or have them take part in a conference call, don't let them battle in front of you.

For starters, this kind of argument smacks of unprofessionalism. It is usually a play for a bigger role on the team, but it is almost guaranteed to have bad outcomes and undermines your confidence in the team members. If they are second-guessing each other, you may start to get nervous about your decisions; in that case, both advisers are diminished.

"There are major wars going on in the financial planning industry— CPAs and attorneys versus financial advisers, people with one credential versus people with another," says Dick Wagner, a principal in the

Denver advisory firm Sharkey, Howes, Wagner and Javer. "That should never spill over into how someone deals with a client. Unless the client has picked a real idiot to do his taxes, everyone should defer to the [accountant] on tax issues, or the financial planner on investment issues.

"If there is conflict, it should happen away from the client—and the client should want it that way, so that the advisers work issues out privately and make combined recommendations, rather than everyone dancing around in the open trying to steal away a little bit of business."

Advisers should question each other in your presence, but it should never deteriorate into one counselor questioning the competency of another.

If your advisers don't agree on a key issue, sit them down individually. You then can hear both sides and be the arbiter, but never let one adviser badmouth another member of your team. Those nasty little arguments build the kind of tension that can sabotage the process and make all of your financial helpers feel uncomfortable.

You also don't want bickering in your presence because your decisions could then give an adviser an idea of what he must do—present forceful arguments and undercut the other experts—to become the most powerful player on the team.

Maintain control

Just because you have multiple advisers working together to meet your interests does not let you off the hook. You still have the ultimate decision-making responsibility.

When you have the team together as a group, ask contrarian questions—"What could go wrong? What IS the worst that could happen?"—so everyone is sure to examine the downside and protect you from it.

Most sports teams not only have a captain, they have a manager. That is your job.

Consider having an outsider review team performance every two or three years

As hard as this may be to believe, even a team approach is no guarantee that you will reach your goals. "Groupthink," in which everyone gets on the same page and overlooks key concerns, is a real possibility, no matter how much you guard against it.

Unless you are comfortable doing this yourself in your role as manager of the team, you may want to get an independent audit. If that's the case, every few years you will want to engage an accountant or financial planner—another quarterback type—to review what your experts have done and to make sure it is comprehensive, performing to expectations and serving your needs.

You also may want outsiders to review the work of team members on an as-needed basis, such as when trusts are drawn up. (You should never sign a trust agreement without a second opinion from a lawyer working at a different firm than the one who drew up the papers.)

If an independent audit turns up problem areas—bases left uncovered or holes in your financial security blanket—you may want to reconvene the team to address those issues, or you may want to make a few trades and kick the underperformers off your squad.

Remember, none of this team stuff is inherently different from what you do when managing each adviser individually. This whole book, after all, has been about managing your managers.

But in the long run, paying that little bit extra for your advisers to function as a unit probably will come back to you in the form of enhanced returns and security. That may not represent the "art of the deal" to Donald Trump, but it should sound pretty good to the rest of us.

22 *Utility infielders; can one adviser handle two jobs?*

Financial advisers of all stripes like to compare their work to that of doctors.

They are, after all, specialists helping to solve and cure a patient's financial ills.

In the medical field, however, failure to refer a patient to a necessary specialist actually can be considered malpractice.

In financial services, failure to refer a client to a specialist is common practice. Specialists in one area—financial planning, banking, accounting or law in particular—often stray into areas that are not their bread-and-butter because their service calls for it.

Your banker, for example, may be able to sell you investments, insurance and offer trust services, services that might otherwise be reserved for a financial planner, insurance agent or lawyer. Some lawyers offer accounting and tax services; others do financial planning beyond establishing trusts and preserving assets. Some accountants, meanwhile, do financial planning, establish trusts and handle certain legal documents. Brokers can offer a lot of bank-lookalike services and (as with insurance agents) may be able to handle your financial planning.

And financial planners can offer practically anything.

As a result of these hazy boundaries, you may someday be faced with one or more of your advisers wanting to cross the traditional borders of their roles, hoping to sell you another product or capture more of your assets under management.

There is nothing particularly nefarious about this. Your current advisers understand your situation, enjoy working with you and believe they have the expertise to help in a secondary area. Essentially, they are offering one-stop shopping, a convenience most people desire.

That's when the problem arises.

A good accountant is not necessarily an outstanding financial planner, or vice versa. Advanced credentials are no guarantee; the fact that a counselor studied for a certificate in another specialty does not make him good at that job, especially if it is no more than a sideline business.

With that in mind, you will have a choice to make if your adviser volunteers to take on an expanded role as your needs grow.

"Unlike medicine, financial planning is too young to have rules about what makes for good practice," says Robert N. Veres of Morningstar Advisor. "You see people trying to wear a lot of different hats, and it is not always the best thing. It takes a lot to be good at any one specialty, let alone trying to practice in two distinct areas. I think it may be asking too much of someone to have them be your expert in two specialties."

The team approach discussed in the previous chapter is another reason to be careful before letting one adviser handle two roles. Because of the natural overlap of each advisory position, you lose the easy opportunity to get a second opinion, to run one adviser's work past another.

Before dismissing the idea of one adviser serve dual roles, however, let's examine the benefits.

The most notable one is convenience or one-stop shopping. The second big benefit is that you already know the adviser (and the adviser knows you); if you have picked that counselor carefully, you can avoid the legwork of choosing a new player for your team.

Don't undervalue convenience. It embodies one of the three qualities most people want in a relationship with a financial adviser—cheap, easy and successful—because it certainly is easy to let one adviser take on an expanded role.

Presumably, the primary relationship with the adviser also has been successful (or why give him more responsibility?), so it's easy to project good things.

The second issue, that his knowledge of you reduces legwork, also applies, to a point.

If you let your guard down and do not perform your due diligence and make sure the adviser is capable of handling your needs in a second arena, you will be unhappy with the results.

You don't have to start from scratch, but you should make sure your adviser is as qualified in his second field as his first. And you should interview at least one other person who specializes in the second field so you can weigh the potential difference in service from someone whose primary business is, say, insurance compared to someone who sells insurance as a sideline.

A good adviser should want you to ask those questions, rather than be offended by your questioning his expertise. Having worked with you—particularly if you put him through the rigorous questioning advocated in this book—he should understand that you are cautious in your approach to advisers and that you want the best possible representation.

If he questions your loyalty or make you feel guilty, re-think the entire relationship. Each of your advisers, no matter his position, should make your best interests his highest priority.

It will always be in your best interest to make sure you have the highest quality representation.

There is something of a parallel between financial advice and baseball. In baseball, a utility infielder is someone who can play more than one position; he gets this opportunity, in many instances, because he isn't good enough to start at any one position.

Any adviser hoping for two positions on your team must have the skill to "start" at both spots.

To determine that, you need an initial interview covering the new territory. You can dispense with the questions that define the relationship because you already know the adviser's manner. But you should ask the what-are-your-qualifications questions—as laid out in the chapters on hiring each specialist—plus any other applicable questions that cover the ground you and the adviser are considering exploring together. In addition to those queries, add the following:

Do you do the (fill-in-the-blank) work yourself?

Many full-service financial firms can take you from cradle to grave, offering planning, accounting, brokerage, insurance and legal services under one roof. You need to know if your adviser truly is expert in more than one specialty, or if he simply plans to farm the work out.

There is nothing wrong with your broker or money manager relying on the insurance expert to do the needs analysis and process your information before making recommendations. You simply want to know upfront who will be dealing with you. If there is another partner in-volved, you should do a background check to make sure he is qualified for the tasks at hand.

What percentage of your clients work with you in both of your specialties?

A basic tenet of any counseling situation is that you want the adviser to be particularly comfortable working with people in your situation. If an adviser takes a dual role with most clients, that makes for ready references and tells you he can function efficiently in both roles.

If, on the other hand, only one in 10 clients actually use this person as a dual adviser, the new specialty is nothing more than a sideline. At that point, you need to question whether the adviser has the expertise of someone who makes your new area of need his primary specialty.

For example, say your accountant sells financial planning services, but only to a few clients. It is reasonable to wonder whether he has the knowledge, expertise and interest offered by the competition, namely a planner who spends all day, every day helping people manage money.

If your needs are minimal, the comfort level you have with your ac-countant could make it easy to hire him for a little financial planning help. If, however, you have a major money management job, the more-expert planner might be your choice.

What percentage of your time do you spend dedicated to the new specialty—and to continuing education in this field—compared to the role in which you are currently my adviser?

Again, you are qualifying the adviser's expertise. You don't want to be a guinea pig.

If the adviser is trying to build a dual clientele and the time spent on this side of the business is growing, that should raise your comfort level; conversely, you might not feel particularly comfortable with a financial planner who is dabbling in estate planning.

Remember, too, that the adviser probably will not cut you a price discount for this work, which means you will pay as much for a part-time specialist as for a full-time expert.

How do you get paid in the new advisory role?

This is absolutely critical, because not every financial specialty bills the same way.

There are, for example, financial planners who use the "fee-only" label as part of their allure. But their work on a flat-fee basis may apply only to planning; if you purchase insurance from them, you could be paying commissions.

Check to make sure there are no pricing surprises.

Why do you want me as a client on this side of your business?

As you learned in the chapter on friends as potential financial helpers, this is a key question for anyone with whom you have a personal relationship. It applies to professional relationships, too.

The adviser who wants two roles on your financial team is jeopardizing the existing relationship. If something goes wrong, he will lose you as a client altogether.

That being the case, inquire about his motives. Are you simply an easy mark, a way to expand and generate some extra business, or does he believe your financial relationship has evolved to the point that you need additional help, notably assistance he is qualified to provide?

If increased fees—rather than expertise or need—seems to be driving his desire to serve you, consider who benefits the most from turning one adviser into a double agent.

Why should I come to you instead of someone specifically dedicated to my new field of interest?

An adviser must convince you that he is the best qualified, most compatible person for each role he wants on your team. If he doesn't have compelling reasons for expanding his territory—i.e., he has the same expert credentials as a full-time practitioner and already is familiar with your finances—you most likely will be better off sticking to the one-field, one-expert line of thinking.

Remember, it may be common practice for an adviser to wear two hats, but it may also border on malpractice if they can't do each job equally well.

23 *Breaking up is hard to do*

In the now-discontinued television sitcom "Caroline in the City," the lead character was never any good at ending relationships.

In one particular episode, Caroline couldn't bring herself to change dry cleaners—no matter the miserable quality of his work—until he died.

At that, she gave the eulogy at his funeral.

Then, rather than tell her hairdresser she was seeking a new look from someone else, she said that she was moving to Norway. He bought it until bumping into her at a party (when she hastily agreed to go rushing back to him).

Of course, Caroline was a fictitious character.

The main difference between a character like her and real people like us is that we could never pull that Norway thing off in the first place.

Ending relationships is never easy. The mere thought smacks of confrontation, hardship, betrayal and a whole range of emotions most of us would rather avoid.

Still, when a member of your financial team is not doing his job and meeting your expectations, you must be stern, express what you want and be prepared to dismiss him if the business side of the relationship does not improve.

When it comes to managing your affairs, remember one rule: Business is business. No matter your personal feelings for someone, he doesn't stay on your team if he can't do the job to your satisfaction.

Even if you don't hire a friend or relative—and Chapter 6 explained why that's a bad idea—separating business from your feelings is hard. Chances are you will become friendly with your advisers as the relationships grow. If you subsequently find they can't meet your business expectations, the budding friendships could make you doubly reluctant to make a change.

Worse yet, you might not be as lucky with a lousy financial planner as Caroline was with her miserable dry cleaner. Your adviser could have a long, healthy life ahead.

Typically, people want to end financial relationships because expectations are not being met. If the real estate agent doesn't sell the house, for example, you might not to renew the listing; that dismissal is easy because the contract is finite, as opposed to the unwritten, use-the-same-person-forever mentality that's part of many banking, accounting, legal and investment relationships.

In Chapter 10 on controlling your players, the mantra you were supposed to repeat was "It's my money." Nowhere is that more applicable than when you are thinking of dumping an adviser.

You might recall the story of Jim (from Chapter 5), the poor sot who lost the investing contest and most of his clients. Until the newspaper contest, his clients let him control their investments; they were following blindly because he was supposed to be the best broker in town. When his dismal contest performance struck a familiar chord, they woke up, retook control and reshaped the relationship, either cutting Jim loose or making sure he understood what they were looking for (which presumably was not a 40 percent loss during an up year for the stock market).

Obviously, you should jettison your adviser if you suspect fraud, wrongdoing or any sort of problem. In those instances, you should not only dismiss the adviser but file complaints and pursue legal remedies to get your money back.

But short of those extreme cases, there are plenty of situations in which an advisory relationship just doesn't work out, when you feel let down by the goods and services offered and believe you would be better off working with someone else.

If a relationship sours for *any reason* and you believe there may be a need to dismiss an adviser, the process is simple and straightforward. You may allow a final chance at redemption, but here are the steps you should follow:

Step 1. At the first sign of trouble—when service does not jive with your expectations—tell the adviser your concerns

If the adviser pooh-poohs them, remind him that "It's my money." For that money, you deserve, at the very least, an explanation of why your expectations are not being met. If no explanation is forthcoming, you know the adviser isn't taking you seriously.

If that's the case, skip Step 2 and go directly to Step 3.

Step 2. Redefine the relationship

You have explained what the trouble is. Now set out to fix it.

Don't change your expectations, but make sure your hopes for the relationship are reasonable. It would be unreasonable to expect a banker to make you a loan for which you are not qualified; it would be reasonable for the banker to suggest alternative means of financing that might suit your needs and to explain how those options work and affect your overall financial health.

It is unreasonable to expect a tax preparer to cut your taxes by taking deductions he isn't comfortable claiming, but it is desirable to discuss all manner of deductions for which you qualify, even if a particular credit or benefit is worth just a few bucks. After all, it's your money.

You can even re-examine the basic levels of service being provided. If—as has happened in my own home—an insurance company raises premiums when they are supposed to go down (due to a clean driving record, for instance), consistently sends incorrect bills and is just plain sloppy, you have a right to ask the agent to clear up the problems. You never would have anticipated these problems when buying coverage, and they are not the agent's fault, but if the agent won't go to bat for you and save you the hassle, you need to redefine the relationship.

One difficult area to redefine is return on investment. Presumably, you and your broker or financial planner set targets based on your investment profile. But many advisers are chastised by customers not for missing return targets but for not "beating the market."

That is particularly ironic because a diversified investment portfolio, by design, will not beat the market. It encompasses more and different types of risk than the simple market baskets—such as the Standard & Poor's 500 Index—that people use as benchmarks.

If you no longer believe the adviser has the acumen to reach the investment targets you set together—and your unhappiness stems from the adviser's actions, and not from a downturn in the market that brings everyone down—then a change is in order. If, however, performance has lagged its targets but has been reasonable given current market conditions, setting new performance standards could be a mistake. (If you tell a financial planner to achieve 25 percent returns in the next year or lose you as a client, you encourage the adviser to gamble. He can go hellbent-for-leather to achieve the gains and keep you as a client by taking extraordinary risks. If the move backfires, you lose a lot of money and he loses you as a client—the exact same outcome he could have achieved by remaining conservative. If you don't believe a team member can hit your targets, find someone who can.)

So the idea in redefining the relationship is to revisit what you were seeking when you first signed on as a client and review how your needs have changed and how you see things differently now that you have had time to get used to having an adviser.

Make a list of what you want from the adviser, including the services you currently receive and the areas in which he or she falls short. Prioritize your wants, giving the adviser a chance to see how the service being provided is not meeting your key needs.

Realize, too, that the adviser may opt to drop you as a client, which is not necessarily a bad outcome, particularly if he refunds some of your payment to salve your dissatisfaction. The adviser may work with all clients on one level, and your desire for something else simply may not fit his profile.

Throughout the hiring process, the idea was to find advisers who wanted to "hire" you as a client. If they no longer value you as a customer, you would be better off knowing now.

If the adviser is willing to refocus his or her efforts to keep you as a client, set a specific trial period. If you are still not satisfied after, say, six months or a year, you will move to:

Step 3. Drop the ax

The moment you are not satisfied with an adviser's performance, start preparing for this action. For an advisory relationship to work, you must trust and have confidence in the adviser and his abilities; if either of those elements is gone, so too is the adviser.

If you have obligations to fulfill—the listing contract with a real estate agent, a management fee with a planner or the unexpired term of a certificate of deposit—you will have to live up to them. If you believe the situation is desperate, examine the cost of an early escape (paying remaining fees or any penalties now but foregoing services due). In some rare cases, it is worth making your changes immediately, rather than letting time compound mistakes.

Before kicking someone off your team, however, do some advance preparation. You may need to have records transferred or to take possession of some securities; you will want a place for those records and securities.

You may also need to be prepared to move some money around. If you leave a brokerage firm, for example, you may need to pull money out of mutual funds run by the house—although you can probably leave the funds in place and the account open until you have hired a new adviser.

Transferring assets is a pain; make sure you know the rules and can avoid screw-ups that could cost you at tax time. Learn the rules involved before making a change; get the necessary information so your new adviser—whenever he is hired—can help you move your money.

The actual dismissal should be clean and concise. If you need to notify the firm in writing, make the note short and say only that you no longer intend to use the adviser's services after a specific date, by which time you want possession of all monies, pertinent records and paperwork.

If the adviser or a supervisor wants to discuss your decision, be brief and firm. This is when the situation can get ugly and emotional, and you don't need that. Worse yet would be to wind up like Caroline and the hairdresser, rushing right back into a situation that you already have deemed untenable. You should not be badgered, pestered or otherwise bothered about making a decision that is clearly in your own best interest.

Having dispatched with the adviser, you are ready for:

Step 4. Hire a replacement

If you did not go through the full-blown, it's-a-lot-of-work process described in this book while picking the departed adviser, change your interview and preparation style.

If you picked the departed helper by the book, you need to start over again and try to figure out how to avoid making the same mistake twice. Ask yourself what went wrong with the relationship and what impressed you during the interviews that failed to materialize later.

Make sure any prospective new adviser knows you are coming out of a bad relationship; express your concerns and describe what went wrong and what you expect from a new counselor.

Ask how he would react in a situation like the one that prompted the decline of your last relationship, and whether he considers your expectations with the previous adviser to have been unreasonable. Be honest about the circumstances so an adviser can pull himself out of the running if you sound like a client he cannot work with. Use the list of your expectations developed under Step 2 of the dismissal process to show prospective replacements your priorities and to help them understand how the relationship soured.

Once you hire a new partner for your financial team, he should review the work of the departed player, keeping whatever is worthwhile. It's especially important he justifies investment changes, as such decisions have tax consequences and may be motivated by self-interest (the new broker gets commissions when you sell the old stocks and purchase new ones, creating an incentive to say stocks purchased under your previous brokerage relationship were dogs).

The new relationship comes with no guarantees that it will be better than the old one, but, if you learn from experience and hire by-the-book, you should not have to go through many advisers to find one you can keep for a lifetime.

Firing and replacing team members will not be fun and should not be entered into lightly, but neither is it enjoyable to feel you aren't getting your money's worth. Ultimately, what will be enjoyable is having an adviser with whom you can have a long and prosperous relationship.

The Last Word

If you have made it this far into the book, you are, if nothing else, persistent.

That, or you took shortcuts.

Either way, it is an appropriate metaphor for the use of this book in your efforts to hire financial helpers.

Your job, in selecting and managing advisers, is to screen out the rogues, scoundrels, incompetents, personality problems and the greedy. What you should be left with are people whose expertise matches your current and future needs, and whose style and manner provide guidance and counsel in a way you desire.

There is no doubt in my mind the selection process proscribed in this book can be overkill. If you are persistent and dogged in your pursuit of the most appropriate financial representation, this book will screen out those advisers who do not have the attention span or desire to meet your demands. It also will weed out the bad guys, since you will no longer be an easy mark; your confidence and trust will be too hard to gain, and there will be easier targets for them to pursue.

At the same time, you do not need to follow every suggestion or ask every last question in order to determine an adviser's qualifications and your comfort level. Just as you may have skipped around in the book to seek out specific bits of information, so can you pick and choose the type of data you want to get from an adviser.

The question is whether you know enough about each adviser—or type of adviser—to leave stones unturned while searching for a helper.

For example, my colleagues at *The Boston Globe* routinely tell me when they have interviewed a financial planner I know. When I ask if they have interviewed—or plan to talk with—other planners before signing up, most say no. At most, they intend to talk to one other planner.

That leaves them short of the recommended level of interviews for choosing a candidate.

Obviously, I would recommend they do the due diligence necessary to be absolutely certain they have made the right choice, but my colleagues—and readers of this book—are busy people. Following all the recommendations of this book before hiring—from all of the questions to references to interviewing three or more candidates—takes time and effort that can be hard to justify if you consider yourself a good judge of character.

I can live with that, and so can you.

There's nothing to say my busy colleagues won't be perfectly happy with the first planner they interview, or that everyone who hires an adviser on the spur of the moment (rather than before the service is necessary) faces disaster.

But, as with everything else in finances, it is a risk-reward tradeoff. You must balance the risk that your judgment and good fortune will not hold up against the reward of the time you save taking a short cut.

Most of the time, things will turn out fine. When they don't, however, the time you saved will not be worth the cost.

So decide which approach you will take, whether it is going completely by the book or adapting the book's approach to your lifestyle, needs and knowledge. Hopefully, you will find a way to undertake this effort properly, but with only minimum disruption to the rest of your life.

My job in writing this book was to develop a way for you to eliminate the bad guys and the bad matches. That meant developing a process that would be hard for laggards to pass.

If you give an adviser the full wax job, I believe you virtually guarantee you will have competent, qualified representation. It may not be the "very best" choice you could make, but it is unlikely to be someone who rips you off or makes you feel abused.

Make the methods in this book work for you. Use as much or as little of each selection process as you believe is necessary, but remember it is better to overqualify advisers than to make assumptions about their abilities.

I can't stress enough that the majority of advisers I meet in all of the specialties are, at a bare minimum, competent and well-intentioned. They may balk at doing so much work to get your business simply because they are not the bad guys.

Still, don't be afraid to make an adviser jump through some hoops. If he won't work hard to win your business, you can only imagine how he might respond once he has it.

Whether you use just a few suggestions from this book or carry your copy into an interview and make an adviser answer every last question, remember one thing: As the prospective client, you are entitled to overkill. You are allowed to worry, fret and sweat the small stuff.

It's your money. Use your knowledge to make the most of it; hire advisers who help you protect it and make more of it.

Appendix 1
State and federal securities regulators

You will want to make two phone calls to find out whether the person you are dealing with—or their firm—has a history of complaints and client troubles. Over a career, a problem or two is not uncommon; more than that should be a big red flag.

Start with your state securities administrator. You will find the addresses and phone numbers listed below. Most can send you background materials on your adviser and tell you about any pending or prior cases or disciplinary actions against both the adviser and the firm. Requests may take a few days to process and there may be a nominal charge for copies of records.

The state securities administrators—along with those from Mexico and the provinces of Canada—all are part of the North American Securities Administrators Association. If you have trouble getting data from your state securities administrator—offices frequently are overwhelmed with requests for information—you might contact NASAA at Suite 310, One Massachusetts Ave. N.W., Washington, DC 20001. Phone 202-737-0900. Web address: www.nasaa.org.

When you have finished with the state agency, put in a precautionary call to the National Association of Securities Dealers public disclosure phone center, 1-800-289-9999, which can tell you whether the NASD if the agency has any complaints or cases pending against member broker-dealers. This is a very quick double-check, which may be helpful if a broker previously worked in another state or has operations in more than one area. Stock brokers generally are NASD members; many financial planners are not.

As this book went to press, NASD Regulation was developing a means to provide ADV and CRD background checks online. For more information, check out www.nasdr.com.

You can also check with the Securities & Exchange Commission (www.sec.gov) to find out if a company is legitimate or if why the agency took action against a broker or firm for wrongdoing (actions that the state securities administrator should have notified you about). Even SEC officials acknowledge, however, that you are likely to get more information from the state authorities; if you want to contact your regional SEC office, you will find the address and phone number listed in the section on filing a complaint.

State and provincial securities administrators:

Alabama

Securities Commission
770 Washington Avenue,
Suite 570
Montgomery, AL 36130-4700
334-242-2984

Alaska

Department of Community &
Economic Development
Division of Banking, Securities,
& Corporations
150 Third Street, Room 217
P.O. Box 110807
Juneau, AK 99811-0807
907-465-2521
www.dced.state.ak.us/bsc/
secur.htm

Arizona

Corporation Commission
1300 West Washington,
Third Floor

Phoenix, AZ 85007
602-542-4242
www.ccsd.cc.state.az.us/
indexNH.html

Arkansas

Securities Department
Heritage West Building—
Room 300
201 East Markham
Little Rock, AR 72201
501-324-9260
www.state.ar.us/arsec

California

Department of Corporations
Suite 750
320 West 4th Street
Los Angeles, CA 90013-1105
213-576-7643
www.corp.ca.gov/srd/
security.htm

Colorado

Division of Securities
1580 Lincoln, Suite 420
Denver, CO 80203
303-894-2320
www.dora.state.co.us/Securities

Connecticut

Department of Banking
260 Constitution Plaza
Hartford, CT 06103-1800
860-240-8230
www.state.ct.us/dob/pages/
secdiv.htm

Delaware

Division of Securities
Department of Justice
820 North French Street,
5th Floor
Carvel State Office Building
Wilmington, DE 19801
302-577-8424
www.state.de.us

District of Columbia

Department of Insurance and
Securities Regulation
Securities Bureau
810 First Street NE, Suite 701
Washington, DC 20002
202-727-8000

Florida

Office of Comptroller
Department of Banking
101 East Gaines Street
Plaza Level, The Capitol
Tallahassee, FL 32399-0350
850-410-9805

Georgia

Office of the Secretary of State
Division of Securities & Business
Regulation
Two Martin Luther King, Jr.
Drive SE
802 West Tower
Atlanta, GA 30334
404-656-3920
www.sos.state.ga.us/securities/
default.htm

Hawaii

Department of Commerce &
Consumer Affairs
1010 Richards Street, 2nd Floor
Honolulu, HI 96813
808-586-2744
www.hawaii.gov/dcca/dcca.html

Idaho

Department of Finance
Securities Bureau
700 West State Street, 2nd Floor
Boise, ID 83720

208-332-8004
www.state.id.us./finance/
sec.htm

Illinois

Office of the Secretary of State
Securities Department
17 North State Street, Suite 1100
Chicago, IL 60601
312-793-3384
Springfield office:
520 South Second Street
Suite 200 Lincoln Tower
Springfield, IL 62701
217-782-2256
www.sos.state.il.us/depts/
securities/secflhome.html

Indiana

Office of the Secretary of State
Securities Division
302 West Washington,
Room E-111
Indianapolis, IN 46204
317-232-6681
www.ai.org/sos/security

Iowa

Insurance Division
Securities Bureau
340 E. Maple
Des Moines, IA 50319-0066
515-281-4441
www.state.ia.us/government/
com/ins/security/security.htm

Kansas

Office of the Securities
Commissioner
618 South Kansas Avenue,
2nd Floor
Topeka, KS 66603-3804
785-296-3307
www.cjnetworks.com/fiksecom
Wichita office:
230 E. William, Suite 7080
Wichita, KS 67202
316-337-6280

Kentucky

Department of Financial
Institutions
1025 Capital Center Drive,
Suite 200
Frankfort, KY 40601
502-573-3390
www.dfi.state.ky.us/security/
Security.html

Louisiana

Securities Commission
3445 North Causeway Blvd.,
Suite 509
Metairie, LA 70002
504-846-6970

Maine

Department of Professional &
Financial Regulation
Securities Division

121 State House Station
Augusta, ME 04333-0121
207-624-8551

Maryland

Office of the Attorney General
Division of Securities
200 Saint Paul Place, 20th Floor
Baltimore, MD 21202-2020
410-576-6360
www.oag.state.md.us

Massachusetts

Secretary of the Commonwealth
Securities Division
One Ashburton Place,
Room 1701
Boston, MA 02108
617-727-3548

Michigan

Office of Financial & Insurance
Services
6546 Mercantile Way
Lansing, MI 48909
517-241-6350
www.cis.state.mi.us/corp

Minnesota

Department of Commerce
133 East Seventh Street
St. Paul, MN 55101
651-296-4026
www.commerce.state.mn.us

Mississippi

Secretary of State's Office
Securities Division
202 North Congress Street,
Suite 601
Jackson, MS 39201
601-359-6371

Missouri

Office of the Secretary of State
600 West Main Street
Jefferson City, MO 65101
573-751-4136
http://mosl.sos.state.mo.us

Montana

Office of the State Auditor
Securities Department
840 Helena Avenue
Helena, MT 59604
406-444-2040

Nebraska

Department of Banking &
Finance
Bureau of Securities
1200 N Street, Suite 311
Lincoln, NE 68508
402-471-3445
www.ndbf.org

Nevada

Secretary of State
Securities Division
555 E. Washington Avenue
5th Floor, Suite 5200
Las Vegas, NV 89101
702-486-2440
www.state.nv.us
Reno office:
1105 Terminal Way, Suite 211
Reno, NV 89502
775-688-1855

New Hampshire

Bureau of Securities Regulation
Department of State
State House, Annex—Room 317A
25 Capital Street
Concord, NH 03301
603-271-1463

New Jersey

Department of Law & Public
Safety
Bureau of Securities
153 Halsey Street, 6th Floor
Newark, NJ 07102
973-504-3600

New Mexico

Regulation & Licensing
Department
Securities Division
725 St. Michaels Drive

Santa Fe, NM 87505-7605
505-827-7140 (general
information)

New York

Office of the Attorney General
Investor Protection Securities
Bureau
120 Broadway, 23rd Floor
New York, NY 10271
212-416-8200
www.oag.state.ny.us

North Carolina

Department of the Secretary
of State
Securities Division
300 North Salisbury Street,
Suite 100
Raleigh, NC 27603-5909
919-733-3924
www.secstate.state.nc.us/secstate/
sos.htm

North Dakota

Securities Commissioner
State Capitol, 5th Floor
600 E. Boulevard
Bismarck, ND 58505-0510
701-328-2910

Ohio

Division of Securities
77 South High Street, 22nd Floor
Columbus, OH 43215

614-644-7381
www.securities.state.oh.us

Oklahoma

Department of Securities
First National Center, Suite 860
120 N. Robinson
Oklahoma City, OK 73102
405-280-7700
www.state.ok.us/fiosc

Oregon

Department of Consumer &
Business Services
Division of Finance and
Corporate Securities
350 Winter Street NE, Room 410
Salem, OR 97301-3881
503-378-4387
www.cbs.state.or.us/external/dfcs

Pennsylvania

Securities Commission
Eastgate Office Building
1010 North 7th Street—2nd
Floor
Harrisburg, PA 17102-1410
717-787-8061
www.psc.state.pa.us/PAflExec/
Securities
Philadelphia office:
State Office Building
Suite 1100
Philadelphia, PA 19130-4088
215-560-2088

Pittsburgh office:
806 State Office Building
Pittsburgh, PA 15222-1210
412-565-5083

Puerto Rico

Commissioner of Financial
Institutions
P.O. Box 11855
Fernandez Juncos Station
San Juan, Puerto Rico 00910-
3855
787-723-3131

Rhode Island

Department of Business
Regulation
Securities Division
233 Richmond Street, Suite 232
Providence, RI 02903-4232
401-222-3048
www.doa.state.ri.us

South Carolina

Office of the Attorney General
Securities Division
Rembert C. Dennis Office
Building
1000 Assembly Street
Columbia, SC 29201
803-734-4731
www.scsecurities.com

South Dakota

Division of Securities
118 West Capitol Avenue
Pierre, SD 57501-2000
605-773-4823
www.state.sd.us/dcr/securities/
security.htm

Tennessee

Department of Commerce &
Insurance
Securities Division
Davy Crockett Tower, Suite 680
500 James Robertson Parkway
Nashville, TN 37243-0575
615-741-2947
www.state.tn.us/commerce/
securdiv.html

Texas

State Securities Board
208 East 10th Street, 5th Floor
Austin, TX 78701
512-305-8300
http://www.ssb.state.tx.us

Utah

Division of Securities
Heber M. Wells Building
160 East 300 South, 2nd Floor
Salt Lake City, UT 84111
801-530-6600
www.commerce.state.ut.us

Vermont

Department of Banking,
Insurance, Securities & Health
Care Administration
Securities Division
89 Main Street, 2nd Floor
Montpelier, Vermont 05620
802-828-3420
www.state.vt.us/bis

Virginia

State Corporation Commission
Division of Securities & Retail
Franchising
1300 East Main Street, 9th Floor
Richmond, Virginia 23219
804-371-9051
www.state.va.us/scc/division/srf

Washington

Department of Financial
Institutions
Securities Division
General Administration Building
210 11th Street
3rd Floor West, Room 300
Olympia, WA 98504-1200
360-902-8760
www.wa.gov/dfi/securities

West Virginia

Office of the State Auditor
Securities Division
Building 1, Room W-100

Charleston, WV 25305
304-558-2257
www.wvauditor.com

Wisconsin

Department of Financial
Institutions
Division of Securities
345 W. Washington Ave.,
4th Floor
Madison, WI 53703
608-261-9555
badger.state.wi.us/agencies/dfi

Wyoming

Secretary of State
Securities Division
State Capitol, Room 109
200 W. 24th Street
Cheyenne, WY 82002-0020
307-777-7370
www.soswy.state.wy.us

CANADA

Alberta

Securities Commission
4th Floor, 300—5th Avenue S.W.
Calgary, Alberta
Canada T2P 3C4
403-297-6454
www.albertasecurities.com

British Columbia

Securities Commission
200-865 Hornby Street
Vancouver, British Columbia
V6Z 2H4 Canada
604-899-6500
www.bcsc.bc.ca

Manitoba

Securities Commission
1130-405 Broadway
Winnipeg, Manitoba
R3C 3L6 Canada
204-945-2548

New Brunswick

Securities Administration Branch
133 Prince William Street,
Suite 606
Harbour Building
Saint John, New Brunswick
E2L 4Y9 Canada
506-658-3060

Newfoundland & Labrador

Department of Government
Services and Lands
Securities Division
2nd Floor, West Block
Confederation Building
St. John's, Newfoundland
709-729-4189

Northwest Territories

Securities Registry
Department of Justice
1st Floor Stuart M. Hodgson
Building
5009 49th Street
Yellowknife, Northwest
Territories
X1A 2L9 Canada
867-873-7490

Nova Scotia

Securities Commission
1690 Hollis Street
2nd Floor, Joseph Howe Building
Halifax, Nova Scotia
B3J 3J9 Canada
902-424-7768

Nunavut

Legal Registries
Bag 9500
5102 50th Avenue, Suite #2
Lower Level, Scotia Center
Yellowknife, NT
X1A 2R3 Canada
867-920-6354
ww.gov.nt.ca

Ontario

Securities Commission
20 Queen Street West, Suite 800
Box 55
Toronto, Ontario
M5H 3S8 Canada
416-597-0681

Prince Edward Island

Department of Community
Services and Attorney General
95 Rochford Street, 4th Floor
Charlottetown, Prince Edward
Island
C1A 7N8 Canada
902-368-4552
www.gov.pe.ca

Québec

Commission des valeurs
mobilières du Québec
800 Square Victoria, 22nd Floor
P.O. Box 246
Tour de la Bourse
Stock Exchange Tower
Montreal, Québec
H4Z 1G3 Canada
514-940-2150
www.cvmq.com

Saskatchewan

Securities Commission
800 1920 Broad Street
Regina, Saskatchewan
S4P 3V7 Canada
306-787-5645

Yukon Territory

Corporate Affairs
2134 2nd Avenue, 3rd Floor
Andrew A. Philipsen Law Centre
Whitehorse, Yukon

Appendix 2
State insurance commissioners/independent insurance agents associations

State insurance regulators maintain oversight of insurers' solvency and market practices. They determine whether an insurance company meets the financial standards necessary to sell insurance in your state, and monitor the activities of both insurers and agents.

Most state insurance commissioner's offices can provide consumer information about prices, products and the financial strength of the companies selling insurance within the state. Most insurance commissioner's offices have some form of consumer telephone service for answering inquiries, distributing information on the complaint history, financial ratings and prices offered by individual insurance companies. Some also maintain databases of information on complaints about individual agents.

As an adjunct to checking in with the insurance commissioner, you might want to check with the state association for independent insurance agents. Those organizations not only can help you find independent agents in your area, but some of them will tell you of an agent's disciplinary history. They also provide a second opinion, where if you hear something fishy from an agent, you can contact the state association and run the situation past them; most will quickly provide an expert to answer your question.

Here are the addresses and phone numbers for state insurance commissioners in the United States, Canada and the territories, as well as contact information and web addresses for the independent insurance agents association for each state.

Alabama

Department of Insurance
201 Monroe Street, Suite 1700
Montgomery, AL 36104
334-269-3550

Alabama Independent Insurance
Agents
2918 Clairmont Avenue
Birmingham, AL 35205
205-326-4129
www.aiia.org

Alaska

Division of Insurance
3601 C Street
Suite 1324
Anchorage, AK 99503-5948
907-269-7900

Alaska Independent Insurance
Agents & Brokers
P.O. Box 241846
Anchorage, AK 99524-1846
907-349-2500
www.aiiab.org

American Samoa

Office of the Governor
Pago Pago,
American Samoa 96799
011-684-633-4116

Arizona

Department of Insurance
2910 North 44th Street,

Suite 210
Phoenix, AZ 85018-7256
502-912-8400

Independent Insurance Agents &
Brokers of Arizona
2828 North 36th
Street, #C
Phoenix, AZ 85008-1303
602-956-1851
www.iiabaz.com

Arkansas

Department of Insurance
1200 West 3rd Street
Little Rock, AR 72201
501-371-2600

Independent Insurance
Agents of Arkansas
P.O. Box 24808
Little Rock, AR 72221
501-221-2444
www.iiaa.org/state/ar.htm

California

Department of Insurance
300 Capitol Mall, Suite 1500
Sacramento, CA 95814
916-492-3500
San Francisco office:
45 Fremont Street, 23rd Floor
San Francisco, CA 94102
415-538-4040
Los Angeles office:
300 South Spring Street
Los Angeles, CA 90013
213-346-6400

Insurance Brokers & Agents of
the West
1000 Broadway, #600
Oakland, CA 94607-4033
510-663-7800
http://public.ibawest.com

Colorado

Division of Insurance
1560 Broadway, Suite 850
Denver, CO 80202
303-894-7499

Professional Independent
Insurance Agents of Colorado
1660 South Albion, #518
Denver, CO 80222-4043
303-512-0627
www.iiaa.org/state/co.htm

Connecticut

Department of Insurance
P.O. Box 816
Hartford, CT 06142-0816
860-297-3802

Independent Insurance Agents of
Connecticut
30 Jordan Lane
Wethersfield, CT 06109-1278
860-563-1950
www.iiaa.org/state/ct.htm

District of Columbia

Department Of Insurance &
Securities Regulation
Suite 701

810 First Street, N. E.
Washington, DC 20002
202-727-8000 x3018

Metro Washington Association of
Independent Insurance Agents
127 South Peyton Street
Alexandria, VA 22314
703-706-5446
www.iiav.com

Delaware

Department of Insurance
Rodney Building
841 Silver Lake Boulevard
Dover, DE 19904
302-739-4251

Independent Insurance Agents of
Delaware
600A N.E. Front Street
Milford, DE 19963-1391
302-424-4081
www.iiaa.org/state/de.htm

Florida

Department of Insurance
State Capitol
Plaza Level Eleven
Tallahassee, FL 32399-0300
850-922-3101

Florida Association of Insurance
Agents
P.O. Box 12129
Tallahassee, FL 32317-2129
850-893-4155
www.faia.com

Georgia

Department of Insurance
2 Martin Luther King, Jr. Drive
Floyd Memorial Bldg.,
704 West Tower
Atlanta, GA 30334
404-656-2056

Independent Insurance Agents
of Georgia
P.O. Box 48386
Atlanta, GA 30362-1386
800-878-6487
www.iiag.org/consinfo.htm

Guam

Department of Revenue &
Taxation
Insurance Branch
P.O. Box 23607
GMF, Guam 96921
671-475-1843

Hawaii

Insurance Division
Department of Commerce &
Consumer Affairs
250 S. King Street, 5th Floor
Honolulu, HI 96813
808-586-2790

Hawaii Independent Insurance
Agents Association
1132 Bishop Street, #1408
Honolulu, HI 96813
808-531-3125
www.iiaa.org/state/hi.htm

Idaho

Department of Insurance
700 West State Street,
3rd Floor
Boise, ID 83720-0043
208-334-4250

Independent Insurance Agents
of Idaho
595 South 14th Street
Boise, ID 83702-6836
208-342-9326
www.iiaa.org/state/id.htm

Illinois

Department of Insurance
320 West Washington St.,
4th Floor
Springfield, IL 62767-0001
217-785-0116
Chicago office:
100 West Randolph Street
Suite 15-100
Chicago, IL 60601-3251
312-814-2420

Professional Independent
Insurance Agents of Illinois
4360 Wabash Avenue
Springfield, IL 62707-7009
217-793-6660
www.piiai.org

Indiana

Department of Insurance
311 W. Washington Street,
Suite 300

Indianapolis, IN 46204-2787
317-232-2385

Independent Insurance Agents
of Indiana
3435 West 96th Street
Indianapolis, IN 46268-1102
317-824-3780
www.bigi.org

Iowa

Division of Insurance
330 East Maple Street
Des Moines, IA 50319
515-281-5705

Independent Insurance Agents
of Iowa
4000 Westown Parkway, #200
West Des Moines, IA 50266
515-223-6060
www.iiaiowa.org

Kansas

Department of Insurance
420 S.W. 9th Street
Topeka, KS 66612-1678
785-296-7801

Kansas Association of Insurance
Agents
815 SW Topeka Blvd.
Topeka, KS 66612-1608
785-232-0561
www.kaia.com

Kentucky

Department of Insurance
215 West Main Street
Frankfort, KY 40602-0517
502-564-6027

Independent Insurance Agents of
Kentucky
10221 Linn Station Road
Louisville, KY 40223-3885
502-426-0610
www.iiak.com

Louisiana

Department of Insurance
950 North 5th Street
Baton Rouge, LA 70802
225-342-5423

Independent Insurance Agents of
Louisiana
9818 Bluebonnet Blvd.
Baton Rouge, LA 70810-6442
225-819-8007
www.iial.com

Maine

Bureau of Insurance
Department of Professional &
Financial Regulation
State Office Building, Station 34
Augusta, ME 04333-0034
207-624-8475

Maine Insurance Agents
Association
432 Western Avenue

Augusta, ME 04330-6014
207-623-1875
www.meiaa.com

Maryland

Insurance Administration
525 St. Paul Place
Baltimore, MD 21202-2272
410-468-2090

Independent Insurance Agents of
Maryland
2408 Peppermill Drive
Glen Burnie, MD 21061-3257
410-766-0600
www.iiamd.org

Massachusetts

Division of Insurance
One South Station, 4th Floor
Boston, MA 02110
617-521-7301

Massachusetts Association of
Independent Agents
137 Pennsylvania Avenue
Framingham, MA 01701-8837
508-628-5452
www.massagent.com/govt.htm

Michigan

Insurance Bureau
Department of Commerce
611 W. Ottawa St.,
2nd Floor North
Lansing, MI 48933-1020
517-373-9273

Michigan Association of
Insurance Agents
P.O. Box 80620
Lansing, MI 48908-0620
517-323-9473
www.michagent.org

Minnesota

Department of Commerce
121 7th Place East, Suite 200
St. Paul, MN 55101-2145
651-296-6025

Minnesota Independent
Insurance Agents
7300 Metro Blvd., #605
Edina, MN 55439-2313
612-835-4180
www.miia.org

Mississippi

Insurance Department
1804 Walter Sillers Building
550 High Street
Jackson, MS 39201
601-359-3569

Independent Insurance Agents of
Mississippi
1818 Crane Ridge Drive
Jackson, MS 39216
601-354-4595
www.msagent.org

Missouri

Department of Insurance
301 West High Street, 6 North

Jefferson City, MO 65102-0690
573-751-4126

Missouri Association of Insurance
Agents
P.O. Box 1785
Jefferson City, MO 65102
573-893-4301
www.missouriagent.org

Montana

Department of Insurance
840 Helena Avenue
Helena, MT 59601
406-444-2040

Independent Insurance Agents
of Montana
1200 North Montana Avenue,
Suite #2
Helena, MT 59601
406-442-9555
www.iiaa.org/state/mt.htm

Nebraska

Department of Insurance
Terminal Building,
Suite 400
941 'O' Street
Lincoln, NE 68508
402-471-2201

Independent Insurance Agents
of Nebraska
P.O. Box 30716
Lincoln, NE 68503-0716
402-476-2951
www.iian.org

Nevada

Division of Insurance
788 Fairview Drive, Suite 300
Carson City, NV 89701-5753
775-687-4270

Nevada Independent Insurance
Agents
310 North Stewart Street
Carson City, NV 89701-4207
775-882-1366
www.niia.org

New Hampshire

Department of Insurance
56 Old Suncook Road
Concord, NH 03301
603-271-2261

Independent Insurance Agents of
New Hampshire
125 Airport Road
Concord, NH 03301-7300
603-224-3965
www.iianh.com

New Jersey

Department of Insurance
20 West State Street CN325
Trenton, NJ 08625
609-292-5360

Independent Insurance Agents
of New Jersey
P.O. Box 3230
Trenton, NJ 08619-0230
609-587-4333
www.iianh.com

New Mexico

Department of Insurance
P.O. Drawer 1269
Santa Fe, NM 87504-1269
505-827-4601

Independent Insurance Agents of
New Mexico
P.O. Box 25447
Albuquerque, NM 87125-5447
505-843-7231
www.iianm.org

New York

Department of Insurance
25 Beaver Street
New York, NY 10004-2319
212-480-2289
Albany office:
Agency Building One
Empire State Plaza
Albany, NY 12257
518-474-6600

Independent Insurance Agents
Association of New York
109 Twin Oaks Drive
Syracuse, NY 13206-1205
315-432-9111
www.iiaany.com

North Carolina

Department of Insurance
P.O. Box 26387
Raleigh, NC 27611
919-733-3058

Independent Insurance Agents of
North Carolina
P.O. Box 10097
Raleigh, NC 27605-0097
919-828-4371
www.iianc.com

North Dakota

Department of Insurance
600 E. Boulevard
Bismarck, ND 58505-0320
701-328-2440

Independent Insurance Agents of
North Dakota
418 East Rosser Avenue
Bismarck, ND 58501-4085
701-258-4000
www.iiaa.org/state/nd.htm

Ohio

Department of Insurance
2100 Stella Court
Columbus, OH 43215-1067
614-644-2658

Independent Insurance Agents
Association of Ohio
P.O. Box 758
Columbus, OH 43216-0758
614-464-3100
www.iiaoh.org

Oklahoma

Department of Insurance
2401 N.W. 23rd Street, Suite 28

Oklahoma City, OK 73107
405-521-2828

Oklahoma Association of
Insurance Agents
1000 NW 50th Street
Oklahoma City, OK 73118
405-840-4426
www.oaia.org

Oregon

Division of Insurance
Department of Consumer &
Business Services
350 Winter Street NE, Room 200
Salem, OR 97310-0700
503-947-7980

Independent Insurance Agents
of Oregon
5100 SW Macadam,
Suite 350
Portland, OR 97201-6102
503-274-4000
www.iiao.org

Pennsylvania

Insurance Department
1326 Strawberry Square,
13th Floor
Harrisburg, PA 17120
717-783-0442

Independent Insurance Agents
of Pennsylvania
2807 North Front Street
Harrisburg, PA 17110

717-236-4427
www.iiaa.org/state/pa.htm

Puerto Rico

Department of Insurance
Cobian's Plaza Building
1607 Ponce de Leon Avenue
Santurce, Puerto Rico 00909
787-722-8686

Rhode Island

Insurance Division
Department of Business
Regulation
233 Richmond Street, Suite 233
Providence, RI 02903-4233
401-222-2223

Independent Insurance Agents of
Rhode Island
2400 Post Road
Warwick, RI 02886-2208
401-732-2400
www.iiari.com

South Carolina

Department of Insurance
1612 Marion Street
Columbia, SC 29201
803-737-6160

Independent Insurance Agents of
South Carolina
P.O. Box 210008
Columbia, SC 29221
803-731-9460
www.iiasc.com

South Dakota

Division of Insurance
Department of Commerce &
Regulation
118 West Capitol Avenue
Pierre, SD 57501-2000
605-773-3563

Independent Insurance Agents of
South Dakota
222 East Capital Street, #17
Pierre, SD 57501-2564
605-224-6234
www.iiasd.org

Tennessee

Department of Commerce &
Insurance
Volunteer Plaza
500 James Robertson Parkway
Nashville, TN 37243-0565
615-741-2241

Insurors of Tennessee
2500 Hillsboro Road, #200
Nashville, TN 37212-5625
615-385-1898
www.insurors.org

Texas

Department of Insurance
333 Guadalupe Street
Austin, TX 78701
512-463-6464

Independent Insurance Agents of
Texas

P.O. Box 684487
Austin, TX 78768-4488
512-476-6281
www.taia.com

Utah

Department of Insurance
3110 State Office Building
Salt Lake City, UT 84114-1201
801-538-3800

Independent Insurance Agents
Association of Utah
4885 S 900 East, #302
Salt Lake City, UT 84117-5746
801-269-1200
www.iiaa.org/state/ut.htm

Vermont

Division of Insurance
Department of Banking,
Insurance & Securities
89 Main Street, Drawer 20
Montpelier, VT 05620-3101
802-828-3301

Vermont Insurance Agents
Association
P.O. Box 1387
Montpelier, VT 05601-1387
802-229-5884
www.iiaa.org/state/vt.htm

Virgin Islands

Division of Banking & Insurance
1131 King Street, Suite 101
Christiansted

St. Croix, Virgin Islands 00820
340-773-6449

Virginia

State Corporation Commission
Bureau of Insurance
P.O. Box 1157
Richmond, VA 23218
804-371-9694

Independent Insurance Agents of
Virginia
8600 Mayland Drive
Richmond, VA 23294
804-747-9300
www.iiav.com

Washington

Office of the Insurance
Commissioner
14th Avenue & Water Streets
P.O. Box 40255
Olympia, WA 98504-0255
360-753-7301

Independent Insurance Agents &
Brokers of Washington
15015 Main Street, #205
Bellevue, WA 98007-5229
425-649-0102
www.iiaa.org/state/WA.HTM

West Virginia

Department of Insurance
P.O. Box 50540
Charleston, WV 25305-0540
304-558-3354

Professional Independent
Insurance Agents of West
Virginia
179 Summers Street at Lee, #321
Charleston, WV 25301
304-342-2440
www.piiawv.org

Wisconsin

Office of the Commissioner of
Insurance
121 E. Wilson
Madison, WI 53702
608-267-1233

Independent Insurance Agents of
Wisconsin
725 John Nolen Drive
Madison, WI 53713-5160
608-256-4429
www.iiaw.com

Wyoming

Department of Insurance
Herschler Building
122 West 25th Street, 3rd East
Cheyenne, WY 82002-0440
307-777-7401

Association of Wyoming
Insurance Agents
P.O. Box 189
Sundance, WY 82729-0189
307-283-2052
www.awia.com

Appendix 3
Tax preparer/CPA organizations

Because anyone who wants to can hang out a sign and operate as a tax preparer, it is not always easy to check a tax preparer's background or expertise.

That being the case, you may decide to pursue an adviser with an advanced credential. Nationally, you can check on advisers with the following agencies:

For enrolled agents:

The National Association of
Enrolled Agents
200 Orchard Ridge Drive,
Suite 302
Gaithersburg, MD 20878-1978
301-212-9608
800-984-4339 for referrals

For accredited tax preparers (ATP) or accredited tax advisors (ATA):

Accreditation Council for
Accountancy and Taxation
1010 North Fairfax St.
Alexandria, VA 22314
703-549-6400

For certified public accountants (CPA):

American Institute of Certified
Public Accountants
1121 Avenue of the Americas
New York, NY 10036-8775
800-862-4272.

In most areas, the state society of CPAs will provide more detail than
the national organization. With that in mind, you are probably better
off contacting the agency for your state; listed below:

Alabama Society of CPAs
P.O. Box 5000
Montgomery, AL 36103-5000
334-834-7310
www.ascpa.org

Alaska Society of CPAs
341 W. Tudor, Suite 105
Anchorage, AK 99503
907-562-4334

Arizona Society of CPAs
2120 N. Central Ave., Suite 100
Phoenix, AZ 85004
602-252-4144
www.ascpa.com

Arkansas Society of CPAs
11300 Executive Center Dr.
Little Rock, AR 72211-5352
501-664-8739
www.arcpa.org

California Society of CPAs
275 Shoreline Drive
Redwood City, CA 94065-1407

650-802-2600
www.calcpa.org

Colorado Society of CPAs
7979 East Tufts Ave., Suite 500
Denver, CO 80237-2843
303-773-2877

Connecticut Society of CPAs
845 Brook St., Bldg. 2
Rocky Hill, CT 06067-3405
860-280-1100
www.cscpa.org

Delaware Society of CPAs
3520 Silverside Rd., Suite 8
Wilmington, DE 19810-4941
302-478-7442

**Greater Washington (DC)
Society of CPAs**
1023 15th St. N.W.,
8th Floor
Washington, DC 20005-2602
202-789-1844
www.gwscpa.org

Florida Institute of CPAs
P.O. Box 5437
Tallahassee, FL 32314-5437
850-224-2727
www.ficpa.org

Georgia Society of CPAs
3340 Peachtree Road N.E.,
Suite 2750
Atlanta, GA 30326-1026
404-231-8676
www.gscpa.org

Guam Society of CPAs
361 South Marine Drive
Tamuning, GU 96911
671-646-3884

Hawaii Society of CPAs
P.O. Box 1754
Honolulu, HI 96806
808-537-9475

Idaho Society of CPAs
250 Bobwhite Court, Suite 240
Boise, ID 83706
208-344-6261

Illinois CPA Society
222 South Riverside Plaza,
16th Floor
Chicago, IL 60606
312-993-0407
www.icpas.org

Indiana CPA Society
P.O. Box 40069
Indianapolis, IN 46240-0069

317-726-5000
www.incpas.org

Iowa Society of CPAs
950 Office Park Road, Suite 300
West Des Moines, IA 50265-2548
515-223-8161
www.iacpa.org

Kansas Society of CPAs
400 Croix Place
Topeka, KS 66611
785-267-6460

Kentucky Society of CPAs
1735 Alliant Ave.
Louisville, KY 40299
502-266-5272
www.kycpa.org

Society of Louisiana CPAs
2400 Veterans Blvd., Suite 500
Kenner, LA 70062
504-464-1040
www.lcpa.org

Maine Society of CPAs
153 US Route 1, Suite 8
Scarborough, ME 04074-9053
207-883-6090
www.mecoa.org

Maryland Association of CPAs
1300 York Rd., Building 10,
Suite C
Luthersville, MD 21093
410-296-6250
www.macpa.org

Massachusetts Society of CPAs
105 Chauncey Street, 10th Floor
Boston, MA 02111
617-556-4000
www.mscpaonline.org

Michigan Society of CPAs
5480 Corporate Dr., Suite 200
Troy, MI 48098
248-267-3700
www.michcpa.org

Minnesota Society of CPAs
N.W. Financial Center, #1230
7900 Xerxes Avenue South
Bloomington, MN 55431
612-831-2707
www.mncpa.org

Mississippi Society of CPAs
246 Highland Village
Jackson, MS 39211
601-366-3473

Missouri Society of CPAs
P.O. Box 419042
St. Louis, MO 63141-9042
314-997-7966
www.mocpa.org

Montana Society of CPAs
P.O. Box 138
Helena, MT 59624-0138
406-442-7301

Nebraska Society of CPAs
635 South 14th St.,
Suite 330

Lincoln, NE 68508
402-476-8482

Nevada Society of CPAs
5250 Neil Road, Suite 205
Reno, NV 89502
775-826-6800
www.nevadacpa.org

New Hampshire Society of CPAs
1750 Elm St., Suite 403
Manchester, NH 03104
603-622-1999
www.nhscpa.org

New Jersey Society of CPAs
425 Eagle Rock Ave.
Roseland, NJ 07068-1723
973-226-4494
www.njscpa.org

New Mexico Society of CPAs
1650 University N.E., Suite 450
Albuquerque, NM 87102
505-246-1699
www.nmcpa.org

New York State Society of CPAs
530 Fifth Ave., 5th Floor
New York, NY 10036-5101
212-719-8300

**North Carolina Association
of CPAs**
3100 Gateway Center Blvd.
Morrisville, NC 27560
919-469-1040
www.ncacpa.org

North Dakota Society of CPAs
2701 South Columbia Rd.
Grand Forks, ND 58201-6029
701-775-7100
www.ndscpa.org

Ohio Society of CPAs
P.O. Box 1810
Dublin, OH 43017-7810
614-764-2727
www.ohio-cpa.com

Oklahoma Society of CPAs
50 Penn Place
1900 N.W. Expressway, #910
Oklahoma City, OK 73118
405-841-3800
www.oscpa.com

Oregon Society of CPAs
P.O. Box 4555
Beaverton, OR 97076-4555
503-641-7200
www.orcpa.org

Pennsylvania Institute of CPAs
1650 Arch Street, 17th Floor
Philadelphia, PA 19103-2099
215-496-9272
www.picpa.org

Colegio de Contadores Publicos Autorizados de Puerto Rico
Edificio Capital Center
Ave. Arterial Hostos #3,
Buzon 1401
Hato Rey, PR 00918
787-754-1950

www.colegiocpa.com

Rhode Island Society of CPAs
One Franklin Square
Providence, RI 02903
401-331-5720
www.riscpa.org

South Carolina Association of CPAs
570 Chris Drive
West Columbia, SC 29169
803-791-4181
www.scacpa.org

South Dakota CPA Society
P.O. Box 1798
Sioux Falls, SD 57101-1798
605-334-3848

Tennessee Society of CPAs
Box 187
Brentwood, TN 37024-0187
615-377-3825
www.tncpa.org

Texas Society of CPAs
512 E. Riverside Dr., Suite 100
Austin, TX 78704-1356
512-445-0044
www.tscpa.net

Utah Association of CPAs
220 E. Morris Ave.,
Suite 320
Salt Lake City, UT 84115
801-446-8022
www.uacpa.org

Vermont Society of CPAs
100 State Street
Montpelier, VT 05602
802-229-4939

Virgin Islands Society of CPAs
P.O. Box 3016
Christiansted
St. Croix, VI 08822-3016
340-773-4305

Virginia Society of CPAs
4309 Cox Road
Glen Allen, 23060
804-270-5344
www.vscpa.com

Washington Society of CPAs
902 140th Ave. N.E.
Bellevue, WA 98005

425-644-4800
www.wscpa.org

West Virginia Society of CPAs
P.O. Drawer 1673
Charleston, WV 25326
304-342-5461
www.wvscpa.org

Wisconsin Institute of CPAs
P.O. Box 1010
Brookfield, WI 53008-1010
262-785-0445
www.wicpa.org

Wyoming Society of CPAs
1603 Capitol Ave., Suite 413
Cheyenne, WY 82001
307-634-7039
www.wyocpa.org

Appendix 4
State Bar Associations

Here is a state-by-state listing of bar associations, including addresses, phone numbers and web sites. There may also be a regional or local bar association that can provide you with more detailed information about lawyers in the community in which you live.

Alabama
415 Dexter St.
Montgomery, AL 36104
334-269-1515
www.alabar.org

Alaska
510 L. St., Suite 602
Anchorage, AK 99501
907-272-7469
www.alaskabar.org

Arizona
111 West Monroe, Suite 1800
Phoenix, AZ 85003-1742
602-252-4804
www.azbar.org

Arkansas
400 W. Markham
Little Rock, AR 72201

501-375-4606
www.arkbar.com

California
180 Howard Street
San Francisco, CA 94105
415-538-2000
www.calbar.org

Colorado
1900 Grant St.,
Suite 950
Denver, CO 80203
303-860-1115
www.cobar.org

Connecticut
30 Bank Street
New Britain, CT 06050-0350
860-223-4400
www.ctbar.org

Delaware
1201 Orange Street,
Suite 1100
Wilmington, DE 19801
302-658-5279
www.dsba.org

District of Columbia
1250 H St. N.W.,
6th Floor
Washington, DC 20005-5937
202-737-4700
www.dcbar.org

Florida
650 Apalachee Pkway.
Tallahassee, FL 32399-2300
850-561-5600
www.flabar.org

Georgia
800 The Hurt Building
50 Hurt Plaza
Atlanta, GA 30303
404-527-8700
www.gabar.org

Hawaii
1132 Bishop St., Suite 906
Honolulu, HI 96813
808-537-1868
www.hsba.org

Idaho
P.O. Box 895
Boise, ID 83701
208-334-4500
www.state.id.us/isb

Illinois
Illinois Bar Center
Springfield, IL 62701
217-525-1760
www.illinoisbar.org

Indiana
230 E. Ohio St.,
4th Floor
Indianapolis, IN 46204-2119
317-639-5465
www.ai.org/isba

Iowa
521 E. Locust St.,
Third Floor
Des Moines, IA 50309
515-243-3179
www.iowabar.org

Kansas
1200 SW Harrison St.
Topeka, KS 66612-1806
785-234-5696
www.ksbar.org

Kentucky
514 W. Main St.
Frankfort, KY 40601-1883
502-564-3795
www.kybar.org

Louisiana
601 St. Charles St.
New Orleans, LA 70130-3404
504-566-1600
www.lsba.org

Maine
124 State St.
Augusta, ME 04332-0788
207-622-7523
www.mainebar.org

Maryland
520 W. Fayette St.
Baltimore, MD 21201
410-685-7878
www.msba.org

Massachusetts
20 West St.
Boston, MA 02111
617-542-3602
www.massbar.org

Michigan
306 Townsend St.
Lansing, MI 48933-2083
517-346-6300
www.michbar.org

Minnesota
600 Nicollet Mall, Suite 380
Minneapolis, MN 55402
612-333-1183
www.mnbar.org

Mississippi
643 N. State St.
Jackson, MS 39225-2168
601-948-4471
www.msbar.org

Missouri
326 Monroe St.
Jefferson City, MO 65101

573-635-4128
www.mobar.org

Montana
P.O. Box 577
Helena, MT 59624
406-442-7660
www.montanabar.org

Nebraska
635 S. 14th St.
Lincoln, NE 68501
402-475-7091
www.nebar.org

Nevada
600 E. Charleston Blvd.
Las Vegas, NV 89104
702-382-2200
www.nvbar.org

New Hampshire
112 Pleasant St.
Concord, NH 03301-2947
603-224-6942
www.nhbar.org

New Jersey
New Jersey Law Center
One Constitution Square
New Brunswick, NJ 08901-1500
732-249-5000
www.njsba.com

New Mexico
P.O. Box 25883
Albuquerque, NM 87125
505-842-6132
www.nmbar.org

New York
One Elk St.
Albany, NY 12207
518-463-3200
www.nysba.org

North Carolina
P.O. Box 25908
Raleigh, NC 27611-5908
919-828-4620
www.ncbar.com

North Dakota
515 1/2 E. Broadway, Suite 101
Bismarck, ND 58501
701-255-1404
www.sband.org

Ohio
1700 Lake Shore Drive
Columbus, OH43204
614-487-2050
www.ohiobar.org

Oklahoma
1901 N. Lincoln Blvd.
Oklahoma City, OK 73152-3036
405-416-7000
www.okbar.org

Oregon
5200 S.W. Meadows Rd.
Lake Oswego, OR 97035
503-620-0222
www.osbar.org

Pennsylvania
100 South St.
Harrisburg, PA 17108-0186

717-238-6715
www.pa-bar.org

Rhode Island
115 Cedar St.
Providence, RI 02903
401-421-5740
www.ribar.com

South Carolina
950 Taylor St.
Columbia, SC 29202
803-799-6653
www.scbar.org

South Dakota
222 E. Capitol Ave.
Pierre, SD 57501-2596
605-224-7554
www.sdbar.org

Tennessee
3622 West End Ave.
Nashville, TN 37205
615-383-7421
www.tba.org

Texas
1414 Colorado
Austin, TX 78711
512-463-1463
www.texasbar.com

Utah
645 S. 200 E.
Salt Lake City, UT 84111
801-531-9077
www.utahbar.org

Vermont
P.O. Box 100
Montpelier, VT 05601-0100
802-223-2020
www.vtbar.org

Virginia
707 E. Main St., Suite 1500
Richmond 23219-2800
804-775-0500
www.vsb.org

Washington
2101 Fourth Avenue,
Fourth Floor
Seattle, WA 98121-2330
206-443-9722
www.wsba.org

West Virginia
2006 Kanawha Blvd. E.
Charleston, WV 25311-2204
304-558-2456
www.wvbar.org

Wisconsin
P.O. Box 7158
Madison, WI 53707-7158
608-257-3838
www.wisbar.org

Wyoming
500 Randall Ave.
Cheyenne, WY 82001
307-632-9061
www.wyomingbar.org

Appendix 5
State Boards of Realtors

When it comes to performing background checks, getting referrals and filing complaints about real estate agents, state and local Boards of Realtors are a focal point of reference. Here are the addresses, phone numbers and web sites for the state boards. To find your local board, contact the Information Central service for the National Association of Realtors at 1-800-874-6500 or check out the group's web site at www.realtor.com.

Alabama Association of Realtors
522 Washington Ave.
Montgomery, AL 36104
334-262-3808
www.alabamarealtors.com

Alaska Association of Realtors
741 Sesame Street, Suite 100
Anchorage, AK 99503
907-563-7133
http://alaskarealtors.com/aar

Arizona Association of Realtors
255 E. Osborn Rd., Suite 200
Phoenix, AZ 85012-2327
602-248-7787
www.aaronline.com

Arkansas Realtors Association
204 Executive Ct. Suite 300
Little Rock, AK 72205
501-225-2020
www.arkansasrealtors.com

California Association of Realtors
525 South Virgil Ave.
Los Angeles, CA 90020
213-739-8200
www.car.org

Colorado Association of Realtors
308 Inverness Way South
Englewood, CO 80112-5818
303-790-7099
www.colorealtor.org

Connecticut Association of
Realtors
111 Founders Plaza,
Suite 1101
East Hartford, CT 06108-3296
860-290-6601
www.ctrealtor.com

Delaware Association of Realtors
9 East Loockerman St.,
Suite 315
Dover, DE 19901
302-734-4444
www.delawarerealtor.com

Washington DC Association of
Realtors
1818 N Street NW, Suite T-50
Washington, DC 20036
202-887-6213
www.gwcar.org

Florida Association of Realtors
P.O. Box 725025
Orlando, FL 32872-5025
407-438-1400
http://fl.realtorplace.com

Georgia Association of Realtors
3200 Presidential Drive
Atlanta GA 30340-3981
770-451-1831
www.garealtor.com

Guam Board of Realtors
P.O. Box 5786
Agana, GU 96910
011-671-477-2081

Hawaii Association of Realtors
1136 12th Ave.,
Suite 220
Honolulu, HI 96816-3793
808-733-7060
www.hawaiirealtors.com

Idaho Association of Realtors
1450 West Bannock St.
Boise, ID 83702
208-342-3585
www.idahorealtors.com

Illinois Association of Realtors
Box 19451
Springfield, IL 62794-9451
217-529-2600
www.illinoisrealtor.org

Indiana Association of Realtors
7301 N. Shadeland
Indianapolis, IN 46250
317-842-0890
www.indianarealtors.com

Iowa Association of Realtors
999 Oakridge Dr.
Des Moines, IA 50314-2197
515-244-2294

Kansas Association of Realtors
3644 S.W. Burlingame Rd.
Topeka, KS 66611
913-267-3610

Kentucky Association of Realtors
161 Prosperous Pl.
Lexington, KY 40509-1804

606-263-7377
www.kar.com

Louisiana Realtors Association
P.O. Box 14780
Baton Rouge, LA 70898
504-923-2210
www.larealtors.org

Maine Association of Realtors
19 Community Dr.
Augusta, ME 04330
207-662-7501
www.mainerealtors.com

Maryland Association of Realtors
2594 Riva Rd.
Annapolis, MD 21401-7406
410-841-6080
www.mdrealtor.org

Massachusetts Association of
Realtors
256 Second Ave.
Waltham, MA 02451
781-890-3700
http://ma.living.net

Michigan Association of Realtors
P.O. Box 40725
Lansing, MI 48901-7925
517-372-8890
www.mirealtors.com

Minnesota Association of
Realtors
5750 Lincoln Dr.
Edina, MN 55436
612-935-8313

Mississippi Association of
Realtors
555 Park Dr., Suite 301
Jackson, MI 39208-8805
601-932-5241

Missouri Association of Realtors
P.O. Box 1327
Columbia, MO 65205
314-445-8400

Montana Association of Realtors
208 North Montana, Suite 105
Helena, MT 59601
406-443-4032
www.mtmar.com

Nebraska Realtors Association
145 S. 56th St., Suite 100
Lincoln, NE 68510-2150
402-488-4303

Nevada Association of Realtors
P.O. Box 7338
Reno, NV 89510-7338
702-829-5911
www.nvrealtors.org

New Hampshire Association of
Realtors
115 A Airport Road, Box 550
Concord, NH 03302-0550
603-225-5549
www.nhar.com

New Jersey Association of
Realtors
P.O. Box 2098
Edison, NJ 08818-2098

732-494-5616
www.njar.com

Realtors Association of New
Mexico
P.O. Box 4190
Santa Fe, NM 87502-4190
505-982-2442
www.nmrealtor.com

New York State Association
of Realtors
P.O. Box 122
Albany, NY 12260
518-463-0300
www.nysar.com

North Carolina Association
of Realtors
901 Seawell Rd.
Greensboro, NC 27407
336-294-1415
www.realtor.org

North Dakota Association
of Realtors
1120 College Dr., Suite 112
Bismarck, ND 58501
701-258-2361

Ohio Association of Realtors
200 East Town St.
Columbus, OH 43215
614-228-6675
www.ohiorealtors.org

Oklahoma Association
of Realtors

9807 N. Broadway
Oklahoma City, OK 73114
405-848-9944
www.oklahomarealtors.com

Oregon Association of Realtors
P.O. Box 351
Salem, OR 97308-0351
503-362-3645
http://or.realtorplace.com

Pennsylvania Association
of Realtors
4501 Chambers Hill Rd.
Harrisburg, PA 17111-2406
717-561-1303
www.parealtor.org

Puerto Rico Association of
Realtors
P.O. Box 8998
Santurce, PR 00910-0998
809-725-1325
www.Prealtor.com

Rhode Island Association
of Realtors
100 Bignall St.
Warwick, RI 02888-1005
401-785-3650
www.riliving.com

South Carolina Association
of Realtors
P.O. Box 21827
Columbia, SC 29221
803-772-5206
http://screaltors.com

South Dakota Association
of Realtors
120 North Euclid
Pierre, SD 57501-2521
605-224-0554
www.sdrealtor.org

Tennessee Association of Realtors
P.O. Box 121149
Nashville, TN 37212-1149
615-321-0515
www.tarnet.com

Texas Association of Realtors
P.O. Box 2246
Austin, TX 78768-2246
512-480-8200
www.tar.org

Utah Association of Realtors
5710 South Green Street
Murray, UT 84123
801-268-4747
www.utahrealtors.com

Vermont Association of Realtors
P.O. Box 1074
Montpelier, VT 05602
802-229-0513
www.vtrealtor.com

Virgin Islands Association of
Realtors
3009 Orange Grove Shopping
Center 13

Christiansted, VI 00820-4313
809-773-1855

Virginia Association of Realtors
10231 Telegraph Rd.
Glen Allen, VA 23059-4578
804-264-5033
www.VARealtor.com

Washington Association
of Realtors
P.O. Box 719
Olympia, WA 98507-0719
360-943-3100
www.warealtor.com

West Virginia Association
of Realtors
2110 Kanawha Blvd. East
Charleston, WV 25311
304-342-7600
www.wvrealtors.com

Wisconsin Realtors Association
4801 Forest Run Rd.,
Suite 201
Madison, WI 53704-7337
608-241-2047
www.wra.org

Wyoming Association
of Realtors
P.O. Box 2312
Casper, WY 82602-2312
307-237-4085

Appendix 6
Online consumer resources

When it comes to finding good financial advisers, researching candidate backgrounds, getting updates on the latest developments or filing complaints against advisers who have done you wrong, there is no place like the Internet, where you can access the organizations that oversee virtually every type of adviser.

What follows are web addresses and descriptions for the various organizations that will help you most in your search for an adviser, either by providing data and information or educational materials. All of these sites are independent and non-commercial, and most are run by industry groups or government agencies. That doesn't mean you can't get good information from any of the thousands of commercial personal finance sites out there, it simply means that these addresses—listed in alphabetical order—should be visited while you work on hiring or firing a financial adviser.

Alliance for Investor Education
www.investoreducation.org
The Alliance for Investor Education is dedicated to facilitating greater understanding of investing, investments and the financial markets among current and prospective investors. It pursues educational initiatives and joins with other groups to develop and provide objective information for consumers.

Certified Financial Planner Board of Standards

www.cfp-board.org

The CFP Board is a professional regulatory group that owns and licenses the CFP credential. Consumers can contact the agency to confirm if a financial planner is currently licensed, to check a CFP's disciplinary history, or to lodge a complaint against a CFP.

Consumer Information Center

www.pueblo.gsa.gov

The federal government and its agencies produce hundreds of consumer publications on all manner of subjects, from how to get good deals on various goods and services to spotting fraud. A large number of publications cover financial planning and investing. At this web site, you can not only see what's available, you can view the ones that interest you for free.

Consumer World

www.consumerworld.org

A public service site, Consumer World has gathered over 1,750 of the most useful consumer resources on the Internet and categorized them for easy access. You can file complaints with government agencies, Better Business Bureaus or a company's consumer affairs department; you also can access hundreds of consumer booklets (many of which were developed by the groups running other web sites listed in this appendix).

Council of Better Business Bureaus

www.bbb.org

This organization runs a network of local and regional agencies that log, file and pursue complaints against business large and small all across the country. It also provides consumer resources both to guard against fraud and, through its filings, to find out if a company or individual has troubled clients before.

You can use this web site to file complaints, but you may want to deal with the local office. You can find the nearest BBB office to your home through a link on the site, or by clicking directly into www.bbb.org/BBBComplaints/lookup.asp.

Commodity Futures Trading Commission

www.cftc.gov

The CFTC was created by Congress in 1974 as an independent agency with the mandate to regulate commodity futures and option markets in the United States. The agency protects market participants against manipulation, abusive trade practices and fraud.

Federal Trade Commission

www.ftc.gov

The Federal Trade Commission enforces a variety of federal antitrust and consumer protection laws. The Commission seeks to ensure that the nation's markets function competitively, and are vigorous, efficient, and free of undue restrictions. From this site, you can e-mail a complaint, learn more about companies you are dealing with and where to find them, get important consumer tips and read all you need to know about this Government agency.

Financial Planning Association

www.fpanet.com

This is the web site of the Financial Planning Association. As such, it offers referrals, as well as consumer information and brochures.

Investing Online Resource Center

www.investingonline.org

The Investing Online Resource Center is a non-commercial organization that tries to provide unbiased help and information to people who invest online or are considering investing online. It has links to independent ratings of online brokerage firms and other consumer-friendly data that will help an investor shop around.

Investment Dealers Association of Canada

www.ida.ca

Loosely speaking, the Investment Dealers Association of Canada is the Canadian equivalent of the National Association of Securities Dealers in the United States. It is a national self-regulatory organization and trade association of the securities industry, regulating the activities of investment dealers in terms of both their capital adequacy and conduct. Investor protection is one of this groups priorities, and the web site helps consumers walk through the complaint process.

Investor Protection Trust

www.investorprotection.org

The Investor Protection Trust (IPT) provides independent, objective information needed by consumers to make informed investment decisions. Founded in 1993 as part of a multi-state settlement to resolve charges of misconduct, IPT has two major functions: serving as an independent source of non-commercial investor education materials and assisting in the prosecution of securities fraud. IPT operates programs under its own auspices and uses grants to underwrite important initiatives carried out by other organizations.

NASD Regulation

www.nasdr.com

NASD Regulation, Inc. is the independent subsidiary of the National Association of Securities Dealers, Inc. charged with regulating the securities industry and The Nasdaq Stock Market. NASD Regulation's jurisdiction extends to over 5,400 firms with more than 58,000 branch offices, and over 505,000 securities industry professionals. Regulation accomplishes this oversight through the registration, education, testing and examination of member firms and their employees, and through the creation and enforcement of rules designed for the ultimate benefit and protection of investors.

NASDR's web site includes its "public disclosure program," where you can do a background check of a broker. As this book went to press, the organization was developing a way to view a financial planner's Form ADV online.

National Association of Personal Financial Advisors

www.napfa.org

This is a membership organization of fee-only financial planners. The web site offers referrals, as well as information on fee-only planning.

National Association of Securities Dealers (NASD)

www.nasd.com

The largest self-regulatory agency in the securities business, the NASD is the parent organization of the Nasdaq-Amex Market Group and also oversees NASD Regulation. It is that regulatory group's web site that is most useful to consumers, but anyone looking for broad market information might look here. In addition, you might check out NASD Individual Investor Services at www.investor.nasd.com.

National Fraud Information Center

www.fraud.org

The NFIC was originally established in 1992 by the National Consumers League, the oldest nonprofit consumer organization in the United States, to fight the growing menace of telemarketing fraud by improving prevention and enforcement. The NFIC helps consumers get advice about telephone solicitations and report possible telemarketing fraud to law enforcement agencies; as such, this is an agency to contact if you are concerned that an adviser's pitch is not on the up-and-up.

In addition to the web site, you can call the NFIC hotline toll-free at 800-876-7060.

National Futures Association

www.nfa.futures.org

The NFA is the self-regulatory agency of the futures industry (it was authorized by Congress). Anyone who is involved with buying or selling futures contracts for the public must be an NFA member. The NFA's purpose is to protect the public and assure high standards of conduct by its members.

North American Securities Administrators Association

www.nasaa.org

NASAA represents securities administrators from throughout North America. As noted in Appendix 1, any complaints you have concerning a financial adviser are likely to go to your state securities administrator. While the state agency's contact information is located in Appendix 1, you can also find it on this web site, along with information on how to pursue complaints and how the dispute resolution process works.

Securities & Exchange Commission

www.sec.gov

The primary mission of the U.S. Securities and Exchange Commission (SEC) is to protect investors and maintain the integrity of the securities markets. The SEC oversees all of the key participants in the securities world, including stock exchanges, corporations, broker-dealers, investment advisors, mutual funds, and public utility holding companies. Central to its mission is fighting securities fraud. To that end, the organization's web site offers a wealth of information; use the SEC's EDGAR database as a background check for securities filings that may be of interest to you.

If you need help or have problems with a financial adviser, be sure to look for the section on investor assistance and complaints.

Index

Accountants, 96. *See also* Tax
    preparers
    audits and, 181
    background checks and, 174
    bankers and, 242
    complaints and, 185
    conflict of interest and, 25
    CPA designation and, 171–172
    dual roles and, 257–258
    financial planning and, 93
    organizations of, 96, 98, 172,
      295–300
    standards and, 63
Account management fees, 124
Account minimums, 145
Accreditation Council for Accoun-
    tancy and Taxation, 173, 295
Accredited Asset Management Spe-
    cialist (AAMS), 96
Accredited Estate Planners (AEP), 96
Accredited Investors, 45, 250
Accredited Tax Advisor (ATA), 171
Accredited Tax Preparer (ATP), 171
Activity letters, 135
Alliance for Investor Education, 313
A.M. Best, 158
American Bar Association, 199, 203
    state associations and, 301–305
American College, 95, 153

American Institute for Chartered
    Property Casualty Underwriters,
    153
American Institute of Certified Public
    Accountants, 96, 98, 172, 296
American Society of Chartered Life
    Underwriters & Chartered Finan-
    cial Consultants, 38
American Trial Lawyers Organization,
    194
Annuities, 116, 118–119
Applegarth, Ginger, 250
Arbitration, 126
Arguments. *See* Complaints
Asset-based fees, 192
Asset Management Program, 96
Asset managers. *See* Brokers
Assets-under-management, 25
Association for Investment Manage-
    ment and Research (AIMR), 95,
    120
Attorneys. *See* Lawyers
Audits, 179, 181–182
    Office of State Auditor, 277, 280
    team building and, 255–256
Auto-mechanic analogy, 26–27

Back-end loans, 118
Background checks, 17–20

Background checks, (cont.)
  bankers and, 239–243
  brokers and, 20, 63, 121–122,
    128–129, 134, 139
  credentials and, 61–66 (*see also* Cre-
    dentials)
  financial planners and, 20, 98–109
  F&R selling and, 40–41
  initial interview and, 54–55
  insurance agents and, 20, 156–164,
    283–293
  lawyers and, 20, 196–204, 301–305
  online resources and, 313–318
  real estate agents and, 20, 216–233,
    307–311
  references and, 75–81 (*see also* Ref-
    erences)
  referrals and, 29–30 (*see also* Refer-
    rals)
  securities regulators, 273–282
  state bar associations, 301–305
  state boards of realtors, 307–311
  state insurance commissioners and,
    283–293
  tax preparers and, 174–184,
    295–300
Bank advisers, 24
Bankers, 2, 14
  affiliation and, 238
  background checks and, 239–243
  communication and, 244
  conflict of interest and, 30
  cooperation and, 242, 250
  credentials and, 238
  do-it-yourself approach and, 237
  dual roles and, 257
  interviews and, 234, 239–243
  loans and, 241
  payment structure and, 24, 233,
    238–241
  personal service and, 44
  references and, 243
  relationships with, 21–22, 233–236,
    243–245
  searching for, 237
  services and, 6, 239–240

standards and, 63, 241
  team building and, 252–253
  things to avoid and, 133
Bauer Financial Reports, 241
Beating the market, 91
Better Business Bureau, 174, 225, 314
Black-box formula, 44, 85
Board of realtors, 225, 230, 307–311
Bonds, 69–80, 118. *See also* Brokers
Boston Globe, The, 55, 270
Brokers, 1
  affiliation and, 117–118
  background checks and, 20, 63,
    121–122, 128–129, 134, 139
  buyer brokers, 212–213, 215, 217,
    229–230
  buying criteria of, 125–126
  clientele and, 122–123, 125–126
  communication and, 124–125
  complaints and, 128–129, 138–139
  control and, 69–80, 128
  cooperation and, 251
  CRD number and, 121–122,
    127–129, 134, 139
  credentials and, 119–120
  discount, 115, 123
  do-it-yourself approach and, 114
  dual roles and, 257, 259
  financial planning and, 93
  firm switching and, 138
  interviews and, 120–133
  online services and, 83, 141–147
  payment structure and, 115,
    118–119, 123–124, 130
  personal service and, 44
  referrals and, 31–32
  relationship with, 134–138
  reputation of, 113
  role of, 116–117
  searching for, 134
  securities holding and, 126–127
  securities regulators and, 273–282
  SIPC and, 129–130
  standards and, 63
  termination and, 128
  transaction questions for, 130–133

types of, 114–116
underlings and, 127–128
Broker's open, 219
Brougham, Lord Henry Peter, 191
Buffet, Warren, 247
Bureau of Insurance, 287
Bureau of Securities Regulation, 278
Business lawyers, 190
Buy-and-hold strategy, 108, 115, 131
Buyer brokers, 212–213, 215, 217, 229–230
Byrne, Brendan, 20–21

Calhoun, Mary, 137–138
Cash management accounts, 124
CBSMarketwatch.com, 84
C-class shares, 23–24
Central Registration Depository (CRD), 99
Certificate of deposit, 249, 252
Certified civil trial lawyer, 194
Certified Divorce Planner (CDP), 96
Certified Employee Benefit Specialist (CEBS), 96
Certified Financial Planner Board of Standards, 63, 95, 314
Certified Financial Planner (CFP), 61–63
brokers and, 120
credentials and, 95
insurance agents and, 153
Certified Fund Specialist (CFS), 96, 120
Certified Investment Management Consultant (CIMC), 96
Certified Public Accountants (CPAs), 96, 171–172
audits and, 181
background checks and, 174
complaints and, 185
organizations of, 96, 98, 172, 295–300
Certified tax lawyers, 194
Certified Trust and Financial Advisers (CTFA), 96–97

CFP Board of Standards, 63, 95, 314
Charitable-remainder trust, 248
Charles Schwab, 105
Chartered Financial Analyst (CFA), 64, 95, 120
Chartered Financial Consultant (ChFC), 95–96, 153
Chartered Life Underwriter (CLU), 95, 153
Chartered Mutual Fund Consultant (CMFC), 96, 120
Chartered Mutual Fund Counselor, 63
Chartered Property Casualty Underwriter (CPCU), 153
Chat-rooms, 84
Clarity, 47–49. *See also* Communication; Information
brokers and, 119–120, 136
control and, 71
credentials and, 61–66
financial planners and, 110–111
ground rules and, 72
interviews and, 58
Clark, Robert, 7, 80
Clientele
brokers and, 122–123, 125–126
dual roles and, 260
F&R selling and, 37–42
family/friends and, 37–42
financial planners and, 101–104, 107
ideal relationship and, 43–50
insurance agents and, 163
lawyers and, 198–200, 202
online services and, 87, 89–90
real estate agents and, 217, 221, 224
tax preparers and, 175–177, 183
team building and, 255
CNNfn.com, 84
Commission des valeurs mobilieres du Quebec, 282
Commissioner of Financial Institutions, 279

Commissions, 23–24. *See also* Payment structure; Price
  bankers and, 238–241
  brokers and, 115, 118–119, 123–124, 130, 142–143
  consultation and, 46
  dual roles and, 260–261
  insurance agents and, 155, 160
  lawyers and, 191–194, 200–202, 205
  real estate agents and, 207, 214–215, 218, 223–224, 228–229
  sales contests and, 108, 117, 124, 131, 136–137, 153
  tax preparers and, 172–173, 177–178
  trailing, 94
  wrap fee and, 94
Commodity Futures Trading Commission, 314
Communication
  bankers and, 244
  financial planners and, 102
  insurance agents and, 162, 165
  lawyers and, 202–205
  real estate agents and, 222, 226–231
  tax preparers and, 182, 184
  team building and, 251–252, 254
  telephones and, 53, 115, 133
  termination and, 263–268
Complaints, 254–255
  brokers and, 128–129, 138–139
  financial planners and, 105–106, 112
  insurance agents and, 163, 166
  lawyers and, 203, 205–206
  online resources and, 317
  real estate agents and, 226–230
  securities regulators and, 273–282
  tax preparers and, 183, 185
  termination and, 263–268
Computers. *See* Online services; Websites
Confidentiality, 75
Conflict of interest, 24–27
  bankers and, 30

  lawyers and, 205
  online services and, 87–88
  real estate agents and, 211, 229–230
  referrals and, 30, 33
  tax preparers and, 25, 30
Confrontations, 74
Consultation. *See* Interviews
Consumer Information Center, 314
Consumer lawyers, 190
Consumer World, 314
Contingent fees, 25, 192
Continuing education, 65
  brokers and, 120–121
  financial planners and, 100
  insurance agents and, 159
  lawyers and, 197
  real estate agents and, 217
  tax preparers and, 176
Control, 67–68
  brokers and, 128
  confrontations and, 74
  financial planners and, 104–105
  ground rules and, 72
  information and, 71–82
  insurance agents and, 164–166
  interviews and, 72–84
  responsibility and, 69–80
  team building and, 255
  termination and, 263–268
  understanding and, 71
Control group, 98
Convenience, 258–259
Corporate Affairs, 282
Corporation Commission, 274
Costs. *See* Price
Council of Better Business Bureaus, 314
Counselors of Real Estate, 213
CPhD, 66
Crash protection, 146
CRD (Central Registration Depository) number, 121–122
  brokers and, 127–129, 134, 139
Credentials, 4
  bankers and, 238
  brokers and, 119–120

continuing education and, 65
earning of, 64–65
exams and, 61–63
financial planners and, 95–97
insurance agents and, 152–153
lawyers and, 194–195
online resources and, 313–318
real estate agents and, 213–214
sanctioning bodies and, 65
specialization and, 65–66
standards and, 62–66. *see also*
    Regulations
tax preparers and, 176
Criminal lawyers, 190
Curry, Tom, 233
cyberinvest.com, 142

Deductions, 179–180
Deep-discount brokers, 115
de facto advice, 1, 76
Demo trades, 147
Department of Banking, 275
Department of Banking & Finance,
    277
Department of Banking, Insurance,
    Securities & Health Care Admin-
    istration, 280
Department of Business Regulation,
    279
Department of Commerce, 277
Department of Commerce & Con-
    sumer Affairs, 275
Department of Commerce & Insur-
    ance, 280
Department of Community & Eco-
    nomic Development, 274
Department of Community Services
    and Attorney General, 282
Department of Consumer & Business
    Services, 279
Department of Corporations, 274
Department of Finance, 275
Department of Financial Institutions,
    276, 280–281
Department of Government Services
    and Lands, 281

Department of Insurance, 284–293.
    See also Division of Insurance; In-
    surance Division
Alabama, 284
Arkansas, 284
California, 284
Connecticut, 285
District of Columbia, 285
Delaware, 285
Florida, 285
Georgia, 286
Idaho, 286
Illinois, 286
Indiana, 286
Kansas, 287
Kentucky, 287
Louisiana, 287
Mississippi, 288
Missouri, 288
Montana, 289
Nebraska, 289
New Hampshire, 289
New Jersey, 289
New Mexico, 290
New York, 290
North Carolina, 290
North Dakota, 290
Ohio, 290
Oklahoma, 290
Puerto Rico, 291
South Carolina, 291
Tennessee, 292
Texas, 292
Utah, 292
West Virginia, 293
Wyoming, 293
Department of Insurance & Securities
    Regulation, 275, 285
Department of Law & Public Safety,
    278
Department of Professional & Finan-
    cial Regulation, 276
Department of Revenue & Taxation,
    286
Department of Securities, 279
Diesslin, David H., 13

DirectAdvice.com, 83
Disagreements, 254–255. *See also*
    Complaints
Discount brokers, 115, 123
Discretionary agreement, 128
Distribution costs, 94, 118
Division of Banking & Insurance, 292
Division of Insurance. *See also* Depart-
    ment of Insurance; Insurance
    Division
  Alaska, 284
  Colorado, 285
  Iowa, 287
  Massachusetts, 288
  Nevada, 289
  Oregon, 291
  South Dakota, 292
  Vermont, 292
  Virgin Islands, 292
Division of Securities, 275, 278,
    280
Divorce attorneys, 190
Do-it-yourself approach, 10–12
  bankers and, 237
  brokers and, 114, 141
  financial planners and, 92
  insurance and, 150–151
  lawyers and, 188–189
  online services and, 83–90, 141
  real estate agents and, 209–212
  tax preparers and, 168–169
Domestic-relations lawyers, 190
Double billing, 199
Dual agents, 229–230, 257–261
Duff & Phelps, 158–159

Education, 16
  brokers and, 120–121
  credentials and, 62–66
  financial planners and, 100
  insurance agents and, 159
  lawyers and, 197
  real estate agents and, 217
  tax preparers and, 176
Einstein, Albert, 169
Eisenhower, Dwight D., 92

Elder lawyers, 190
Emotional discipline, 92
Enrolled agents, 30, 171, 174.
    See also Tax preparers
  organizations and, 295–300
Estate planning
  lawyers, 190
  relationships and, 50
  team players and, 46–47
Excessive requests, 48

Family and friends, 18
  advice from, 1, 15, 50
  business with, 37–42
  initial interview and, 54–56
  insurance agents and, 155
  references and, 79
  referrals and, 29–31, 34
  trust and, 56–57
Family lawyers, 190
F&R selling, 37–42
Fear of offending, 2–3
Federal law, 63
Federal securities regulators,
    273–282
Federal Trade Commission, 315
Fees. *See also* Price
  account management, 124
  asset-based, 192
  bankers and, 233
  contingent, 25, 192
  fee-for-service payments, 191
  fee-off-set, 94
  flat, 24, 115, 173, 191
  F-O credential, 64, 97
  percentage, 192
  referral, 194, 198
  12b-1, 94, 118
  wrap, 94, 119
Fidelity, 105
Financial advisers, 9, 269–271. *See
    also* Background checks; Hiring
  commissions and, 23–24
    (*see also* Commissions)
  conflict of interest and, 24–27, 30,
    33, 87–88, 205, 211, 229–230

control and, 67–84, 104–105, 128,
    164–166, 255, 263–268
credentials and, 4, 61–66, 95–97,
    119–120, 152–153, 194–195,
    213–214, 238
dual roles and, 229–230, 257–261
friends and, 37–42
interviews and, 18, 51–60 (*see also*
    Interviews)
online resources and, 1, 5, 83–90,
    141–147, 273–293, 296–318
payment structure and, 24 (*see also*
    Payment structure)
references and, 75–81 (*see also* Ref-
    erences)
referrals and, 19–20, 29–35, 41–42,
    97–98
relationships with, 43–50 (*see also*
    Relationships)
securities regulators and, 273–282
state boards of realtors, 307–311
team building and, 46–47, 247–256
termination and, 90, 106, 128,
    163–164, 183, 203, 223–224,
    263–268
timing and, 17–22
financialengines.com, 83, 85, 88
Financial planners, 91
    background checks and, 20, 98–99,
        109
    clientele and, 101–104, 107
    complaints and, 105–106
    credentials and, 63, 95–97, 314
    dual roles and, 257
    firm switching and, 111
    interviewing of, 99–109
    online resources and, 314–315
    payment structure of, 93–94,
        101–102
    relationship with, 109–111
    research and, 105
    restitution and, 112
    rogue, 105, 109
    role of, 92–93
    searching for, 97–98
    termination and, 106

things to avoid, 109–111
transaction questions for, 107–109
Financial Planning Association, 98,
    315
Firing. *See* Termination
First Financial Trust, 250
Flat-fee, 24
    brokers and, 115
    lawyers and, 191
    tax preparers and, 173
Florida Association of Insurance, 285
F-O (fee-only) credential, 64, 97
Form ADV, 55
    financial planners and, 99–101,
        105–106
    online services and, 89
Freebies, 146
Friends. *See* Family and friends
Full service brokers, 114–116, 123

General Motors Corporation, 99
Goldinger, S. Jay, 69
Governmental lawyers, 190
Gurney, Edward, 167
Gut feeling, 4

H&R Block, 4, 170
Hand, Learned, 179
Happiness letters, 135
Hiring, 269–271
    accountants and, 167–186
    background checks and, 17–20 (*see
        also* Background checks)
    bankers and, 233–245
    brokers and, 113–147
    deadlines and, 17
    do-it-yourself approach and, 10–12,
        83–92 (*see also* Do-it-yourself ap-
        proach)
    F&R selling and, 37–42
    financial planners and, 91–112
    friends and, 37–42
    insurance agents and, 149–166
    lawyers and, 187–206
    online resources and, 1, 5, 83–90,
        141–147, 273–293, 296–318

Hiring, (cont.)
  price and, 2–3. *see also* Price
  privacy and, 15
  procrastination and, 9–10
  quality and, 3–4, 6–8
  real estate agents and, 207–231
  references and, 75–81 (*see also* References)
  a replacement, 267–268
  tax preparers and, 167–186
  time and, 15–22
House funds, 111

Immigration lawyers, 190
Independent Insurance Agents (state organizations of). *See also* Insurance Brokers & Agents of the West
  Alabama, 284
  Alaska, 284
  Arizona, 284
  Arkansas, 284
  Colorado, 285
  Connecticut, 285
  Delaware, 285
  Florida, 285
  Georgia, 286
  Hawaii, 286
  Idaho, 286
  Illinois, 286
  Indiana, 287
  Iowa, 287
  Kansas, 287
  Kentucky, 287
  Louisiana, 287
  Maryland, 288
  Massachusetts, 288
  Metro Washington, 285
  Michigan, 288
  Minnesota, 288
  Mississippi, 288
  Missouri, 289
  Montana, 289
  Nebraska, 289
  Nevada, 289
  New Hampshire, 289

  New Jersey, 289
  New Mexico, 290
  New York, 290
  North Carolina, 290
  North Dakota, 290
  Ohio, 290
  Oklahoma, 291
  Oregon, 291
  Pennsylvania, 291
  Rhode Island, 291
  South Carolina, 291
  South Dakota, 292
  Tennessee, 292
  Utah, 292
  Virginia, 293
  Washington, 293
  West Virginia, 293
  Wisconsin, 293
  Wyoming, 293
Information, 1–2, 269–271. *See also* Background checks
  conflict of interest and, 24–27
  control and, 71–82
  credentials and, 61–66
  insurance agents and, 164–165, 283–293
  interviews and, 51–60
  online services and, 83–90, 313–318
  references and, 75–81 (*see also* References)
  securities regulators and, 273–282
  state bar associations, 301–305
  state boards of realtors, 307–311
  state insurance commissioners, 283–293
  tax preparer/CPA organizations, 295–300
  team building and, 251–252, 254
  understanding and, 47, 49
Inheritance, 1, 9, 17, 25
Inside information, 136
Instant trust, 33–34
Institute for Investment Management Consultants, 96
Institute of Certified Bankers, 97

Insurance Administration, 288
Insurance agents, 1–2, 9, 11, 149
  alternate choices to, 151–152
  associations of, 283–293
  background checks and, 20,
    156–164, 283–293
  clientele and, 163
  communication and, 162
  complaints and, 163, 166
  continuing education and, 159
  control and, 164–166
  credentials and, 152–153
  disputed claims and, 161–170
  do-it-yourself approach and,
    150–151
  dual roles and, 257, 259
  financial planning and, 93
  interviews and, 18, 156–164
  licensing and, 159–160
  payment structure and, 155,
    160–161
  personal service and, 44–45
  policy types and, 154–155
  references and, 164
  relationship with, 153, 166
  searching for, 155–156
  standards and, 63
  state commissioners and, 283–293
  termination and, 163–164
  types of, 151
Insurance Brokers & Agents of the
  West, 285
Insurance Bureau, 288
Insurance Department, 288, 291
Insurance Division. *See also* Department of Insurance; Division of
  Insurance
  Hawaii, 286
  Iowa, 276
  Rhode Island, 291
Intellectual property lawyers, 190
Interest-only mortgages, 236
Internal Revenue Service (IRS), 4–5,
  167–186
International Foundation of Em-
  ployee Benefit Plans, 96

Internet, 1, 5, 83–84, 315. *See also*
  Websites
  brokers and, 141–147
  clientele and, 87
  conflict of interest and, 87–88
  interaction and, 88
  online brokers and, 141–147
  payment structure and, 86–87
  personal services and, 88–89
  references and, 89
  securities regulators and,
    273–282
  standards and, 89
  termination and, 90
  traditional advice and, 85–86
Interviews, 18, 46, 270
  background checks and, 53–55
    (*see also* Background checks)
  bankers and, 234, 239–243
  brokers and, 120–133
  control and, 73–84
  dual roles and, 259–261
  family and, 55–56
  financial planners and, 99–109
  initial, 51–60
  insurance agents and, 156–164
  lawyers and, 46, 196–204
  price and, 58 (*see also* Price)
  real estate agents and, 216–225
  references and, 59–60 (*see also*
    References)
  reservations and, 58
  scheduling of, 53–54
  services and, 57–58
  Social Security number and, 122
  tax preparers and, 18, 175–184
  telephone and, 53
Investing Online Resource Center,
  315
Investment consultants. *See* Brokers
Investment Counsel Association of
  America, 98
Investment Dealers Association of
  Canada, 315–316
Investments. *See* Brokers; Financial
  planners

Investorama.com, 142
Investor Protection Trust, 316
IRS, 4–5, 167–186

Junk bonds, 69–80
Justification, 30, 32

Kiplinger's Personal Finance, 26

Labor lawyers, 190
Lawsuits, 206
Lawyers, 2, 9, 187
    arbitration and, 126
    background checks and, 20,
        196–204, 301–305
    clientele and, 198–200, 202
    communication and, 202–203
    complaints and, 203, 205–206
    conflict of interest and, 25
    continuing education and, 197
    credentials and, 194–195
    do-it-yourself approach and,
        188–189
    dual roles and, 257
    interviews and, 46, 196–204
    payment structure and, 191–194,
        200–202, 205
    relationships and, 204–206
    responsibilities of, 189–190
    searching for, 195–196
    specialization and, 197
    state bar associations of, 301–305
    team building and, 46–47, 252
    termination and, 203
    training and, 16
    types of, 190–191
    underlings and, 199
Legal Registries, 282
Levin, Ross, 45, 250
Licensed Independent Network of
    CPA Financial Planners (LINC), 97
Licensing. *See* Credentials
Life insurance, 116, 154–155. *See also*
    Insurance agents
Life Insurance Advisers Association,
    152

Loans, 1, 241
Local box, 218

Margin accounts, 146
Market, 249. *See also* Brokers
    beating of, 91
    online brokers and, 141–147
    online resources and, 315–318
Marketing and distribution costs, 94,
    118
Market-maker, 144
Market specialist, 144
Merrill Lynch, 117
Million Dollar Round Table, 153
Money magazine, 168
Money managers, 116, 119. *See also*
    Brokers
Money market accounts, 145
Moody's Investors Service, 158
Morgan, J. Pierpont, 196
Morgan Stanley Dean Witter, 117
Morningstar, 70, 77, 80, 258
Muller, Todd, 162–163
Multiple jobs, 257–261, 229–230
Multiple Listing Service, 209, 213,
    219
Munger, Charles, 247
Mutual funds, 23–24, 62, 83, 249. *See
    also* Brokers
MyCFO.com, 83
MyMoneyPro.com, 83

Nasdaq, 144
NASD Regulation, 99, 131, 273–274
    brokers and, 134
    CRD number and, 122
    online resources and, 316–317
National Association of Enrolled
    Agents, The, 174, 295
National Association of Estate Plan-
    ners and Councils, 96
National Association of Life Under-
    writers (NALU), 153
National Association of Personal Fi-
    nancial Advisors (NAPFA), 13, 64,
    97–98, 316

National Association of Real Estate
    Brokers, 214
National Association of Realtors, 208,
    214, 307
National Association of Securities
    Dealers (NASD), 99, 131, 273–274
    brokers and, 134
    CRD number and, 122
    online resources and, 316–317
National Endowment for Financial
    Education, 96, 119–120, 175
National Fraud Information Center,
    317
National Futures Association, 317
Networking. See Team building
New York Stock Exchange, 249.
        See also Brokers
    beating of, 91
    online brokers and, 141–147
    online resources and, 315–318
North American Securities Adminis-
    trators Association (NASAA), 273,
    317–318
Noyes, Harry Clarke, 32

Office of Comptroller, 275
Office of Financial & Insurance Ser-
    vices, 277
Office of the Attorney General,
    277–279
Office of the Commissioner of Insur-
    ance, 293
Office of the Insurance Commis-
    sioner, 293
Office of the Secretary of State,
    275–277
Office of the Securities Commis-
    sioner, 276
Office of the State Auditor, 277,
    280
1–800-MUTUALS, 83, 86
One-stop shopping, 258
Online services, 1, 5, 83–84, 315. See
        also Websites
    brokers and, 141–147
    clientele and, 87

    conflict of interest and, 87–88
    interaction and, 88
    online brokers and, 141–147
    payment structure and, 86–87
    personal services and, 88–89
    references and, 89
    securities regulators and, 273–282
    standards and, 89
    termination and, 90
    traditional advice and, 85–86

Patent attorneys, 190
Payment structure, 23
    bankers and, 24, 233, 238–241
    brokers and, 115, 118–119,
        123–124, 130
    conflict of interest and, 24–27
    credentials and, 64
    dual roles and, 260–261
    financial planners and, 93–94,
        101–102
    insurance agents and, 155, 160–161
    lawyers and, 191–194, 200–202,
        205
    online services and, 86–87,
        142–143
    real estate agents and, 24, 207,
        214–215, 218, 220, 223–224,
        228–229
    sales quotas, 108, 117, 124, 131,
        136–137, 153
    tax preparers and, 24, 172–173,
        177–178
Percentage fees, 192
Perks, 146
Personal Financial Specialist (PFS), 63,
    96, 98
Personal injury lawyers, 190–191
Personal service, 44–45
    online services and, 83–90
Pre-dispute correspondence, 126
Price, 2–3, 13–14, 80
    account management and, 124
    affordability and, 5–6
    asset-based, 192
    bankers and, 24, 233, 238–241

Price, (cont.)
  brokers and, 115, 118–119,
    123–124, 130
  conflict of interest and, 24–27
  contingent, 25, 192
  do-it-yourself approach and, 10–12
  dual roles and, 260–261
  fee-off-set and, 94
  financial planners and, 101–102
  flat fees, 24, 115, 173, 191
  F-O credential, 64, 97
  insurance agents and, 155, 160–161
  interviews and, 58
  lawyers and, 191–194, 200–202,
    205
  marketing costs and, 94
  online services and, 86–87,
    142–143
  percentage and, 192
  performance and, 23
  real estate agents and, 207,
    214–215, 220, 223–224
  referrals and, 194, 198
  sales quotas and, 108, 117, 124,
    131, 136–137, 153
  spread and, 109, 118, 132
  tax preparers and, 172–173,
    177–178
  trailing commissions and, 94
  12b–1 fee and, 94, 118
  wrap fee and, 94, 119
Privacy, 14–15
Prizes for sales quotas, 108, 117, 124,
    131, 136–137, 153
Procrastination, 9
  do-it-yourself approach and, 10–12
  family and, 15
  fear of scams and, 12–13
  price and, 13–14
  privacy and, 14–15
  timing and, 15–22
Prudential Securities, 117

Quality, 6, 23, 144
Quarterbacks, 253–254
Quota bait, 108, 117, 124, 131,
    136–137, 153

Real estate agents, 9, 14, 208
  affiliation and, 213
  background checks and, 20,
    216–230, 307–311
  broker's open house and, 219
  brokers vs. agents, 212–213, 215,
    217, 229–230
  clientele and, 217, 221, 224
  communication and, 222, 231
  complaints and, 226–230
  conflict of interest and, 211,
    229–230
  continuing education and, 217
  cooperation, 250–251
  credentials and, 213–214
  do-it-yourself approach and,
    209–212
  financing and, 221–222
  interviews and, 216–225
  payment structure and, 24, 207,
    214–215, 218, 220, 223–224,
    228–229
  references and, 226
  relationship with, 207, 226–230
  searching for, 230–231
  standards and, 63
  state boards of, 307–311
  termination and, 223–224
Real estate lawyers, 191
Reality check, 222
Realtist, 214
References, 42, 270
  bankers and, 243
  brokers and, 126
  de facto, 76
  financial planners and, 104
  good answers from, 75–81
  insurance agents and, 164
  interviews and, 59–60
  online services and, 89
  questions for, 77–81
  real estate agents and, 226
  tax preparers and, 183–184
  vs. referrals, 33, 42
Referrals, 19–20, 35
  conflict of interest and, 30
  family and friends, 29–31

fees for, 194, 198
financial planners and, 97–98
self justification and, 30, 32
trust and, 33–34
vs. references, 33, 42
written contracts and, 41
Registered Financial Consultants
    (RFC), 97
Registered Investment Adviser (RIA),
    64, 120
Registered representative, 120
Regulation & Licensing Department,
    278
Regulations, 62–66, 95. *See also* Cre-
    dentials
    bankers and, 241
    CRD and, 99
    financial planners and, 95–97
    insurance agents and, 158–159,
        283–293
    lawyers and, 194–195, 301–305
    NASD and, 99, 122, 134, 273–274,
        316–317
    online resources and, 89, 313–318
    real estate agents and, 307–311
    securities and, 273–282
    tax preparers and, 173–174,
        295–300
Relationship oriented specialists,
    20–22
    bankers and, 234–236
    personal service and, 44–45
Relationships, 269–271
    background checks and, 17–20
    bankers and, 21–22, 233–236,
        243–245
    brokers and, 134–138
    consultation and, 46
    dual roles and, 257–261
    estate and, 50
    family/friends and, 37–42 (*see also*
        Family and friends)
    financial planners and, 109–111
    ideal, 43–50
    instructions and, 48–49
    insurance agents and, 153, 166
    lawyers and, 204–206

online services and, 83–90, 147
personal service and, 44–45
real estate agents and, 207, 226–230
redefining, 265–266
tax preparers and, 184–186
team players and, 46–47
termination and, 263–268 (*see also*
    Termination)
tolerance and, 48
underlings and, 50
understanding and, 47, 49
Reputation, 3–4
Research, 1–2. *See also* Background
    checks; Interviews
    conflict of interest and, 24–27
    financial planners and, 99–109
    online services and, 83–90, 146
    referrals and, 34–35
    team building and, 251–252
Restitution, 112. *See also* Complaints
Retainers, 193
Rogue brokers, 126
Rogue planners, 105, 109
Ruane, Bill, 247

Sales load, 118
Sales quotas, 108, 117, 124, 131,
    136–137, 153
Savings, 11–12
Scams, 12–13, 116
Secretary of State, 277–278, 281
Secretary of the Commonwealth, 277
Securities Administration Branch, 281
Securities & Exchange Commission,
    64, 274, 318
Securities Commissions (state), 274,
    276, 278–279, 281–282
Securities Investor Protection Corpo-
    ration (SIPC), 129–130
Securities Registry, 282
Securities regulators, 273–282
Selling pressures, 117
Sequoia Fund, 247
Series exams, 119–120
Services, 6–8
    brokers and, 114–116, 123
    changes in, 113

Services, (cont.)
  financial planners and, 102
  insurance agents and, 165–166
  interviews and, 57–58
  personal, 44–45, 83–90
  questions for, 78–89
  relationships and, 44–45
Shares, 23–24, 118, 132. *See also* Brokers
Sharkey, Howes, Wagner & Javer, 47, 255
Sharpe, William, 85
Sharpe Index of Performance, 62–63
Sheshunoff Ratings Services, 241
Shopping. *See* Hiring
Sliding scale arrangements, 193
Snowdon, Mike, 175
Social Security Number, 122
Society of Financial Professionals, 96
Society of Financial Service Professionals, 156
Specialization
  dual roles and, 257–261
  financial planners and, 103
  insurance agents and, 157
  lawyers and, 197
  tax preparers and, 176
Spread, 109, 118, 132
Standard & Poors Corp., 158–159, 265
Standards, 62–66, 95, 314. *See also* Credentials; Regulations
State Corporation Commission, 280, 293
State securities regulators, 273–282
Stock analysts, 64
Stock market, 249. *See also* Brokers
  beating of, 91
  online brokers and, 141–147
  online resources and, 318
Stupid questions, 48
Suing, 206
Sweeps, 145

Tax lawyers, 172, 181, 191
Tax preparers, 2, 9, 167
  audits and, 181–182
  background checks and, 174–184, 295–300
  clientele and, 175–177, 183
  communication and, 182, 184
  complaints and, 183, 185
  conflict of interest and, 25, 30
  continuing education and, 176
  control and, 70
  credentials and, 176
  deductions and, 179–180
  do-it-yourself approach and, 168–169
  interviews and, 18, 175–184
  organizations of, 295–300
  payment structure and, 24, 172–173, 177–178
  references and, 183–184
  relationships with, 184–186
  searching for, 173–174
  termination and, 183
  training and, 16
  types of, 169–172
Team building, 46–47, 247–250
  communication and, 251–252
  control and, 255
  disagreements and, 254–255
  dual roles and, 257–261
  group meetings and, 254
  leadership and, 253–254
  review and, 255–256
  role defining and, 252–253
  termination and, 263–268
Telephones, 53, 115, 133
Termination
  brokers and, 128
  communication and, 265
  financial planners and, 106
  hiring a replacement and, 267–268
  insurance agents and, 163–164
  lawyers and, 203
  online services and, 90
  real estate agents and, 223–224
  redefining relationship and, 265–266
  tax preparers and, 183
  team building and, 263–268

Term insurance, 154
TheRightAdvisor.com, 83
Timing, 15–22
Tolerance, 48
Trailing commissions, 94
Transaction oriented specialists,
    20–21
    bankers and, 234, 236
    online services and, 83–90
    personal service and, 44–45
Trump, Donald, 247
Trust, 33–34, 56–57
Tuccillo, John A., 208
Twain, Mark, 17, 22
12b–1 fee, 94, 118

Underlings
    brokers and, 127–128
    insurance agents and, 162
    lawyers and, 199
    relationships and, 50
    tax preparers and, 179
Understanding, 47–49. *See also*
    Communication; Information
    brokers and, 119–120, 136
    control and, 71
    credentials and, 61–66
    financial planners and, 110–111
    ground rules and, 72
    interviews and, 58
Universal life insurance, 154
Use asset, 208

Vanguard.com, 84
Variable life insurance, 154
Veres, Robert N., 77, 258
Veri-banc, 241
Vermont Insurance Agents Associa-
    tion, 292
Vest, H. D., 61, 63, 66
Wagner, Dick, 47, 254
Websites
    Alliance for Investor Education,
        313
    CBSMarketwatch.com, 84
    Certified Financial Planner Board of
        Standards, 314

CNNfn.com, 84
Commodity Futures Trading Com-
    mission, 315
Consumer Information Center, 314
Consumer World, 314
Council of Better Business Bureaus,
    314
cyberinvest.com, 142
DirectAdvice.com, 83
Federal Trade Commission, 315
financialengines.com, 83, 85, 88
Financial Planning Association,
    315
insurance agents associations,
    283–293
Investing Online Resource Center,
    315
Investment Dealers Association of
    Canada, 315–316
Investorama.com, 142
Investor Protection Trust, 316
MyCFO.com, 83
MyMoneyPro.com, 83
National Association of Personal Fi-
    nancial Advisors, 316
National Association of Securities
    Dealers (NASD), 316
National Futures Association, 316
North American Securities Admin-
    istrators Association, 317–318
Securities & Exchange Commission,
    318
state bar associations, 301–305
state boards of realtors, 307–311
state insurance commissioners,
    283–293
tax preparer/CPA organizations
    and, 296–300
TheRightAdvisor.com, 83
Vanguard.com, 84
Weiss Research, 158–159
Wilde, Oscar, 113
Wilson, Charles, 99
Wrap fee, 94, 119
Written contracts, 41